D1327360

WEST INDIAN IMMIGRANTS

WEST INDIAN IMMIGRANTS

A Black Success Story?

SUZANNE MODEL

Russell Sage Foundation • New York

The Russell Sage Foundation

The Russell Sage Foundation, one of the oldest of America's general purpose foundations, was established in 1907 by Mrs. Margaret Olivia Sage for "the improvement of social and living conditions in the United States." The Foundation seeks to fulfill this mandate by fostering the development and dissemination of knowledge about the country's political, social, and economic problems. While the Foundation endeavors to assure the accuracy and objectivity of each book it publishes, the conclusions and interpretations in Russell Sage Foundation publications are those of the authors and not of the Foundation, its Trustees, or its staff. Publication by Russell Sage, therefore, does not imply Foundation endorsement.

Library of Congress Cataloging-in-Publication Data
Model, Suzanne.
West Indian Immigrants : a black success story? / Suzanne Model.
    p.   cm.
  Includes bibliographical references and index.
  ISBN 978-0-87154-631-9
  1. West Indian Americans—Social conditions.   2. West Indian
  Americans—Economic conditions.   3. Blacks—United States—Social
  conditions.   4. Blacks—United States—Economic conditions.
  5. Immigrants—United States—Social conditions.   6. Immigrants—
  United States—Economic conditions.   7. Success—United States.
  8.   United States—Race relations.   I. Title.
  E184.W54M63 2008
  305.800973—dc22   2007049694

Text design by Suzanne Nichols.

RUSSELL SAGE FOUNDATION
112 East 64th Street, New York, New York 10021
10   9   8   7   6   5   4   3   2   1

Contents

About the Author

Suzanne Model is professor of sociology at the University of Massachusetts, Amherst.

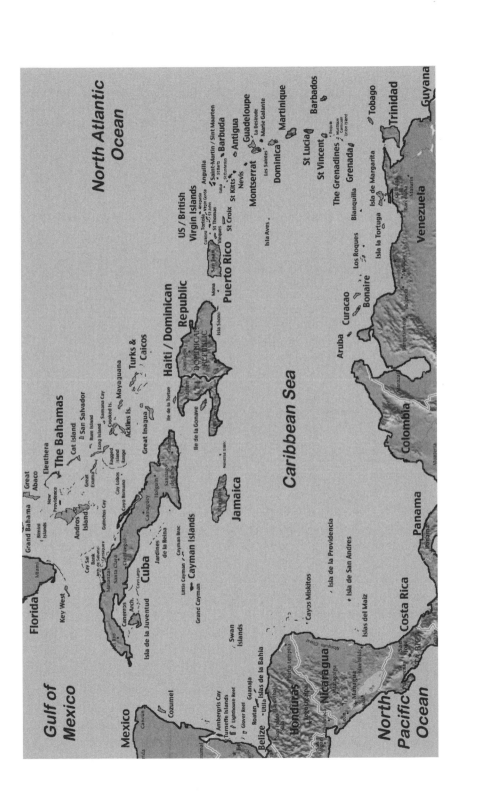

Acknowledgments: Intellectual Debts and Personal Debts

The chronology of my fascination with West Indian immigrants is a good way of conveying my intellectual debt. The story begins in 1980, when I was a graduate student writing a "comps" paper on African American and Chinese organizations. Researching this topic led me to Ivan Light's book *Ethnic Enterprise in America* (1972). Light wanted to explain why Chinese, Japanese, and West Indian immigrants are over-represented as entrepreneurs, while African Americans are not. His argument hinged on a cultural practice known as "rotating credit associations." Because savings banks are reluctant to lend to foreigners, Light concluded that lack of capital is one of the biggest problems facing immigrant entrepreneurs. Rotating credit associations compensate for this deficiency by making relatively large sums of money available to participants in a short period of time.

Light noted that rotating credit associations are well established in China, Japan, and West Africa; they are also active among immigrants of Chinese descent, Japanese descent, and African descent in the West Indies, but *not* in the southern United States. This difference he attributed to variations in the effects of slavery in the Western Hemisphere. Slavery on the U.S. mainland was more destructive of culture than slavery in the Caribbean. As a result, American blacks lost their rotating credit associations but West Indian blacks did not. This difference, Light argued, explains why West Indian immigrants are so much more entrepreneurial than African Americans.

But are they? Consulting tabulations that were published in 1973 but based on the 1970 U.S. census, I found that 3.2 percent of adult males born in the "other West Indies" (such as "other than Cuba") were self-employed. This was not an impressive figure; it was practically identical to the 3.4 percent rate among native-born "Negro" men with native-born parents. Evidently, familiarity with rotating credit associations was not the sine qua non of ethnic entrepreneurship. Further research indicated that Mexicans also had rotating credit but rates of entrepreneurship among them were low, while Jews did not have rotating credit but did have high rates of entrepreneurship.

Why, then, are West Indians considered entrepreneurial at all? As I explain in chapter 2, West Indian immigrants were first described as entrepreneurial in 1909, and the hype continues today. By extension, observers like Nathan Glazer and Daniel Patrick Moynihan (1963) were painting West Indians as a "model minority." This is a label for an ethnic minority whose members encounter discrimination but who nevertheless attain social and economic "success." As the wording suggests, the implicit message is that discrimination is not the insurmountable hurdle that African Americans claim. The minority most frequently used to discount the power of discrimination is Asian Americans. Obviously, a more compelling case is made if the minority is of African origin.

I soon found evidence that West Indians are a model minority. The numbers in Thomas Sowell's edited volume *Essays and Data on American Ethnic Groups* (1978a) demonstrated that first- and second-generation West Indians hold several advantages over African Americans. In explaining why, the economist Sowell, like the sociologist Light, displayed a penchant for culturally based interpretations. Drawing on differences originating in slavery, Sowell argued that whites gave blacks many more opportunities to profit from industry and initiative in the West Indies than in the American South. Consequently, West Indians know far better how to capitalize on contemporary economic opportunities than do African Americans. What's more, Sowell discredited several alternative interpretations. Noting that second-generation West Indians are indistinguishable from African Americans but still have stronger labor market outcomes, he concluded that whites' alleged preference for Caribbean blacks is not a causal factor. As for the argument that movers are more talented than stayers, Sowell believed that so many West Indians had left the Caribbean that positive selection could no longer apply.

Yet selectivity theory was alive and well in the 1970s among more quantitatively oriented economists. In 1977, Barry Chiswick claimed that the positive selectivity of migration is so strong that even the sons of immigrants profit from it. Two years later, in an article entitled

"Some Universal Patterns Among Immigrants," he argued that *all* economically motivated immigrants are more ambitious and industrious than their non-immigrant compatriots. Black immigrants were one of the groups he selected to illustrate this "universality." In a far more sophisticated comparison than Sowell had undertaken, Chiswick showed that, after eleven years in this country, the earnings of black immigrant males equaled those of similarly qualified African Americans. Thereafter, the immigrants earned more.

Of course, it was possible that both culture and selectivity contributed to this result; perhaps culture gave West Indians an initial boost, and selectivity yet another.

The year 1979 brought yet another critical insight to the study of West Indians. According to Nancy Foner, West Indians in London were more occupationally successful than West Indians in New York. Noting that West Indians in the two destination cities shared the same cultural background and the same initiative to relocate, she speculated that U.S. West Indians were profiting from the presence of a large, visible "native" black community. Benefits might accrue, for instance, if African Americans patronize West Indian businesses or become the constituents of West Indian politicians. Citing Sowell's discovery that accentless, second-generation West Indians likewise outperformed African Americans, Foner doubted that white favoritism was responsible for the difference.

I was not convinced. First, I was pretty sure that West Indian entrepreneurialism had been exaggerated. Second, positive selectivity and white favoritism are not mutually exclusive. Noting that Foner relied on published tabulations, I wondered what more sophisticated comparisons of West Indians in Britain and the United States would show. And did not West Indians settle in other destinations? If white favoritism contributed to West Indians' advantage over African Americans, then West Indians in the United States should have been outperforming not only their compatriots who settled in England but also those who migrated elsewhere.

To sum up, already in the early 1980s I was thinking about cross-national comparison as a strategy to test the idea that an African American presence contributes to West Indian success. Yet over a decade passed before I undertook such comparisons. One reason I let the matter lapse was that studies based on the 1980 census found *no* significant differences between the earnings of West Indian-born and U.S.-born black men. There seemed little point in focusing on a pseudo-problem. Indeed, I might never have returned to the question if David Ladipo had not telephoned me from England in 1994. A graduate student at Cambridge University, David wanted to come to New York to undertake comparisons of West Indians in the United States and the United Kingdom. His enthusiasm rekindled my interest. Eventually our collaborative effort detected an occupational advantage for West Indians in New York relative to London. This time I stayed hooked until I solved the puzzle to my satisfaction.

Beyond my intellectual debts are certain personal debts as well. My thanks go to the Russell Sage Foundation for supporting my initial research on New York City, which included collecting data on West Indian attainment. Contributing to that effort were Dan Kryder, Andrew Schlewitz, Gretchen Stiers, and Eleanor Weber. For help with data analysis, I am, as always, indebted to Gene Fisher.

My expeditions to collect data on West Indian immigrants led me to several countries. In Britain, I thank Brendan Burchell for hosting me at Cambridge and Angela Dale for hosting me at the University of Manchester's Cathie Marsh Centre for Census and Survey Research. That first journey could not have been undertaken without a University of Massachusetts Healey Endowment Grant; a Simon Research Fellowship underwrote the second. Particularly memorable in England was the trip that Faye Arnold and I took to the University of Warwick to find out more about the British hierarchy of discrimination. In Paris, I thank Roxane Silberman for obtaining a Poste Rouge for me with CNRS and Annick Kieffer and Irene Fournier for their research assistance. Justus Veenman kindly hosted me at Erasmus University in Rotterdam, where Edwin Martens provided invaluable research assistance and Marjolijn Distelbrink provided welcome companionship. I learned a lot about Dutch Antilleans from Frank Bovenkirk and much about the Surinamese from Mies van Niekerk.

Additional thanks go to Leonard Adams and Bill Thompson at the DuBois Library of the University of Massachusetts; to mapmaker Eric Poehler of the Department of Anthropology, University of Masssachusetts; and to the staff of the Integrated Public Use Microdata Series (IPUMS), especially Matt Sobek. Portions of the analysis in this book were presented at meetings of the American Sociological Association and of Research Committee 28 of the International Sociological Association. At Robert Lucas's invitation, the entire argument was presented at the Myron Weiner Seminar Series on International Migration at MIT. I thank the participants at these many gatherings for their insightful questions and comments.

My long acquaintance with Leonard Coard continues to nurture my curiosity about the West Indies. His response to an earlier version of this manuscript and the comments of Richard Alba and Roger Waldinger were invaluable. For over two years, Suzanne Nichols guided this project through the review process. Her confidence turned it into an RSF publication. My debt to her cannot be measured.

At the personal level, this volume represents the book my father never wrote. Though I did not follow in his footsteps, I think he would have been satisfied with what I have done professionally. In this context, I am reminded of an insight Harriet Zuckerman once shared with me. A researcher of women in science, Professor Zuckerman observed that the fathers of many successful women are very ambitious for their daughters, but not so ambitious for their wives. Luckily, my husband Frank is an exception to this generalization. He has always been at least as ambitious for me as for our daughter and son. I thank Frank for this support, as well as for his tolerance for solitude, without which this book could not have been written.

· Chapter 1 ·

Why Study West Indians?

Why do black immigrants do so much better than blacks who are born in America? It is an unpopular question, but one that demands an answer.
—"Black Like Me," *The Economist*, May 11, 1996, 57

Not long after the United States government released the results of the 2000 census, a headline in the *Boston Globe* proclaimed: "Study Shows U.S. Blacks Trailing." The article revealed that black immigrants were receiving higher household incomes and suffering less unemployment than U.S.-born blacks (Rodriguez 2002). Two years later, the *New York Times* reported a similar finding in the educational realm: blacks at Harvard and other elite colleges were disproportionately the offspring of foreign-born parents (Rimer and Arenson 2004).

In fact, assertions that black immigrants have more favorable social and economic outcomes than African Americans are old news. For about one hundred years, American journalists and scholars have been rediscovering that black immigrants have stronger socioeconomic outcomes than African Americans. Beyond the truism that Americans have short memories, why does this "discovery" attract so much attention?

There are several reasons. One is that black immigrant success sends the message that racial discrimination is not the handicap that African Americans claim. Black immigrants have dark skin, yet they succeed. As *The Economist* (1996, 57–58) states: "Figures like these suggest that racism does not account for all, or even most, of the difficulties encountered by native-born blacks." Second, black immigrant achievement sends the message that African American economic shortfalls are the result of African American behavioral shortfalls. As the Jamaican-born sociologist Orlando Patterson (2006) argues, if young African American men are to obtain well-paying jobs, they should begin by accepting the low-wage jobs that black immigrants do. Then they would acquire the skills to move up. In other words, black immigrant success lets whites off the hook and places the responsibility for African American problems squarely on African American shoulders.

1

This logic leads to the third and perhaps most compelling reason why black immigrant achievement attracts so much attention. If racial bias is not the cause of African American disadvantage, then affirmative action programs are not the remedy. Since the late 1960s, many employers and even more college admissions officials have been complying with affirmative action directives. These directives require gatekeepers to offer more opportunities than they might otherwise extend to applicants from disadvantaged groups. Opponents of affirmative action have advanced a number of arguments to discredit this policy. Black immigrant achievement constitutes one of the most compelling. After all, affirmative action is a program designed to redress the injustices of white racism. But if white racism is responsible for black disadvantage, then why do black immigrants fare so well?

Before moving on, a clarification is needed. Media hype to the contrary, not all black immigrants have stronger outcomes than African Americans. Black immigrants from the Hispanic Caribbean and Haiti do not; black immigrants from Africa do not. The immigrants responsible for the favorable numbers cited by reporters come overwhelmingly from the English-speaking West Indies, that is, from Britain's colonies and former colonies in the Caribbean (Dodoo 1997; Kalmijn 1996; Rong and Brown 2001). This situation is hardly surprising. Though commonly labeled "West Indians," the language and culture of English-speaking West Indians are far more compatible with the language and culture of Americans than are the languages and cultures of sub-Saharan Africans or of non-English-speaking West Indians. Because the great majority of black immigrants are English-speaking West Indians, journalists mistakenly attribute their prosperity to black immigrants as a whole.[1]

Limiting the "success" to West Indian blacks does not explain it, however. Although researchers know that West Indians have better outcomes than African Americans, they disagree about why. The explanations offered so far can be divided into three broad categories: culture, selectivity, and favoritism. The first rationale asserts that West Indian immigrants and African Americans differ in values, attitudes, and behaviors. West Indians are diligent, self-sacrificing, and determined; they put a premium on education. African Americans are indolent, self-indulgent, and apathetic; they view schools as institutions of oppression. One justification for these claims is that black Caribbean slaves received greater rewards for their labor than black slaves in the United States. This situation imbued the former with a stronger work ethic than the latter. Another justification is that socialization in an "all-black society" brought advantages unavailable to blacks raised in a "white-dominated society." As for education, under British rule it was the primary means for occupational advancement; hence, even today English-speaking West Indians prize degrees (*Time* 1985). Arguments such as these are here considered versions of the "cultural superiority" hypothesis.

The second rationale attributes West Indian advantage to the positive selectivity of immigration rather than to the superiority of culture. Positive selectivity refers to the idea that people who migrate are more capable than people who do not, both in terms of easily measured characteristics like education and in terms of less easily measured characteristics like ambition. C. J. Stevens (2004) puts it this way: "Those who took the time and possibly-extreme risk to leave their home countries and head to new countries naturally have more drive than people who are content to stay in their poor situations." Thus, not all West Indians are as hardworking as those who move, and movers are more industrious than stayers. This line of reasoning is here called the hypothesis of "positive selection."

The last rationale denies that there are perceptible differences in the behavior of the two groups of blacks. Rather, white Americans imagine that West Indians are superior to African Americans. Several reasons for this positive image have been proposed; for instance, one idea is that West Indians trigger associations with Britain, a nation that white Americans greatly admire. Another idea is that, in their dealings with whites, West Indians project themselves as "good blacks," in contrast to African Americans, who are "bad blacks." Whatever the mechanism, the resulting positive image motivates white American employers to hire and promote West Indians more frequently than their native black counterparts. This third explanation might be called the "white favoritism" hypothesis.

This volume was conceived in the spirit of finding out whether the economic disparities between African Americans and West Indians are primarily a consequence of culture, selectivity, or favoritism. In the pages that follow, these three explanations are subjected to a battery of statistical tests. The results support the conclusion that selectivity is the main cause of West Indian advantage; people who emigrate from the West Indies constitute a positively selected population. Thus, the answer to the question posed by the book's title is that West Indians are not a black success story but an *immigrant* success story.

Readers will gain a fuller appreciation of these implications if they understand how West Indians became embroiled in the affirmative action debate in the first place. The next section sketches this background, looking first at employment and then at education.

West Indians Enter the Debate over Affirmative Action

Although West Indians began arriving in the United States in the early 1900s, their presence did not spark debate until the 1970s. Three factors converged to put them in the public eye. The first was the effort to enforce affirmative action.

Employment

Although President Kennedy had already issued an executive order mandating affirmative action in 1961, not until 1970 did the Equal Economic Opportunity Commission (EEOC) require most firms doing business with the government to meet numerical goals and timetables (Rose 1994). The second factor was passage of the Immigration and Nationality Act of 1965 (Hart-Celler Act), which greatly increased the number of Caribbean nationals eligible to immigrate legally to the United States. The third factor was the introduction of statistical methods to measure discrimination, coupled with the availability of data on which to undertake those measurements. In 1965 the U.S. Department of Commerce introduced its first "public use sample" of a U.S. census, a set of computer tapes that any researcher could purchase and analyze. Ultimately, these developments converged. Thomas Sowell, an opponent of affirmative action, undertook a statistical analysis of the 1970 public use sample and concluded that West Indians had better job outcomes than African Americans. Interpreting this finding as evidence that whites did not discriminate against blacks, he argued for an end to affirmative action.

To appreciate how West Indian attainment could be put to such use, it is necessary to understand how experts define and measure discrimination. The Nobel Prize–winning economist Gary Becker (1971) has offered perhaps the most frequently cited definition: the existence of wage differentials in excess of what might be expected on the basis of productivity-related characteristics. However, little progress was made in measuring discrimination until the introduction of multivariate statistical models. One reason was that African Americans tended to be less educated than white Americans. In addition, blacks were overrepresented in the South, a region of limited economic opportunities, and they were less likely to be married (Farley and Allen 1987; Mare and Winship 1991). As a result, it was easy to refute charges of discrimination on the grounds that black applicants had weaker productivity-related characteristics than white.

In 1965 the sociologist Paul Siegel struck a blow at the tendency to blur qualifications and race by publishing a multivariate analysis of black-white earnings differences. According to Siegel, previous attempts at controlling for differences in the qualifications of the two races had not been possible because "prior to the publication of the 1960 Census of Population, simultaneous tabulations of income by education *and* occupation were not available" (Siegel 1965, 42, emphasis in original). Working algebraically from the published figures, Siegel defined "the cost of being a Negro" as the gap between the earnings of whites and nonwhites who had similar amounts of schooling, who worked in similar occupations, and who resided in or out of the South. Before he took these factors into account, nonwhites earned $2,852 less than whites. Siegel's analysis attributed 61.5 percent of this amount, or $1,755, to nonwhites' shorter schooling, poorer occupations, and propensity to live in the South. The remaining $1,097 he "interpreted as reflecting the money costs to nonwhites of *discrimination*, though they may to some extent be influenced by quality differences in education or occupation which are too fine to be discerned by our gross measures" (54, emphasis added).

This work has served as the model for numerous studies in what has come to be called the "residual method" of measuring discrimination (Smith 2003). Statistical techniques make blacks and whites "the same" on as many measurable job-related characteristics as possible, and the difference that remains between the two races is interpreted as a measure of discrimination.

There are, however, some obstacles to making people the same on as many measurable job-related characteristics as possible. One year of schooling for a white student may impart more skills than one year of schooling for a black student. This is what Siegel means by "quality differences . . . too fine to be discerned by our gross measures." Another problem is that many job-related characteristics are unmeasurable, or at least hard to measure. Most data sets do not contain measures of work attitudes, for instance. If black and white workers were "made the same" on work attitudes, would the cost of being black diminish? After all, the cost of being black declines when black and white workers are "made the same" on job experience or on region of residence. What would happen if black and white workers were made the same on work attitudes? Would this adjustment diminish the cost of being black? Would it raise the cost? If so, by how much?

As in the school quality example, the answer depends on how "work attitudes" relate to race. If race has nothing to do with work attitudes—if the proportion of lazy whites is the same as the proportion of lazy blacks—then adding indicators of these characteristics to analyses of economic outcomes would have no effect on the cost of being black.

If, on the other hand, a higher proportion of blacks than whites are lazy, then adding indicators of these characteristics would decrease the cost of being black.

The opinion that poor work attitudes are the main cause of African American economic disadvantage has a long history. Already in the late nineteenth century, black leaders like Booker T. Washington were advocating that blacks "soft-pedal" their grievances against whites and look to their own behavior as the cause of their low status (Meier 1963). Others, particularly W. E. B. Du Bois, disagreed, maintaining that white racism was the primary obstacle (Broderick and Meier 1965). And in the main, this opinion has prevailed, as can be seen by the perspective of civil rights leaders. But the civil rights movement focused primarily on racism in the political arena, not the economic arena. After the passage of the Civil Rights Act of 1964, the issue of discrimination in the workplace again rose to the fore.

Of the many legacies of the civil rights movement, affirmative action proved the most controversial. Statistical studies of the kind undertaken by Paul Siegel showed that blacks earned less than similarly qualified whites. Liberals maintained that discrimination was the cause of this shortfall. Conservatives maintained that the cause was a lack of diligence on the part of blacks; multivariate analyses, they argued, did not control for the difference in work ethic between the two races. Neither side brought new evidence to the debate until studies of West Indian "success" began to appear. That this discovery was a blow to the proponents of the discrimination argument and a windfall for the opponents of affirmative action the following remarks make clear.

In 1978, Thomas Sowell (1978b, 41–42) wrote: "West Indian Negroes in the United States have long had higher incomes, more education, higher occupational status, and proportionately far more business ownership than American Negroes. Both their fertility rates and their crime rates have been lower than those of native blacks—or native whites." Using 1970 census data on West Indians, he showed that they "earned 94 percent of the average income of Americans in general, while native blacks earned only 62 percent. Second-generation West Indians in the United States earned 15 percent more than the average American" (Sowell 1983, 107).

Sowell's writings had an impact not only because his figures were news to many Americans but also because his interpretations were news. Drawing a dichotomy between successful and unsuccessful minorities, he asserted that

the Jews, the Japanese-Americans and West Indian Negroes emphasized such traits as work, thrift, and education—more generally achievements involving planning and working for the future; implying the emotional control for self-denial in the present and emphasizing the logical and mundane over the emotional, the imaginative, and the heroic. The opposite characteristics can be seen among the Irish and the Negroes, where advancement has been achieved in emotional and imaginative areas, such as oratory, lyric literature, and music, and which have produced many dramatic "leaders and heroes." . . . A high value on immediate "fun," "excitement," and emotionalism has characterized the less successful minorities. For both the Irish and the Negroes, Saturday night acquired a great importance as time to release emotions in music, lively social activities, and fighting. (Sowell 1975, 130–31, 146)

What is the evidence for these disparate value systems? On what grounds does Sowell conclude that West Indians exhibited attitudes and behaviors that spurred success, while African Americans exhibited attitudes and behaviors that fostered failure? His empirical evidence is primarily an examination of outcomes. Arguing from effects to causes, Sowell reasons that *because* West Indians have been more prosperous than African Americans and *because* the Islanders have had fewer social problems than American blacks, the attitudes and behaviors of the two groups must differ in ways that have an impact on economic and social outcomes. To be sure, demonstrating that a set of work-related attitudes produces specific on-the-job behaviors, which in turn affect the size of economic rewards, is an extremely difficult task. Rather than attempt it, Sowell turns to history for the source of these attitudinal differences. As he reads the historical record, differences between the Caribbean slave experience and the American slave experience were sufficiently great to produce highly disparate value systems (Sowell 1975, 1978b, 1981, 1983).

Delaying until chapter 3 a synopsis of Sowell's interpretation of history, it is immediately apparent that there is a problem with his logic. Would not the attitudes and behaviors that blacks developed under slavery change after abolition? Clearly Sowell thinks they remained the same. Consider, for example, his description of the consequences of slavery in the United States: "Many generations of such dependency depressed initiative, so slaves developed foot-dragging, work-evading patterns that were to remain as a cultural legacy long after slavery itself had disappeared. Duplicity and theft were also pervasive patterns among antebellum slaves and these too remained long after slavery ended" (Sowell 1981, 187). Evidently, inertia was responsible for propagating values and behaviors that were no longer useful. Again, to quote Sowell, "History shows new skills being rather readily acquired in a few years, as compared to generations—or centuries—[being] required for attitude changes. Groups today plagued by absenteeism, tardiness, and a need for constant supervision at work or in school are typically descendants of people with the same habits a century or more ago" (Sowell 1981, 284).

In the context of the affirmative action debate, the implication of these remarks is clear. African American culture contributes more to black economic disadvantage than does white discrimination. In statistical jargon, adding indicators of work motivation to analyses of job outcomes would greatly reduce "the cost of being African American" but would have no effect on "the cost of being West Indian."

And what are the implications of this conclusion for social policy? The sociologist William Beer summarized its implications well in a 1986 *Wall Street Journal* editorial:

> People in favor of affirmative action assume that the low rate of upward mobility of black Americans is largely due to racial discrimination. West Indians are black, and they presumably must be targets of bigotry as much as black Americans. . . . Yet, the percentages of blacks from the Caribbean who are successful in business and the professions surpass those of many white ethnic groups, and the group's jobless rate is lower than the national average. Its stunning success contradicts the claim that the dismal situation of black Americans is largely due to racial discrimination, thus calling into question the whole rationale for preferential treatment. (Beer 1986, 12)

In this way did West Indian prosperity become proof that cultural deficiencies, not job discrimination, lay behind African American disadvantage.

Higher Education

Although university administrators began implementing affirmative action in the 1970s, West Indians had no place in early discussions about the policy's implications for education. The reason is probably that, until recently, relatively few West Indians were of college age. In those early years, admissions committees devised their own strategies for maximizing student body diversity. The medical school at the University of California at Davis reserved sixteen of its one hundred spaces for members of targeted groups. When it twice rejected Allan Bakke but admitted students of color with lower test scores and grades, Bakke sued. The consequence of his suit, which reached the Supreme Court in 1978, was that explicit quotas became illegal. At the same time, the Court agreed that some steps could be taken to enhance the representation of disadvantaged groups in institutions of higher learning.

In the years that followed, many admissions committees utilized a points system. They gave additional points to members of targeted groups, as well as to persons from particular geographic areas, children of alums, musicians, athletes, and so on. Undergraduates applying to the University of Michigan received 20 additional points out of a maximum of 150 if they belonged to a targeted group. The university's law school, however, engaged in a "whole file review": each applicant was evaluated on the basis of all the information available. In addition, the law school aimed to produce not a fixed percentage but a "critical mass" of underrepresented minorities. In June 2003, the Supreme Court heard suits against both these policies. In the end, it struck down the numerically driven undergraduate policy by a vote of six-to-three, but endorsed the subjective approach developed at the law school five-to-four. In defending the latter, the majority opinion supported affirmative action on the ground that a diverse student body enhanced learning (Harvard Civil Rights Project 2003).

Interestingly, West Indian achievement played no part in the Michigan lawsuit, perhaps because colleges and universities had little information about the heritage of their black students.[2] Nonetheless, research had been accumulating that showed that heritage has consequences. An inquiry into the ancestries of Harvard undergraduates revealed that only 38 percent of a sample of black students identified as African American. Twenty-three percent described themselves as Caribbean (Haynie 2002). Others identified as African, as biracial, or as bi-ethnic. A more rigorous study, this one of blacks at twenty-eight elite colleges and universities, revealed that black immigrants and their offspring accounted for just over 40 percent of these schools' black students (Massey et al. 2003). This is more than four times their proportion in the black population (*Harvard Magazine* 2004).

The *New York Times* reported these findings in June 2004, just after they were presented at a reunion of Harvard's African American alumni. A storm of controversy followed, primarily because these discoveries raised the question: "Who Really Benefits from Colleges' Affirmative Action?" (McNamee 2004). Were the children of black immigrants benefiting at the expense of the children of African Americans (Onwuachi-Willig, forthcoming)? Opponents of affirmative action, such as University of California at Berkeley regent Ward Connerly, interpreted the Harvard finding as further evidence that low-income native blacks were not benefiting (Johnson 2005). Even supporters of affirmative action agreed that the people for whom the policy was originally intended were being neglected. For example, the sociologist

Philip Kasinitz commented that the Harvard findings were "a victory of diversity over justice," adding that "the traditional mission of affirmative action seems to be eclipsed" (quoted in Kline 2005). Others used it as a basis for accusing black middle class parents of neglecting their children's intellectual development (Kline 2005). One of the strongest of these indictments came from Henry Louis Gates, chair of Harvard's African and African American Studies Department. "We need to learn what the immigrants' kids have so we can bottle it and sell it," he said, "because many members of the African-American community, particularly among the chronically poor, have lost that sense of purpose and values which produced our generation" (quoted in Rimer and Arenson 2004). So here again West Indian immigrants were identified as a model for African Americans to follow.

The Organization of the Book

Chapter 2 presents some basic information about West Indian immigrants, past and present, as well as some important findings: West Indian immigrants have stronger measurable job-related characteristics than West Indians who remain in the Caribbean; West Indian immigrants have stronger measurable job-related characteristics than African Americans; and when West Indians are assigned the (weaker) job-related characteristics of African Americans, the immigrants still have stronger economic outcomes than African Americans. Chapter 3 offers a detailed discussion of the three most popular explanations for these findings—cultural superiority, positive selectivity, and white favoritism—with a focus on the precise causal mechanisms associated with each explanation. In some cases, there is more than one such mechanism. To help conceptualize the relationships among them, the chapter concludes with a path diagram that depicts the causal linkages among all three explanations.

Chapters 4, 5, and 6 are each devoted to testing one of the three hypotheses. Selectivity is considered first, then culture, and finally white favoritism. Each chapter begins by summarizing previous research relevant to the hypothesis. In the case of selectivity, most of that research is statistical; in the case of culture, it is predominantly historical; in the case of white favoritism, it is both ethnographic and statistical. Each of the hypotheses is then subjected to a battery of statistical tests. Most of these tests utilize the public use samples of the last four U.S. decennial censuses, but a few draw on data from other destinations that West Indian immigrants have chosen: Canada, Britain, and the Netherlands. To the extent that statistical analyses of census data can provide an answer to the question of why West Indians have better economic outcomes than African Americans, the results of these tests support selectivity.

Chapter 7, the final chapter, assesses the implications of these findings. It acknowledges the limitations of statistical analyses and concedes that other research strategies might identify additional sources of West Indian advantage. The discussion then turns to the meaning of the statistical results for African Americans, for West Indians, and for affirmative action. The results also have some general implications, particularly for immigration policy. The chapter closes by proposing that research on black immigrants from sub-Saharan Africa would constitute a useful supplement to the present undertaking.

At the end of the book is a methodological appendix that provides details about data quality and model construction. Readers who want to understand the technical challenges associated with the statistical analyses will find this section useful.

• Chapter 2 •

Documenting the Difference Between West Indians and African Americans

THIS chapter examines the labor market outcomes of West Indian immigrants, especially those who arrived before 1925 (the first wave) and those who arrived after 1965 (the third wave). Inadequate numbers preclude an in-depth analysis of the second wave. The chapter opens with a comparison of the measurable job-related characteristics of first-wave West Indian movers versus those who stayed home. In all these comparisons, movers emerge as stronger than stayers, which means that the former are positively selected. Yet another question is whether West Indian movers have stronger measurable job-related characteristics than African Americans. With respect to first-wavers, a comparison of West Indians and African Americans uncovers few differences, but extending the exercise to third-wavers reveals a substantial West Indian advantage.

Four indicators of labor market outcomes are examined: labor force participation, unemployment, occupational prestige, and earnings. The first-wave comparisons yield very few statistically significant differences between the two groups of blacks. Third-wave comparisons, however, reveal several significant West Indian advantages. The West Indian strength on measurable job-related characteristics provides one explanation for West Indians' superior labor market outcomes. But strong measurable job-related characteristics do not fully explain the advantageous labor market outcomes of the third wave. When third-wave West Indians are assigned the (somewhat weaker) job-related characteristics of African Americans, the size of the West Indian advantage is reduced but not eliminated.

Although this kind of labor market advantage has been noted before, no previous effort has compared the two groups of blacks, both male and female, on four economic outcomes, across four decennial censuses (Butcher 1994; Chiswick 1979; Kalmijn 1996; Simmons 2003). This compelling advantage motivates the remainder of this book, which seeks to find the reason for it.

The First Wave of West Indian Immigrants

Ever since 1834, when Britain emancipated the black slaves in its Caribbean colonies, West Indians have been "on the move." Better opportunities lured many from regions of population surplus and underemployment, such as Barbados, to regions of population shortage and job opportunity, such as Trinidad. The most labor-intensive nineteenth-century project was the French attempt to build a canal across the Isthmus of Panama. Some fifty thousand West Indian workers contributed to this 1880s undertaking, which eventually failed.

Arrival in the United States

In 1898 the United States became the dominant power in the Caribbean by defeating Spain in the Spanish-American War. Two consequences of this victory paved the way for British West Indian immigration to the United States. The first was the development of a new export: bananas. Jamaica was a key producer, though Central America also provided substantial acreage. These investments produced sea links on which first freight and later passengers traveled. By the early twentieth century, "banana boats" were bringing tourists to the Caribbean and emigrants to the Northeast, especially New York (Palmer 1995).

The second development was America's decision to build a canal connecting the Pacific and the Caribbean. At first, a route through Colombia was considered, but in 1903 the American government decided on a route through Panama. Purchasing the materials that the French had abandoned there, the Isthmian Canal Commission developed a construction plan that took more than a decade to complete. With respect to labor, the plan was unambiguous. Caribbean workers were preferred. Their advantages were several:

> Firstly, they were nearby. . . . Secondly, the proverbial willingness of Barbadians and Jamaicans to emigrate in search of remunerative employment was well known. Thirdly, . . . it cost the commission a mere $10 a

head to import labourers. . . . Fourthly, . . . the canal companies knew
that they could pay West Indians low wages without incurring the wrath
of a political power. (Newton 1987, 109)

The single most important source of Panama labor was Barbados,
where a recruiting station was established in 1905. Successful candidates were promised round-trip passage, five hundred days of work at
$1.10 daily, medical care, and quarters without furniture (Richardson
1985). What they got was considerably less: dangerous working conditions, unsanitary tenement housing, and an introduction to Jim Crow.
Nevertheless, the desire for "Panama money" was so great that thousands of West Indians headed for the Canal Zone at their own expense.
Before the project was over, about forty-five thousand Barbadians had
arrived as recruits; another one hundred thousand came on their own
(Conniff 1985).

With ocean transport connecting Panama, the West Indies, and the
United States, the infrastructure for mass migration was in place.
Scholars disagree on what percentage of West Indian arrivals in the
United States had previous experience working in Panama. Some
claim that "the level of wages enjoyed by workers in the Canal Zone
. . . was much higher than the rate to which they were accustomed. . . .
Consequently few were content to return to the island on the completion of the work at Panama but went further afield" (Roberts 1957,
136). Dissenters point out that a minority of canal laborers had the resources to afford a trip to the United States. The type of West Indian
most likely to head for the United States, they argue, had good manual
or mental skills and "usually held high expectations that a wider range
of life-improving possibilities would be available" (Watkins-Owens
1996, 18).

Figure 2.1 plots the annual number of blacks who, according to the
U.S. Immigration Commission, arrived from anywhere in the West Indies between 1900 and 1930. Unfortunately, the commission's figures
do not take birthplace into account. They include immigrants from
Spanish-, French-, and English-speaking areas; they do not distinguish
women from men.[1] From a few hundred brave pioneers in 1900, these
newcomers increased to more than ten thousand in 1924, the year before the Johnson-Reed Act massively curtailed entry from abroad. The
figure shows a modest peak in 1914, consonant with the idea that the
United States replaced the Panama Canal as a destination once the wa-
terway was completed. But the reason why the Johnson-Reed Act
brought about a radical drop in West Indian immigration is unclear. To
be sure, the 1924 law was the last and most punitive of the immigration restrictions passed in the nativist atmosphere of the post-World

Figure 2.1   Cuban and West Indian Black Immigrants Arriving in the United States, by Year

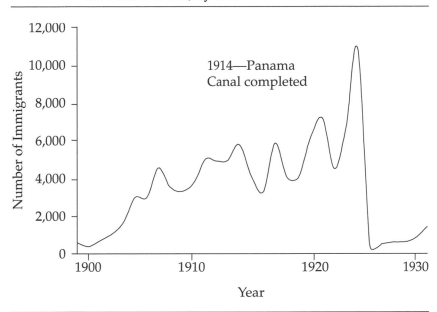

Source: U.S. Department of Labor (1900–1933).

War I era. To regulate the number of arrivals from different places, immigration officials assigned each sending country a quota. In the British case, the quota was extremely generous; indeed, many slots went unfilled.[2] Because the 1924 law grouped Western Hemisphere colonies with their respective mother countries, West Indians should have qualified for entry as British subjects. But as figure 2.1 clearly reveals, they did not.

Another 1924 innovation might explain the hiatus. In order to immigrate, an applicant had to obtain a visa from an American consulate. Roger Daniels (2004, 53) writes: "There is no thorough study of how the consular service actually regulated the issuance of visas, but it is quite clear that officials such as Wilber J. Carr, who directed the consular service from 1909 to 1937, saw their roles to be gatekeepers and that Carr and many of his subordinates were nativists. There is also a great deal of anecdotal evidence that individual consuls often used their authority to impose their own agendas." In short, if consul officials did not wish to grant visas to black West Indians, there was no authority that would require them to do so.

Who Left: The Skills of the First Wave

The great majority of English-speaking West Indians who arrived before the Depression settled in New York City. Some historians claim that the average newcomer from the West Indies was a typical canal worker—that is, "a black male, usually an unskilled agricultural labourer or town dweller between 20 and 35 years of age, and with little formal education" (Newton 1987, 106). Others contend that a "high proportion of their number . . . held, in their country of origin, professional, white-collar and skilled jobs"; in other words, they were "positively selected" (James 2001, 413).

Schooling is a useful indicator of selectivity. If movers are more educated than stayers, they are positively selected on this characteristic. Unfortunately, until 1940 the main source of educational data in America, the U.S. census, inquired about literacy, not about schooling. According to Winston James (2001), illiteracy rates averaged 19 percent for West Indians entering between 1899 and 1910, 16.7 percent for those entering from 1911 to 1917, and 1.2 percent for those disembarking during the 1918 to 1924 period.[3] These figures leave no doubt that West Indian immigrants to the United States were more literate than the compatriots they left behind. For instance, the Jamaican government reported that, in 1911, 47.2 percent of its citizens who were five or more years of age could read and write.

Additional evidence of the positive selection of the first wave can be found by comparing the premigration occupations of arriving West Indian immigrants with the occupations of Jamaicans as a whole. Table 2.1 presents the numbers, which are arranged to facilitate comparison with the Jamaican censuses of 1911 and of 1921. Differences between the American and Jamaican occupational categories are sufficiently great that only the professional and commercial categories are reasonably comparable. However, this restriction in no way diminishes the conclusion that departing immigrants were disproportionately from the upper tiers of Jamaica's occupational structure. In 1921, 4.6 percent of Jamaicans held commercial jobs like manager or bookkeeper, while 11.3 percent of West Indians arriving in the United States between 1916 and 1925 reported holding such jobs.

Positive selection on literacy and premigration occupation, of course, does not mean that first-wave West Indian immigrants had stronger job-related skills than African Americans. The demographer Everett Lee (1966) predicts that the skills of movers fall somewhere between the skills of persons at origin and the skills of persons at destination. But which persons at destination? Given the racial barri-

Table 2.1   Occupational Distribution of Foreign-Born Blacks in the
United States and Jamaica, 1901 to 1925

Country and Year(s)	Professions	Commerce	Industry	Other[a]	Number
United States, 1901 to 1915	2.9	8.5	28.0	60.6	50,677[b]
Jamaica, 1911	2.2	4.8	17.6	75.3	410,900
United States, 1916 to 1925	4.0	11.3	34.1	50.6	48,601[c]
Jamaica, 1921	2.6	4.6	16.6	76.2	443,900

Source: Roberts (1957); Reid (1939/1969).
[a] This category consists mainly of unskilled labor: agricultural workers, servants, and so on.
[b] The West Indies were the previous residence of 75.1 percent of foreign-born blacks in the United States during this period.
[c] The West Indies were the previous residence of 76.6 percent of foreign-born blacks in the United States during this period.

ers of the period, African Americans would seem the appropriate benchmark. But which African Americans? According to calculations based on public use samples of the U.S. census available from the Integrated Public Use Microdata Series (IPUMS), between 1920 and 1930 southern-born blacks increased from 57.6 percent of New York's African American population to 74.5 percent (Ruggles et al. 2004). Since, according to Lee's theory, southern black migrants should have been less skilled than northern-born blacks, any calculations of job-related skills should distinguish the birthplaces of native-born blacks.

With respect to literacy, calculations based on IPUMS data show that, in 1920 and again in 1930, over 97 percent of New York's black adults were able to read and write. Nor were there any statistically significant differences among northern-born, southern-born, and Caribbean-born blacks. In 1940, when figures on schooling became available, two significant distinctions emerged. Foreign-born West Indian men had significantly more education than southern-born black men (7.9 years versus 7.0 years), and foreign-born West Indian women had significantly less education than northern-born black women (7.6 years versus 8.7 years). All other comparisons were insignificant. Taken together, these numbers say that the average West Indian adult was a little less educated than his or her northern-born black counterpart and a little more educated than his or her southern-born counterpart.[4] These differences are in the direction that Everett Lee would predict but small in magnitude.

Unfortunately, a comparison of the occupations of West Indians and African Americans in New York, unlike a comparison of the occupations of West Indian movers and stayers, cannot provide insight into the selectivity of Caribbean migration. Postmigration occupation is affected not only by factors that operate at origin, like selectivity and schooling, but also by factors that operate at destination, like racism and culture shock. Postmigration occupation is an example of a labor market outcome and hence is considered in the next section.

The Labor Market Outcomes of the First Wave

A substantial literature chronicles West Indians' adaptation to Harlem and Harlem's adaptation to West Indians. In terms of labor market outcomes, most contemporary observers describe West Indians as faring better than African Americans, though both groups of blacks encountered racism at every turn. One of the earliest attempts to include the immigrants is George Haynes's 1912 study *The Negro at Work in New York City* (1912/1968). Counting entries in the Negro Business Directory of 1909, Haynes (1912/1968, 58) concludes that one-fifth of the business owners were West Indians, though the immigrants made up only about 10 percent of the population. A footnote adds: "Among 94 Negro men in New York in 1907 who claimed to know a trade, 57 or 61% were West Indian." A Columbia University master's thesis (Moore 1913, 26) in the same period observes: "It is frequently said that the West Indian is the only Negro that can withstand the competition of the Jew. There is no doubt that he is successful in small business." Yet again, W. A. Domingo (1925, 649), a well-known Jamaica-born journalist and political activist, wrote: "West Indian representation in the skilled trades is relatively large; this is also true of the professions, especially medicine and dentistry. Like the Jew, they are forever launching out in business, and such retail businesses as are in the hands of Negroes in Harlem are largely in the control of the foreign-born."

Amazingly, there is little empirical support for the claim that West Indians were more entrepreneurial than African Americans. As part of a larger study, the U.S. Immigration Commission obtained information on the 1908 employment situations of household heads in one of New York's poorest neighborhoods. "The occupations of 166 African American men were identified; six were proprietors. The occupations of 110 foreign-born black men were identified; none were proprietors"

(Model 2001, 56–57). Calculations based on the New York State censuses of 1905, 1915, and 1925 yield self-employment rates of under 2 percent for both groups of black males (Gutman 1976; Holder 1998). Calculations based on the IPUMS for the New York metropolitan area produce the following percentages of self-employed West Indian men: 5.1 percent in 1920, 4.6 percent in 1930, and 9.1 percent in 1940. The analogous percentages for African American men are 6.0 percent in 1920, 4.3 percent in 1930, and 3.9 percent in 1940. Differences between the northern- and southern-born are trivial. Thus, historical narratives to the contrary, only the 1940 census describes West Indians as significantly more entrepreneurial than African Americans. To be sure, narratives of the late 1930s do celebrate West Indian entrepreneurship (McKay 1940/1968; Ottley and Weatherby 1967; Reid 1939/1969). Yet by 1970 the self-employment rate was down to 3.9 percent. Thus, self-employment was a significant West Indian activity for only a brief period of time. Therefore, it is not a labor market outcome of interest to this study.

What about West Indian–African American differences on other labor market outcomes? This question is addressed here using IPUMS data for New York in 1920, 1930, and 1940. The 1920 census provides only two outcomes: labor force participation and occupational prestige. Later years add unemployment rates and earnings.[5] This book relies on ratios to convey whether or not West Indians do better than African Americans on a selected labor market outcome. The first step is to calculate the West Indian average and the African American average.[6] Then the West Indian average is divided by the African American average. The resulting quotient or ratio summarizes the performance of West Indians relative to African Americans. A ratio of 1.00 indicates that the two groups' averages are the same; a ratio smaller than 1.00 indicates that the West Indian average is smaller than the African American average; a ratio greater than 1.00 indicates that the West Indian average is larger. Because low unemployment is desirable, on unemployment a number below 1.00 implies a West Indian advantage.

The results appear in table 2.2. Some ratios are quite close to 1.00, and some diverge considerably. For instance, in 1920 the labor force participation rate of West Indian women was 16 percent higher than the rate for African American women. Does this indicate a West Indian advantage? Not necessarily. Because these numbers are based on samples, they may not be identical to the numbers that would be produced if the calculations included all of New York's West Indians and African Americans. Luckily, statisticians have a solution to this problem: they test for statistical significance. As a rule, if statistical tests show that the potential error of the sample-based result is no more than 5 percent,

Table 2.2   Ratio of Foreign-Born West Indian Observed Means to African American Observed Means on Four Economic Indicators: Residents of the New York Metropolitan Area

Year	Labor Force Participation		Unemployment		Occupational Prestige		Annual Earnings	
	Men	Women	Men	Women	Men	Women	Men	Women
1920	1.03	1.16	n.a.	n.a.	1.03	0.95	n.a.	n.a.
1930	1.02	0.94	0.85	0.96	1.03	0.97	n.a.	n.a.
1940	1.01	0.77*	0.79	1.33	1.31*	0.84	1.13	0.96

Source: Author's calculations based on the 1920, 1930, and 1940 Integrated Public Use Microdata Series (IPUMS).
* Statistically significant at the .05 level or better.

scholars accept the sample-based result as descriptive of the population it represents. In this book, asterisks appear when a statistically significant difference between West Indians and African Americans is found.

To continue with the example of women's labor force participation, there is no asterisk affixed to the ratio 1.16. This means that the West Indian advantage may be due to chance. Interestingly, in 1940 the labor force participation of West Indian women was 23 percent lower than African American women's. Since this ratio carries an asterisk (.77*), scholars are reasonably confident that there is a real difference between the two groups. Only one other ratio meets this criterion: in 1940 the occupational prestige of West Indian men was 31 percent higher than that of African American men.

There are at least two reasons why only two ratios are significant for this first-wave analysis. First, in any given year the number of foreign-born West Indians is small—one hundred to two hundred in most cells. The smaller the sample, the harder it is to attain statistical significance. Second, the parameter of interest is the ratio of two means. The more these means vary, the greater the likelihood that there is a significant difference between them. Because racism was so virulent in this early period, the variation around a black mean is comparatively modest. To take men's occupational prestige as an example, in 1930 the black variance was 92.0, while the white variance was 151.0. In short, economic differences among blacks were so small that the effect of birthplace is barely perceptible.

Supplementary analyses (not shown) distinguished between blacks born in the North and the South. This approach unearthed four additional contrasts that attained significance: three of them favored West Indians over northern-born blacks; one favored southern-born blacks over West Indians. Of course, the numbers underlying these results are small, but the trend suggests that New York's black migrants, both southern and Caribbean, surpassed the city's black natives more often than the reverse. This is consonant with the hypothesis that migrants are a "positively selected population." In other words, one reason there are few significant differences between first-wave West Indian immigrants and African Americans is that a high proportion of the latter were positively selected migrants from the South.

Since this analysis does not support the well-known "fact" that first-wave West Indians fared better economically than African Americans, why do so many accounts of black New York remark on it? One reason might be visibility. The owner of Antillean Realty, the copublisher of the *Amsterdam News*, the originator of the numbers "racket," and the founder of a funeral parlor chain were all West Indian (Anderson 1981). West Indians were extremely active in left wing politics, black nationalist organizations, union drives, and so on (James 1998; Watkins-Owens 1996). Several were well-known street orators; many created and contributed to the myriad of political and literary journals of the period. Without their prose, poetry, and plays, the Harlem Renaissance might not have occurred (Parascandola 2005). This prominence may explain why so many accounts depict West Indians favorably even though statistics do not.

Alternatively, Violet Johnson (2006, 3–4) proposes, the prominence of Harlem's West Indians may have been an illusion fostered by immigrant leaders themselves. They sought to "amplify" their strengths in order "to establish their legitimacy as the brokers of Black advancement" rather than cede that role to their native-born counterparts. Noting that this kind of self-promotion did not "encourage a great deal of scholarly objectivity," Johnson might well expect a gap between the statistical and the rhetorical reality.

The Second Wave of West Indian Immigrants

The year 1924 marks the official closing date for membership in the first wave. A reasonable definition of the second wave is the wave of immigrants who arrived after 1924, when the Johnson-Reed Act took effect, and before 1967, when the Hart-Celler Act took effect. Approximately 84,000 people fit this description (U.S. Department of Labor 1932; U.S. Immigration and Naturalization Service, *Annual Report*, 1968; U.S. Immigration and Naturalization Service, *Statistical Yearbook*,

1999). Most were English-speakers, most arrived after 1945, and one-third of them arrived after 1961. An unknown proportion were return migrants—West Indians who had journeyed previously to "the States," gone home, and ventured back again.

Several factors combined to reduce the size of the second wave. The unwelcoming atmosphere symbolized by the 1924 law was reinforced first by the Great Depression, which motivated many to return home, and then by the Second World War, which motivated many to stay there. However, when the postwar economic boom did little to enhance Caribbean living conditions, West Indians were again on the move. That the United States did not immediately emerge as a destination for English-speakers was mainly due to the passage of a second punitive immigration law, the McCarran-Walter Act (1952). This legislation, passed over President Truman's veto, set an annual quota of one hundred from each colony in the Western Hemisphere. Spouses and children of citizens were exempt from the quota, as were tourists, students, and temporary farm workers. Doubtless some students and farm workers entered, then dropped from view after their visas expired. But mass migration was out of the question. A second, less compelling reason the United States did not immediately emerge as a destination is that Britain did. In 1948 Britain passed the Nationality Act, under which residents of the Commonwealth could enter Britain at will. By 1951 over seventeen thousand West Indian blacks had taken advantage of this offer (Peach 1996). Yet Britain's welcome was brief. By 1962 some admission restrictions were in place; by 1969, 95 percent of Jamaican immigrants were dependents of previous arrivals (National Planning Agency 1969). The number of Caribbean-born persons counted in the British census peaked in 1971 (304,070); further population growth resulted from the emergence of a second generation, not from the expansion of a first (Peach 1996).

The Third Wave of West Indian Immigrants

While England was becoming more restrictive, the United States was becoming less so. Already in his 1959 book *A Nation of Immigrants*, John F. Kennedy had expressed dissatisfaction with the ethnocentric bias of American immigration policy. Six years later, Lyndon Johnson signed the Immigration and Nationality Act of 1965, commonly known as the Hart-Celler Act. This legislation scrapped the provisions that favored immigrants from Britain and northern Europe in favor of generous, hemisphere-wide quotas. As soon as the Western Hemisphere quota went into effect in 1967, America became a magnet for Caribbean movers. To be sure, to British colonials the United States lacked some of England's allure. Nevertheless, for most people contemplating a move, the United States was the first-choice destination (Reitz 1998).

Arrival in the United States

Between 1968 and 1976, when the law again changed, Western Hemisphere countries could send a total of 120,000 persons per annum; Eastern Hemisphere countries could send 170,000. One difference between the two hemispheres was that no single Eastern Hemisphere country could send more than 20,000 quota immigrants, whereas no Western Hemisphere country faced a ceiling of this kind. The motive for the distinction was to facilitate the entry of Mexicans, large numbers of whom had previously entered under the Bracero Program, which expired at the end of 1964. A second difference was that Eastern Hemisphere applicants were subject to a new preference system. It was less skill-based and more kin-based than the preference system mandated by McCarran-Walter. Under Hart-Celler, 20 percent (later 30 percent) of quota visas were reserved for persons with particular skills; those entering under these preferences had to be certified by the U.S. Department of Labor. The remaining 80 percent (later 70 percent) of quota visas were reserved for relatives of American citizens or relatives of permanent residents of the United States (Ngai 2004).[7]

At first glance, West Indians' exemption from preferences seems an advantage. Yet, if they were not parents, spouses, or children of American citizens, if they did not qualify for a preference, and if they were not refugees, Hart-Celler required that they obtain certification from the U.S. Department Labor (Gudeon 1986). Two occupations in which it was easy to obtain labor certification were nurse and domestic servant (Colen 1990; Palmer 1974). Partly for this reason, 61 percent of prime-age West Indians counted in the 1970 census were female.

An idea of the magnitude of the current wave of West Indian immigration can be obtained from the annual reports of the U.S. Immigration and Naturalization Service (INS), though these figures have several limitations. As official enumerations, they only recognize legal immigrants. In addition, the year in which an individual mover is officially admitted is the year when he or she became a legal permanent resident. Increasingly, this is not the year in which he or she initially arrived because some "aliens already living in the United States, including certain undocumented immigrants, temporary workers, foreign students, and refugees, file an application for adjustment of status (to legal permanent residence) with I.N.S." (U.S. Immigration and Naturalization Service 1999, 14). Finally, INS tabulations ignore race.

Figure 2.2 estimates black immigration from the West Indies as a

Figure 2.2   Annual Black West Indian Immigration to the United States, 1967 to 2004

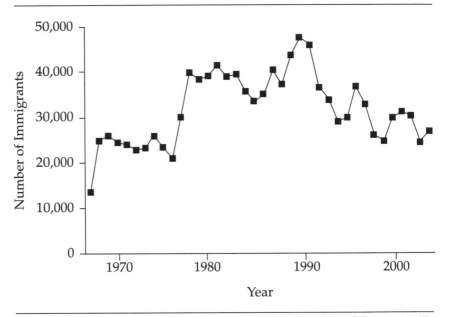

Source: U.S. Immigration and Naturalization Service, *Annual Report* (1967–1977); U.S. Immigration and Naturalization Service, *Statistical Yearbook* (1978–2001); U.S. Department of Homeland Security (2002–2004).

whole from 1967 to 2004. The totals have been adjusted to exclude the significant proportion of emigrants from Trinidad and Guyana who were of Indian rather than African descent.[8] Clearly, the implementation of Hart-Celler produced a large increase in West Indian arrivals. At no point have fewer than twenty thousand entered annually.

In 1976 Congress passed further amendments to the Hart-Celler Act in order to reduce immigration from Mexico. This was achieved by extending to the Western Hemisphere the limit of twenty thousand persons per country that had previously applied only to the Eastern Hemisphere. As a result of this change, relatively more visas went to Caribbean nations than before. In addition, Western Hemisphere applicants now joined Eastern Hemisphere applicants in being subject to the preference system. Because West Indians had now been resident in the United States long enough to take advantage of kinship preferences, their numbers increased. Indeed, figure 2.2 shows not only little subsequent decline but a substantial bulge between 1989 and 1991. This bulge is the result of the 1986 Immigration Reform and Control Act

(IRCA), which granted amnesty to undocumented immigrants who could demonstrate continuous residence in the United States since 1982. From the point of view of the INS, these were new entrants. In fact, however, IRCA beneficiaries had lived in the United States for at least four years, and many considerably longer. Thus, the numbers recorded as arriving between 1989 and 1991 are inflated (Daniels 2004; Vialet 1997). Also noticeable is a modest but perceptible decline after 1991. This might seem surprising since the Immigration Act of 1990 increased admissions by creating several new visa categories. But relatively few West Indians have entered under these categories. A more compelling reason to be skeptical about the post-1991 decline is that INS counts exclude the undocumented, a group that represents an increasing proportion of the West Indian population (Costanzo et al. 2001).

Additional insights into the composition of America's West Indian population can be gained by distinguishing among sending countries. Four nations send over three-quarters of all English-speaking West Indians: Jamaica, Guyana, Trinidad and Tobago, and Barbados. Figure 2.3 shows the number of legal immigrants from each of these four countries between 1968 and 2004. Jamaica, the largest English-speaking Caribbean country, sends far and away the most, while Barbados sends the least. Interestingly, during both the 1960s and the late 1990s, Trinidad and Tobago led Guyana, but in the 1970s and 1980s Guyana sent the larger number. These are, of course, raw figures. Were they adjusted for the size of the sending country's population, the rankings would be different. Guyana would rank first. Between 1967 and 2000, of every 10,000 black Guyanese nationals, an average of 121 moved annually to the United States, compared to 75 from Jamaica, 69 from Trinidad, and 64 from Barbados.[9]

Another noteworthy feature of West Indian immigration is that slightly more women than men have arrived. Analysis of the census data available to this study indicates that, since 1970, about 55 percent of prime-age West Indian immigrants have been female. Moreover, attention to the gender ratio by arrival year (not shown) indicates that this imbalance is not only a result of the surfeit of women who arrived in the late 1960s in response to immigration laws favoring nurses and household servants, but that 54 percent of those arriving in 1999 were women. The gender imbalance is in part a consequence of the matrifocal family structure in the West Indies. In meeting their family's needs, women count less on men than on themselves and their female kin (Barrow 1986). But the gender imbalance is also a consequence of the American labor market, which has long welcomed black female (im)migrants more enthusiastically than their male counterparts.[10]

Figure 2.3   Black Immigration to the United States from Barbados, Jamaica, Trinidad and Tobago, and Guyana, 1967 to 2000

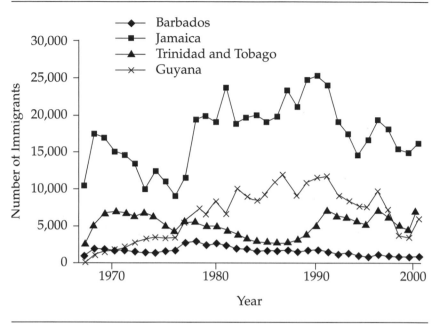

Source: U.S. Immigration and Naturalization Service, Annual Report (1965–1977); U.S. Immigration and Naturalization Service, Statistical Yearbook (1978–2000).

Who Left: The Skills of the Third Wave

Totaling the official figure for the years 1967 to 2004, some 1.2 million West Indian blacks immigrated legally to the United States. Doubtless, several thousand more arrived clandestinely. Were these third-wave movers, like their first-wave counterparts, positively selected on measurable job-related skills like literacy or job outcomes like premigration occupation? To explore this important issue, this study compares West Indian movers and stayers in terms of years of education and premigration occupation. The comparison of education uses U.S. census data to describe West Indian immigrants and Robert Barro and Jong Lee's (1996) cross-national data on education to describe residents of the four major West Indian sending countries: Barbados, Jamaica, Trinidad, and Guyana.

Figure 2.4 graphs the ratio of the mean years of schooling of West

Figure 2.4   Ratio of Movers' Education to Stayers' Education, Four Caribbean Countries, 1966 to 1995

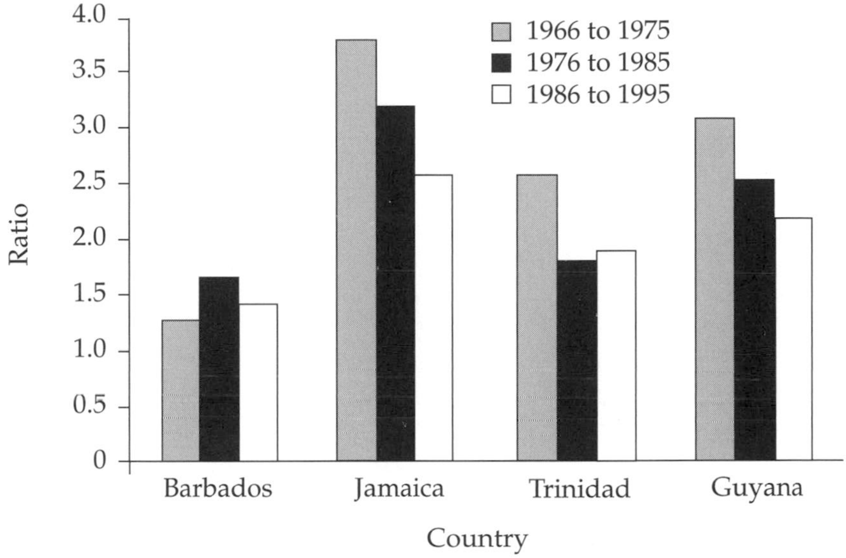

Source: Author's calculations based on the 1970 to 2000 Public Use Microdata Series (PUMS); Barro and Lee (1996).

Indians age twenty-five to sixty-four who immigrated to the United States after age twenty-four and the mean years of schooling of all West Indian residents over age twenty-four. Ratios above 1.0 indicate that movers have more education than residents; ratios below 1.0 indicate that movers have less education than residents. All ratios are above 1.0, which is to say that positive selection obtains across the board.

But there are variations in the size of the ratio within and among countries. With respect to within-country variations, it is plausible to expect "early birds" to be more educated than "latecomers."[11] One reason is that pioneers have fewer compatriots to cushion their adjustment. Another is that United States immigration officials accorded more weight to schooling in the 1967 to 1976 period than they did thereafter.[12] Jamaica, Guyana, and to a lesser extent Trinidad fit this expectation, but not Barbados. There those who arrived in the middle years (1976 to 1985) were more positively selected than their predecessors or followers. One possibility is weakness in the data. Barbados is the only country in figure 2.4 for which Barro and Lee (1996) report lower average schooling in 1980 than before or after. If this figure is incorrect, so is the spike it produces.

Indeed, even if the data are correct, comparing the mean years of schooling of movers and stayers is a simplistic strategy. As Cynthia Feliciano (2006) has shown, a sophisticated comparison would control for age and would compare educational distributions rather than means. Implementing this approach on a sample of thirty-two places, she finds that arrivals from everywhere save Puerto Rico were more educated than those they left behind. Jamaica, the only English-speaking West Indian nation in her study, was tied with Japan as the sixth most educationally selective sending country in the sample.

Another way of evaluating the hypothesis of positive selection is to compare the occupational distributions of movers and stayers. Such a comparison is possible because the Immigration and Naturalization Service publishes information on the occupational categories of new admissions annually, and Caribbean governments publish such information occasionally. INS publications distinguish eight major occupational groups, plus a "no occupation" category that includes "homemakers, students, unemployed or retired persons, and others not reporting or with an unknown occupation" (U.S. Immigration and Naturalization Service 1999, 69).

To determine the direction and degree of selectivity, the percentage of emigrants who held upper-white-collar posts (professional, technical, executive, or managerial occupations) prior to admission is compared to the percentage of residents holding such jobs in their respective homelands. Two sets of figures are offered. Both use the INS figures described earlier, but the first uses continuous data published by the Jamaican government to describe residents, while the second uses decennial census data to characterize residents of Barbados, Jamaica, Trinidad, and Guyana.

Figure 2.5 graphs the ratio of upper-white-collar emigrants to upper-white-collar residents for Jamaica from 1967 to 2001. In 1967, 3.2 white collar workers left Jamaica for every 1 who stayed; as the years passed, the ratio slowly declined, then spiked sharply in the late 1970s. The spike coincided with the introduction of democratic socialism in Jamaica 1977. According to Ramón Grosfoguel (2003), the U.S. government responded to this development with tactics that heightened insecurities among white collar workers, motivating an increase in their departure. Others maintain that "the overzealous, redistributive policies of the Manley administration were driving the better educated and better trained members of the work force out of the country"[13] (Cooper 1985, 728). Whatever the reason, after Manley left office in 1980, the

Figure 2.5   Ratio of the Percentage of Upper-White-Collar Jamaican Immigrants in the United States to the Percentage of Upper-White-Collar Workers in Jamaica, 1967 to 2001

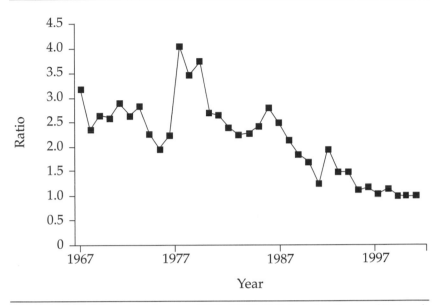

Source: National Planning Agency (1980–1999); U.S. Immigration and Natural-ization Service (1980–2001); U.S. Department of Homeland Security (2002).
Note: Because of missing data, these data points were interpolated for the United States: upper-white-collar ratio for 1967, 1968, 1969, 1971, 1972, 1979, 1980, 1981, 1983, 1985, and 1989.

proportion of white collar departures resumed its decline. In 1997, about as many white collar workers left Jamaica as remained. This pattern is consistent with the expectation that early birds are more positively selected than latecomers.

Figure 2.6 conveys the ratio of upper-white-collar emigrants to upper-white-collar residents for Barbados, Jamaica, Trinidad, and Guyana in 1970, 1979, 1990, and 2000.[14] The figure depicts sixteen ratios, two of which fall below 1.0: Barbados in 1990 (.65) and Jamaica in 2000 (.96). In addition, in 1990 Trinidad lost nearly as many white collar workers as it retained (1.07), though in 2000 white collar workers were again overrepresented among those leaving Trinidad. These exceptions aside, upper-white-collar workers are overrepresented as West Indian emigrants to the United States. But this propensity does not decline with year of departure, as selectivity theory predicts.

Figure 2.6   Ratio of the Percentage of Upper-White-Collar Movers to the Percentage of Upper-White-Collar Stayers, Four Caribbean Countries, 1970 to 2000

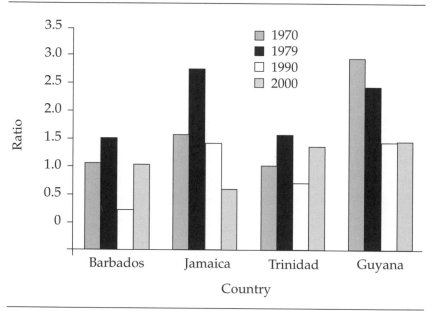

Source: U.S. Immigration and Naturalization Service, *Annual Report* (1970–1977); U.S. Immigration and Naturalization Service, *Statistical Yearbook* (1978–2000).

To sum up this inquiry into who leaves the Caribbean and who stays, immigrant adults are more positively selected on education, and immigrant workers are more positively selected on occupation than their nonmigrant compatriots. However, the expectation that early migrants are more positively selected than latecomers receives more support in terms of education than occupation. This disparity may arise because the two outcomes are not calculated on precisely the same cases: the education figures exclude those under age twenty-five, and the occupation figures exclude those who did not report a job.[15] Then, too, if a special situation obtains when a decennial census is under way, discrete data (only four data points) may mislead. For example, Jamaican emigrants display the expected decline in educational selectivity over time, but this decline is far more obvious in the continuous (figure 2.5) than in the decennial results (figure 2.6). Time trends aside, the key point is that the great majority of West Indian movers have been more skilled than those who stayed at home.

As with first-wavers, the positive selectivity of West Indian migrants motivates the question: do third-wavers have stronger measurable job-related characteristics than African Americans? Recent censuses being much richer than earlier ones, the two groups can be compared on many more characteristics. Today's studies of economic outcomes usually distinguish three types of measurable job-related characteristics: skill (human capital), family responsibilities, and geography. Within recent U.S. censuses, indicators of skill have included age (which is a proxy for job experience), education, years in the United States (for immigrants), and the presence of a disability that limits employment; indicators of family responsibilities have included household headship, marital status, and, for women, number and ages of children; indicators of geography have included whether resident in a metropolitan area, whether resident in New York City, and whether resident in the South, as well as the male (female) unemployment rate in each man's (woman's) state of residence. Table 2.3 conveys how West Indians and African Americans fare on these characteristics, separately by gender, across four census years. Readers interested in how these characteristics were constructed should consult table 2A.2 at the end of this chapter.

As table 2.3 reveals, West Indians are slightly older than African Americans, suggesting greater work experience. In terms of years of schooling, West Indian men have a strong but declining advantage, and West Indian women a modest, more stable advantage. The more consequential comparison is in postsecondary degrees, information on which was first collected in 1990. In that year, about 3.5 percent more West Indian than African American men were college graduates, an edge that fell to 2 percent in 2000. For West Indian women, the respective figures were about 2.5 percent more bachelor's degrees in 1990 and 3 percent more in 2000. Advanced degrees display trends of smaller magnitude.[16] As for health, until 2000 African American rates of work-related disability were higher, but in that census year West Indian rates nearly quadrupled, pushing the immigrant rate above the African American rate.[17] With regard to family responsibilities, West Indian men are more likely to be household heads and to be married, with their spouse present, than are African American men. After 1970, West Indian women were less likely to be household heads and more likely to be married, with their spouse present, than African American women. West Indian women also consistently report fewer children. In addition, West Indian geography is more favorable than African American geography. The immigrants are much more likely to live in a metropolitan area, especially New York, and less likely to live in the South. Finally, in only three of eight comparisons is the average West Indian

Table 2.3 Descriptive Statistics for Job-Related Characteristics of Foreign-Born West Indians and African Americans, by Sex and Year, 1970 to 2000

	West Indian Men, 1970	West Indian Women, 1970	African American Men, 1970	African American Women, 1970	West Indian Men, 1980	West Indian Women, 1980	African American Men, 1980	African American Women, 1980
Age	41.3	40.6	37.5	37.4	36.4	36.5	35.4	36.3
Percent at school	8.97	7.91	8.90	7.51	14.6	18.0	11.8	11.7
Years of school	11.6	10.2	9.43	10.0	13.7	13.7	13.1	13.4
Postmigration years	13.1	13.5	n.a.	n.a.	11.4	11.0	n.a.	n.a.
Percent married or spouse present	69.8	37.1	37.1	51.0	55.5	41.6	44.1	39.6
Percent household head	84.7	28.1	68.6	27.1	65.4	35.3	57.8	36.9
Child ever born	n.a.	1.70	n.a.	2.63	n.a.	1.94	n.a.	2.29
Percent child under age five	n.a.	22.6	n.a.	36.5	n.a.	23.1	n.a.	25.7
Percent disabled	8.73	9.36	n.a.	n.a.	4.42	4.63	12.6	12.9
Percent metro residence	99.0	99.8	83.9	89.0	96.8	98.3	81.1	81.2
Percent New York City residence	63.7	73.4	9.3	11.0	60.0	67.7	8.30	9.29
Percent South residence	8.39	4.10	52.2	51.0	17.7	12.5	50.7	51.1
Percent unemployed in state	3.44	4.65	3.48	5.07	6.54	6.74	6.23	6.80
Unweighted N	1,224	1,683	4,416	5,302	7,680	9,355	6,232	7,353

	West Indian Men, 1990	West Indian Women, 1990	African American Men, 1990	African American Women, 1990	West Indian Men, 2000	West Indian Women, 2000	African American Men, 2000	African American Women, 2000
Age	36.9	37.3	36.	36.8	39.2	39.6	37.6	38.1
Percent at school	17.5	21.6	12.1	15.0	13.3	17.7	12.0	14.1
Years of school	12.2	12.5	11.9	12.3	12.4	12.9	12.4	12.8
Percent BA	9.78	9.96	6.33	7.29	9.80	12.9	7.78	9.80
Percent MA or PhD	4.67	4.10	2.22	3.09	4.77	5.77	3.02	4.65
Postmigration years	13.4	13.5	n.a.	n.a.	16.8	16.9	n.a.	n.a.
Percent married or spouse present	49.3	38.7	36.5	30.8	49.6	42.6	35.8	32.1
Percent household head	57.1	38.3	48.9	45.0	55.0	45.0	48.6	49.4
Child ever born	n.a.	1.86	n.a.	2.12	n.a.	1.07	n.a.	1.03
Percent child under age five[a]	n.a.	18.9	n.a.	20.3	13.7	14.6	8.60	15.2
Percent disabled	4.94	4.61	12.7	10.8	19.0	18.0	17.0	15.8
Percent metro residence	97.9	99.0	86.6	87.8	92.0	94.2	63.1	66.9
Percent New York City residence	53.8	57.9	7.41	8.70	49.6	45.5	6.57	7.62
Percent South residence	26.0	23.6	53.8	53.8	31.8	30.4	57.9	57.1
Percent unemployed in state	6.62	6.13	6.20	6.47	6.22	6.32	5.64	5.97
Unweighted N	10,472	13,044	3,803	3,811	19,806	25,374	14,839	17,460

Source: Author's calculations based on the 1 percent and 5 percent Integrated Public Use Microdata Series (IPUMS).

Note: Limited to persons age eighteen to sixty-four. Means and percentages are weighted, except in 1970.

[a] In 1990 this calculation conveys the percentage of parents residing with one or more children under six years of age.

exposed to a higher state unemployment rate than the average African American.

In sum, table 2.3 shows that, on most job-related characteristics, West Indians are more favorably endowed than African Americans. They are more skilled, the gender distinctions in family responsibilities tilt in their favor, and they are more likely to live in economically desirable regions of the country. This conclusion raises the possibility that any economic advantage West Indian immigrants achieve relative to African Americans is due to their more favorable characteristics.

The Labor Market Outcomes of the Third Wave

So far no systematic West Indian advantage has been detected. An analysis of several outcomes in New York City in 1920, 1930, and 1940 uncovered a single West Indian edge: 1940 male occupational prestige. The discussion now pursues this question using national data obtained from the last four decennial censuses. The results appear in table 2.4. As in the first-wave comparisons, the results are presented as ratios. A ratio of 1.00 indicates that the outcomes of the two groups are the same; a ratio below 1.00 indicates that the West Indian outcome is smaller than the African American; a ratio larger than 1.00 indicates that the West Indian outcome is greater. Readers curious about the actual means and rates used to calculate these ratios should consult table 2A.3 at the end of this chapter.

The rows in table 2.4 present two kinds of results: observed and adjusted. The present discussion focuses exclusively on the observed results. As before, asterisks convey statistical significance at the .05 level or better. All entries in the "observed" rows are significant save one. The 1980 earnings of West Indian men are just below (at 99 percent of) African American earnings—a difference that is not statistically significant. This situation may reflect the exceptionally strong commitment to affirmative action at that historical moment. Thirty-two of thirty-three observed ratios favor West Indians. Further, the size of the West Indian advantage is greater on labor force participation and unemployment than on occupational prestige or earnings. In addition, on women's labor force participation and men's occupational prestige, the size of the West Indian advantage diminishes over time. Nevertheless, West Indians have secured stronger economic outcomes than African Americans for these thirty years.

Why? One explanation has already been proposed: relative to African Americans, West Indians have stronger skills, family responsi-

Table 2.4 Ratio of Foreign-Born West Indian Means to African American Observed Means on Four Economic Indicators: West Indian Means Both Observed and Adjusted

Year	Labor Force Participation		Unemployment		Occupational Prestige		Log Hourly Earnings	
	Men	Women	Men	Women	Men	Women	Men	Women
1970								
Observed	1.16*	1.46*	0.70*	0.32*	1.18*	1.08*	1.16*	1.23*
Adjusted[a]	1.08*	1.29*	0.73*	0.77*	1.05*	1.04*	1.04	0.94
1980								
Observed	1.12*	1.23*	0.62*	0.61*	1.10*	1.10*	0.99	1.09*
Adjusted[a]	1.07*	1.10*	0.55*	0.67*	1.06*	1.07*	0.98*	1.00
1990								
Observed	1.15*	1.18	0.82*	0.62*	1.09*	1.07*	1.13*	1.17*
Adjusted[a]	1.05*	1.09*	0.85*	0.74*	1.05*	1.06*	1.01	1.03*
2000								
Observed	1.20*	1.09*	0.62*	0.71*	1.06*	1.04*	1.12*	1.14*
Adjusted[a]	1.10*	1.07*	0.60*	0.74*	1.06*	1.04*	1.00	1.02*

Source: Author's calculations based on the 1 percent and 5 percent Integrated Public Use Microdata Series (IPUMS).

[a] See the methodological appendix for the variables used in the adjustment and for the restrictions placed on the analysis.

* Statistically significant at the .05 level or better.

bilities that are more conducive to economic success, and a more favorable geographic distribution. However, additional analysis is needed before it can be concluded that these characteristics wholly account for West Indians' advantage on the four economic outcomes presented in table 2.4.

The previous chapter discussed how Paul Siegel addressed this problem. He found that black men's average earnings were $2,852 less than white men's in 1960—a statistically significant shortfall. Using a method called standardization, he attributed $1,755 of that difference to disparities in the two racial groups' educational attainment, place of residence, and so on. But he could not attribute the remaining $1,097 to any observed, job-related characteristic. Siegel labeled this difference "the cost of being black."

Today the most common method for equating groups on observed, job-related characteristics is not standardization but regression. Regression results provide a basis for calculating the mean outcome that West Indians would obtain if they had the characteristics of African Americans. This hypothetical outcome is called the adjusted mean (Farley and Allen 1987; Xie and Goyette 2005). In this book, adjusted means are calculated by giving West Indians the characteristics of African Americans because scholars have found that West Indians have slightly stronger job-related characteristics than African Americans do. Thus, they want to know whether these characteristics fully explain West Indian advantage or whether West Indians would retain an advantage even if they had the slightly weaker job-related characteristics that African Americans do.[18] The final step is to calculate the ratio of the adjusted mean of West Indians to the actual mean of African Americans.

Turning now to the rows in table 2.4 that are labeled "adjusted," note how often a West Indian advantage obtains. Only in the earnings column do some of the results fail to favor West Indians. An asterisk in the "adjusted" row means that the difference between West Indians and African Americans is statistically significant. Of the thirty-two comparisons, eight are insignificant. Two of the eight involve men's unemployment; the other six involve earnings. Later, in chapter 4 (where the analyses incorporate the effect of time spent in the United States on adjusted earnings), it will become evident that, after many years in the United States, West Indians do out-earn African Americans. For present purposes, the appropriate conclusion is that West Indians' stronger job-related characteristics wholly account for their earnings advantage over African Americans.

On most economic indicators, the adjusted means are smaller than their observed counterparts. This confirms that their more favorable characteristics are one reason West Indians fare better than African Americans. But the entries in the adjusted rows also show that job-related characteristics rarely account fully for the differential. Far more often West Indian immigrants do better in the labor market than similarly qualified African Americans.

Findings such as these have led some observers to conclude that blacks no longer experience labor market discrimination. If West Indians do so well, something other than skin color must be responsible for African American disadvantage. But just how well are West Indians doing? Are they, as George Gilder (1981) once claimed, doing better than whites? This is a fair question and one the previous analysis does not answer. At first glance, a sound way to answer it would be to compare the attainment of West Indian immigrants to the attainment of native-born non-Hispanic whites. If racial discrimination has disappeared, West Indian immigrants should do as well as their native white counterparts. Yet, foreign birth might be a handicap in its own right. If so, a better strategy would be to compare foreign-born West Indians to foreign-born non-Hispanic whites. Unfortunately, this approach too is problematic. Non-Hispanic whites are more culturally and linguistically diverse than West Indians. Many don't speak English. Which white national-origin group is the most appropriate benchmark?

There being no perfect strategy for ascertaining the relative success of West Indian immigrants, the approach here uses native-born non-Hispanic whites as the benchmark against which to juxtapose three groups: foreign-born, English-speaking West Indians; foreign-born non-Hispanic whites; and African Americans. The results of these comparisons appear in table 2.5. Within each census year, the first row conveys ratios of foreign-born West Indian adjusted attainment to native-born non-Hispanic white attainment; the second row reports the analogous ratios for foreign-born non-Hispanic whites and the third row the analogous ratios for African Americans.

Looking first at West Indians, observe that men are significantly disadvantaged on thirteen of the sixteen comparisons, and women on five. Moreover, while West Indian men never secure a significant advantage over native white men, West Indian women have significantly higher labor force participation in every year (though their edge is diminishing), and in 1990 and 2000 they have significantly higher earnings than native-born white women. Also of interest are the time trends. For both West Indian men and women, relative rates of labor force participation and unemployment have become more worrisome, while occupational prestige and earnings have improved.

The second row within each census year communicates how much of a disadvantage foreign-born whites experience relative to native-

Table 2.5 Ratios of Minority Adjusted Means to Native-Born Non-Hispanic White Observed Means on Four Economic Indicators

Year	Labor Force Participation		Unemployment		Occupational Prestige		Log Earnings	
	Men	Women	Men	Women	Men	Women	Men	Women
1970								
Foreign-born white	1.06	1.06	1.30	1.39	1.05*	0.97	0.99	1.04
Foreign-born West Indian	0.98	1.39*	0.92	0.98	0.91*	0.90*	0.88*	0.92*
African American	0.97*	1.20*	1.64*	1.30*	0.85*	0.88*	0.91*	0.95*
1980								
Foreign-born white	0.97	0.97	1.42	1.53	1.06	0.95	1.00	1.03
Foreign-born West Indian	0.99*	1.19*	1.07	1.39	0.93*	0.99*	0.93*	1.01
African American	0.94*	1.11*	1.71*	1.79*	0.88*	0.93*	0.96*	1.02
1990								
Foreign-born white	0.97*	1.00	1.09	0.93	1.00	0.99	0.99	1.01
Foreign-born West Indian	0.96*	1.10*	1.57*	1.87*	0.96*	1.00	0.95*	1.04*
African American	0.94*	1.08*	1.88*	2.07*	0.94*	0.97*	0.96*	1.02
2000								
Foreign-born white	0.95*	0.90*	0.73	1.44	1.00	0.98*	1.01	1.03
Foreign-born West Indian	0.90*	1.02*	1.65*	1.60*	0.98*	1.00	0.96*	1.04*
African American	0.88*	0.97*	2.57*	2.11*	0.94*	0.97*	0.96*	1.02

Source: Author's calculations based on the 1 percent and 5 percent Integrated Public Use Microdata Series (IPUMS).
Note: See the methodological appendix for the variables used in the adjustment and for the restrictions placed on the analysis.
* Statistically significant at the .05 level or better.

born whites. Very few ratios are statistically significant. This is partly because of a shortage of cases, but other studies have also shown that non-Hispanic white immigrants incur few labor market penalties (Farley 1996; Model and Fisher 2007).[19] Comparing the West Indian immigrant ratios with the foreign-born white ratios provides insight into the consequences of race, since both groups are foreign-born. Looking first at males, note that West Indian immigrants fare substantially worse than white immigrants, evidence that race is a serious handicap. Very occasionally West Indian men do better on labor force participation or unemployment, but the gap in occupational prestige and earnings consistently favors white immigrants. Notice that, on these last two outcomes, foreign-born white men hardly suffer a penalty at all. When the results for West Indian immigrant females are compared to those for white immigrant females, a more complex picture emerges. West Indian women consistently report higher labor force participation. Initially they also had lower unemployment rates. But in 1990 they lost that advantage. On both occupation and earnings, the opposite situation obtains: after 1980, West Indian–born women performed slightly better than foreign-born white women. These results imply that, since 1970, West Indian women's race has been an obstacle primarily in terms of unemployment. In sum, the results for West Indian women are more consistent with the notion that racial discrimination is declining than are the results for West Indian men.

Additional light can be shed on this interpretation by examining how African Americans perform when compared to native whites. African American men are significantly disadvantaged on all sixteen comparisons, and women on ten. African American women also have significantly higher labor force participation in three of the four years. Thus, the gender interaction found in the West Indian case also operates in the African American case. Indeed, for over twenty years census data have shown African American women suffering a lower "within-gender" penalty than African American men (Farley 1996; Farley and Allen 1987). Since the economic outcomes of West Indian–born women are more favorable than those of African Americans, it is hardly surprising that the economic outcomes of West Indian women sometimes surpass those of native-born whites.

Several explanations for African American women's relatively strong showing have been proposed. Field research has shown that employers view black males negatively but have few reservations about black females (Kirschenman and Neckerman 1991). Others propose that these stereotypes have some basis in reality; for instance, the precariousness of black male employment may motivate black women to increase their effort and geniality (Moss and Tilly 2001). Still others wonder whether African American women's relatively strong showing is not an illusion (Neal 2004). One ground for the objection is that black women without jobs are disproportionately single and poorly schooled, a fact that imparts an upward bias to the earnings of employed black women; white women without jobs are disproportionately married and well educated, a fact that imparts a downward bias to the earnings of employed white women. Yet, not all scholars agree that these biases seriously distort calculations of the wage gap (Antecol and Bedard 2002). Another ground for objection is the failure of census data to incorporate questions about work experience. This means that the ratios in table 2.5 do not control for racial differences on this important characteristic. Again, however, scholars disagree about the consequences of this omission (Kilbourne, England, and Beron 1994).

These disagreements aside, a large body of qualitative and quantitative research indicates that, regardless of ethnicity, black women encounter less labor market discrimination than black men. This means that citing the experience of West Indian women as evidence that racial discrimination has ended is equivalent to citing the experience of African American women as evidence that racial discrimination has ended. In sum, West Indian advantage provides no basis for concluding that persons of African descent no longer encounter labor market discrimination.[20]

A Pseudo-Question?

The goal of this volume is not to identify the causes of white advantage over black but to identify the causes of West Indian advantage over African American. Before proceeding further, there are two challenges that could render this goal superfluous: one is methodological, the other substantive. The methodological challenge is that census data may paint an idealistic picture of West Indians. If so, their advantage over African Americans is an artifact of the data selected for study. The substantive challenge is that many West Indians who arrive as children may be assimilating into the black underclass rather than the black middle class; such a situation would represent a significant caveat to the West Indian success story. As the inquiries below reveal, both objections are red herrings.

Flawed Data

Censuses undercount immigrants and minorities. This would not be a problem if all blacks had an equal chance of being missed. But West Indian immigrants and African Americans are undercounted at different rates. Both groups are likely to be undercounted because they are black, but only immigrants are likely to be undercounted because they are illegal. Therefore, West Indians might be exhibiting an advantage over African Americans because their economically least successful members are less likely to appear in the census than are African Americans' least successful members.[21] Complicating matters further, between 1970 and 2000 the undercount of African Americans diminished, while the undercount of West Indians increased. These changes reflect improvement in African American coverage, but also considerable growth in the number of West Indians settling in the United States illegally.

Luckily, the geography of illegal immigration provides a strategy for assessing the seriousness of the problem. Undocumented immigrants are more likely than documented immigrants to settle where their compatriots are already established (Fernandez and Robinson 1994; U.S. Immigration and Naturalization Service 1999; U.S. Census Bureau 2004). Estimates by Jeffrey Passel and Karen Woodrow (1984) and by Passel and Rebecca Clark (1998) indicate that about three-quarters of Caribbean undocumented immigrants live in New York, New Jersey, or Florida. A simple way of determining whether an undercount of the undocumented is responsible for the advantageous adjusted means reported in table 2.4 is to reestimate them on data that exclude states where that undercount is high. If West Indians still maintain an edge, it is real rather than an artifact of census data.

Table 2.6 presents ratios of West Indian to African American adjusted means for an analysis identical to the previous one except that the sample omits residents of New York, New Jersey, Connecticut, and Florida. The results of tables 2.4 and 2.6 are very similar. In both, eight adjusted means fail to attain significance; in both, six of these eight describe earnings, and the remaining two do not. In sum, there are no significant differences in the economic outcomes of a sample containing few undocumented West Indians and the national sample used in table 2.4. Thus, the increasing proportion of undocumented West Indians absent from recent national samples does not bias the results.

Segmented Assimilation

When scholars began examining the experiences of the many non-European immigrant groups arriving after 1965, a new perspective captured the imagination of some researchers (Portes and Zhou 1993). This new perspective, called "segmented assimilation," is relevant to the present study because it predicts that, rather than outperform the

Table 2.6   Ratio of Foreign-Born West Indian Adjusted Means to African American Observed Means on Four Economic Indicators: Residents of All States Except New York, New Jersey, Connecticut, and Florida

Year	Labor Force Participation		Unemployment		Occupational Prestige		Logged Earnings	
	Males	Females	Males	Females	Males	Females	Males	Females
1970	1.04	1.31*	0.65*	1.85	1.05*	1.01*	1.10	0.93
1980	1.11*	1.13*	0.48*	0.65*	1.06*	1.08*	0.99	1.01
1990	1.07*	1.11*	0.79*	0.66*	1.07*	1.07*	1.03	1.04*
2000	1.14*	1.06*	0.60*	0.80*	1.06*	1.03*	1.01	1.03*

Source: Author's calculations based on the 1 percent and 5 percent Integrated Public Use Microdata Series (IPUMS).
Note: See the methodological appendix for the variables used in the adjustment and for the restrictions placed on the analysis.
* Statistically significant at the .05 level or better.

average African American, a significant number of West Indian young people will display the traits associated with the most disadvantaged of black Americans: the so-called underclass. This term was popularized by William Julius Wilson (1980) to describe a subculture that endorses behaviors such as dropping out of high school, being irregularly employed, engaging in criminal activity, and becoming a teenage parent.[22]

The sociologist Herbert Gans (1992) was the first to link immigrants of color to the underclass. His argument is based on several interrelated observations. Since the 1970s, the number of well-paying, low-skilled jobs has been declining. Today a middle class livelihood requires more than a high school diploma. Yet in some high schools, particularly those located in central-city ghettos, large proportions of the student body do not graduate; of those who do, few go on to college (Jaynes and Williams 1989). What is more, phenotypically black Americans are least able to choose where they live. Although the middle class black suburb has come into its own, large numbers of working class and poor blacks—both native- and foreign-born—live in central-city neighborhoods that are overwhelmingly black (Crowder 1999; Crowder and Tedrow 2001; Logan and Deane 2003; Rosenbaum and Friedman 2007).

Many studies have demonstrated the importance of peers to adolescents (Paulle 2005; Waters 1999). While West Indian youth residing in black middle class neighborhoods go to school mostly with middle class African Americans, West Indian youth raised in ghetto environments go to school partly with underclass African Americans. To be sure, parental values matter too. And there is much evidence that West Indian parents tell their children that a Caribbean heritage is culturally superior to an African American one (Arnold 1996; Johnson 2000; Waters 1999). But segmentationists suspect that this message is conveyed more successfully in the suburbs than in the inner city. In the ghetto, the attractions of underclass peers overwhelm the admonitions of immigrant parents. John Ogbu (1991, 14–15) explains that underclass adolescents, believing "that it requires more than education, individual effort and hard work to overcome the barriers against them," develop an adversarial stance toward school and embrace instead a subculture of "sports, entertainment, hustling, drug dealing and the like."

Confirmation that a significant number of West Indian youth raised in the inner city had joined the underclass would constitute an important exception to the results presented earlier in this chapter. So far the research devoted to this question is inconclusive. Scholars have found that U.S.-raised West Indian males in New York and Miami have higher rates of incarceration than other immigrants, but lower rates than African Americans. On other indicators, however, the experience of U.S.-raised West Indians is unremarkable (Mollenkopf 2005; Portes, Fernández-Kelly, and Haller 2005). Given the relevance of segmented assimilation to the present undertaking, it seems appropriate to subject the hypothesis to additional tests. For this reason, an analysis is offered below on a sample of West Indian and African American young adults taken from the 2000 Public Use Microdata Series (PUMS). This census year is chosen because it was the first to contain an adequate number of foreign-born West Indians who arrived both before the age of thirteen and after the passage of the Hart-Celler Act. These restrictions ensure that they meet the requirements outlined by Gans (1992): they attended secondary school in the United States, and they entered the labor market at a time when unskilled jobs were in decline.[23]

The results are presented again as ratios of West Indian to African American adjusted means. To test segmentationists' expectation that West Indian and African American outcomes are closer within central cities than outside them, each adjusted mean is estimated separately by residential location. The first row of figures in table 2.7 reports ratios in non-central-city areas; the second row reports ratios in central-city areas. Comparing each column reveals that the disparity between the two groups of blacks is generally greater inside than outside central cities. For instance, on male labor force participation, outside cen-

Table 2.7   Ratio of Foreign-Born West Indian Adjusted Means to African American Observed Means on Four Economic Indicators Within and Outside the Central City: Persons Under Age Thirty-Four

Location	Labor Force Participation		Unemployment		Occupational Prestige		Logged Earnings	
	Males	Females	Males	Females	Males	Females	Males	Females
Central city	1.04	1.04	0.56*	0.81	1.07*	1.05*	0.99	1.03
Non-Central city	1.06*	1.12*	0.64*	0.69*	1.10*	1.03	1.00	1.02

Source: Author's calculations based on the 1 percent and 5 percent Integrated Public Use Microdata Series (IPUMS) from the 2000 census.
Note: See the methodological appendix for the variables used in the adjustment and for the restrictions placed on the analysis. Immigrants are limited to persons who arrived under the age of thirteen.
* Statistically significant at the .10 level or better.

tral cities the West Indian adjusted mean is 4 percent greater than the African American adjusted mean, but inside central cities it is 6 percent greater. This pattern holds for six of the eight comparisons. Looked at another way, outside central cities three of the comparisons significantly favor West Indians, whereas within central cities five of the comparisons do so.[24] This is the reverse of the pattern expected by segmentationists.

At the same time, inside or outside central cities, this subsample of West Indians in 2000 reaped fewer advantages than the larger sample from which it is drawn (see the last row in table 2.4). This pattern suggests that, relative to their foreign-born parents, immigrant children experience some downward mobility. Perhaps the disparity is even greater when foreign-born parents and native-born children are compared. But this type of downward mobility is compatible with positive selectivity, not segmented assimilation. As chapter 3 explains, selectivity theorists see economically motivated immigrants as able individuals who pass on to their children only a portion of their endowments. As a result, their offspring do not fare quite as well as their parents do. At the same time, even those in the central city do not turn into layabouts or freeloaders either. In short, segmented assimilation does not apply to West Indian immigrant children—at least in terms of the labor outcomes examined in this study. Accordingly, the question that motivates this book still requires an answer.

Appendix

Table 2A.1   Definitions of Economic Outcome (Dependent) Variables

Variable	Description	Values
Labor force participation[a]	Worked for one hour with pay, for fifteen hours as unpaid family worker or seeks work	0 and 1
Unemployment[b]	Jobless but seeks work	0 and 1
Occupational prestige[c]	Treiman prestige score	6 to 78
Logged hourly earnings[d]	Natural log of hourly earnings	–1.87 to 8.80

Source: Author's calculations based on the Integrated Public Use Microdata Series (IPUMS) U.S.A. website, accessed February 1, 2008 at http://usa.ipums.org/usa/.

[a] In 1920 and 1930, anyone reporting an occupation was coded as in the labor force. Thereafter, the variable refers to the activities described here the week before the census.

[b] Refers to the activity described here the week before the census.

[c] Refers to primary occupation or, for the unemployed, most recent occupation. For 2000, Treiman prestige scores were obtained by assigning 1950 occupational codes to each occupational title and recoding these as Standard International Occupational Prestige (SIOPs) scores (Treiman 1977; Treiman and Ganzeboom 1996). For 1970, prestige scores were obtained from Hauser and Featherman (1977); for 1980 and 1990 from Nakao and Treas (1994).

[d] Based on pre-tax earnings from wages, salary, and/or self-employment in the year preceding the census. To obtain hourly earnings, annual earnings are divided by the product of weeks worked per year and hours worked per week. All earnings results are limited to persons earning at least $500 annually.

Table 2A.2   Measureable Job-Related Characteristics (Independent Variables)

Variable	Description	Range
Age	Age in years	18 (25) to 64
	Square of age in years	324 (625) to 4,096
Education	Currently attending school	0 and 1
	Number of grades completed	0 to 20
	College degree (1990 and 2000 only)	0 and 1
	Master's or PhD degree (1990 and 2000 only)	0 and 1
Time since migration[a]	Years lived in the United States	0 to 63
	Square of years lived in the United States	0 to 3,969
Census year[b]	1970	0 and 1
	1980	0 and 1
	1990	0 and 1
	2000 (omitted category)	
Cohort of arrival[b]	Period of arrival in the United States	
	Before 1953	0 and 1
	1953 to 1966	0 and 1
	1967 to 1976	0 and 1
	1977 to 1985	0 and 1
	1986 to 2000	0 and 1
Family relationships	Head of household	0 and 1
	Married, spouse present	0 and 1

Table 2A.2   *(Continued)*

Variable	Description	Range
Children (women only)	Number of children ever born (1970, 1980, 1990)	0 to 13
	Number of own children under age eighteen at home (2000)	0 to 9
	Number of own children under age five at home	0 to 7
Health	Has a disability of any kind	0 and 1
Region	Lives in a metropolitan area	0 and 1
	Lives in the greater New York area	0 and 1
	Lives in the South	0 and 1
Unemployment rate	Percent of same sex unemployed in same state	1.5 to 11.9
Percent African American[c]	Percent of African Americans of same sex in labor force of individual's metropolitan area	0 to 48.5

Source: Author's calculations based on the 1 percent and 5 percent Integrated Public Use Microdata Series (IPUMS).
[a] This variable appears in all models after chapter 3.
[b] This variable appears in the model described in table 4.2.
[c] This variable appears only in the model described in table 6.3.

Table 2A.3 African American and West Indian Rates or Means on Four Economic Indicators, by Sex and Year

Gender and Year	Labor Force Participation[a]		Unemployment[a]		Occupational Prestige[b]		Annual Earnings[c]	
	African Americans	West Indians	African Americans	West Indians	African Americans	West Indians	African Americans	West Indians
Men								
1920[d]	95.1	97.9	n.a.	n.a.	28.3	29.1	n.a.	n.a.
1930[d]	94.3	96.5	n.a.	n.a.	27.9	28.6	n.a.	n.a.
1970	76.6	89.2***	6.18	4.31***	32.5	38.5***	$5,755	$6,701***
1980	76.0	85.5***	12.2	7.58***	35.1	38.7***	22,460	22,290
1990	75.1	86.3***	11.6	9.55***	36.3	39.7***	21,612	24,454***
2000	66.3	79.4***	12.5	7.79***	37.8	40.2***	32,043	35,880***
Women								
1920[d]	55.9	64.9	n.a.	n.a.	23.3	22.0	n.a.	n.a.
1930[d]	60.2	56.4	n.a.	n.a.	22.8	22.2	n.a.	n.a.
1970	53.4	78.1***	7.25	2.34***	31.9	34.6***	3,566	4,388***
1980	61.9	76.0***	11.5	7.04***	37.9	41.6***	14,841	16,245***
1990	68.5	80.6***	11.4	7.04***	40.7	43.6***	17,057	20,028***
2000	68.8	74.8***	10.6	7.53***	42.3	44.0***	26,279	29,874***

Source: Author's calculations based on the Integrated Public Use Microdata Series (IPUMS) web site, accessed at http://usa.ipums.org/usa.

*** West Indian means are significantly greater than African American means; statistically significant at the .001 level or better.

[a] Numbers are percentages; they are estimated for persons eighteen to sixty-four years of age.

[b] Numbers are average Treiman (1977) prestige scores; they are estimated for persons twenty-five to sixty-four years of age.

[c] Numbers are average real dollars earned in the year previous to the census by persons twenty-five to sixty-four years of age earning at least $500.

[d] Figures for 1920 and 1930 for the New York City metropolitan area only. The remainder are national figures.

• Chapter 3 •

Three Explanations for the Difference Between West Indians and African Americans

HAVING demonstrated that even those West Indian immigrants with the same skills, family responsibilities, and residential location as African Americans do better in the labor market than African Americans, the narrative now takes up the question of why. As pointed out earlier, three types of explanations have been offered: those that emphasize culture, those that emphasize selectivity, and those that emphasize white favoritism. Although they are presented here sequentially, they are not mutually exclusive; one, two, or all three of these explanations may be correct.

The Cultural Superiority Hypothesis

The cultural superiority hypothesis comes in two versions: one is primarily historical, the other entirely contemporary. The historical argument rests on Thomas Sowell's claim that Caribbean black slaves had several advantages over American black slaves (Sowell 1975, 1978b, 1981, 1983). They had more chances for rebellion and escape and more opportunities to grow and sell food. Because of their large numbers, both during and after emancipation, Caribbean blacks had greater access to occupations requiring skill and responsibility. These conditions taught them diligence, self-control, and future orientation, whereas conditions in the United States produced just the opposite characteristics in American blacks.

The contemporary argument emphasizes only the demographic difference. W. A. Domingo (1925, 347–48) explains: "Forming a racial majority in their own countries and not being accustomed to discrimination expressly felt as racial, they rebel against the 'color line' as they find it in America." In other words, because blacks predominate in the West Indies, whites cannot monopolize all the occupations requiring skill and responsibility. Note that both versions emphasize the racial composition of the population, but for Sowell past matters more than present. In addition, Sowell's version is multifaceted: he considers demographic composition to be one of several reasons for the West Indian advantage.

The Historical Arguments of Thomas Sowell

West Indians: Sowell's Positive Story As indicated in chapter 1, Sowell (1975, 1978b, 1981, 1983) presents a two-sided coin: a West Indian positive story and an African American negative story. West Indians' upward mobility results from their diligence, self-control, and future orientation. One source of these traits is their history as rebellious slaves. Several factors contributed to making revolt and escape more common in the Islands than in the States. Because the white population was small, escaped slaves were less easily discovered. The jungle and mountain terrain provided food and facilitated concealment. West Indian blacks and whites were equally ignorant of that terrain. Island winters were not severe. In the American South, on the other hand, long-term subsistence in the wild was extremely difficult. Securing food and staying warm were major problems. The mechanisms through which southern plantation owners discouraged escape included a deliberate policy of keeping slaves ignorant and of meeting their food and clothing needs. Sowell (1981, 187) cites the historian Herbert Gutman's description of how owners thought they should treat slaves: "Create in him a habit of perfect dependence on you" and "prevent him from learning to take care of himself." To this end, each week the master or his agent distributed food rations. In contrast, Caribbean slave owners gave their chattel the time and space to engage in subsistence agriculture—the so-called provision ground system. Sowell attributes this policy to the monoculture of the Islands and to their very large slave populations, which left no hands available for food production. Growing and marketing food for both blacks and whites became the task of slaves and free blacks.

As for regional differences in the position of free blacks, in both regions some slaves were manumitted, and thus a class of "free persons of color" gradually arose. However, the economic status of free blacks was higher in the Islands. Sowell attributes this to regional differences in racial composition. With no white working class, there were simply not enough whites to fill all the skilled and supervisory posts generated by the economy. As a result, more free persons of color—and later blacks in general—secured desirable jobs in the Caribbean than was possible for free blacks in the United States.

Sowell contends that the attitudinal and behavioral consequences of these two slave systems were very different. Caribbean blacks responded to their economic autonomy and better chance of escape with initiative, diligence, and, perhaps most important, the ability to develop a rational plan that demanded self-denial today in order to secure a brighter tomorrow. American blacks responded to their economic dependency and low probability of escape with "evasion of work, half-done work, unpredictable absenteeism, and abuse of tools and equipment" (Sowell 1981, 200). Moreover, after emancipation, blacks were such a large proportion of the Caribbean population that whites again had no choice but to grant blacks a wide range of job options. And with these options came the values necessary for success in a free market economy.

One problem with this interpretation is its failure to specify the mechanisms through which values are transmitted over a 150-year period. While transmission is not impossible, Sowell's argument would be stronger if it identified the mechanisms of transmission or cited evidence for the ongoing utility of the behaviors central to his interpretation. Even if their slave heritage transmitted a strong work ethic to many West Indians, in the post-emancipation period the structure of opportunity changed. Of this era, Sowell (1978b, 47) writes: "Peonage virtually re-enslaved the black population of the West Indies, as in the southern United States." If so, would not these changes have affected Caribbean blacks' values? This logic leaves Sowell's readers wondering under what conditions people adopt new values and under what conditions they retain old ones.

Another problem with his interpretation is that he paints a very homogenous picture of West Indian culture. Evidently, because their history at one time accorded them opportunities to gain from diligence, most West Indians are "frugal and hard-working" (Sowell 1981, 219). This formulation leaves no room for cultural differences that might result from regional variations in the history, geography, economy, or demography of West Indian locales (Premdas 1995).

Chapter 5 assesses Sowell's claims. Among its discoveries is that social and economic conditions varied substantially across the Caribbean. In particular, provision grounds were not universally provided.

Nearly all the arable land on Barbados was in sugar, leaving no room for provision grounds. As a result, Richard Sheridan (1995, 64) predicted, "much light can be shed on the merits and demerits of the provision ground system by comparing the radically different systems of subsisting slaves in Barbados and Jamaica." This variation paves the way for a test of "the positive story." Put simply: if some West Indian slaves had the opportunity to participate in a market economy, would not their descendants be more prosperous than the descendants of West Indian slaves who did not have this opportunity? This question is answered empirically in chapter 5.

African Americans: Sowell's Negative Story   As already pointed out, Sowell's interpretation of African American history is a crucial part of his explanation for West Indian advantage. North American slavery offered little incentive to work, save that of avoiding punishment. Most slaves were wholly dependent on their owners for food; rebellion or escape brought death or recapture. The emancipation of slaves in the United States changed these incentives only slightly because most freedmen and their families labored under a system of debt peonage. Landlords not only disproportionately appropriated the fruits of their tenants' labors but also obstructed their freedom of movement by duplicity and usury.

This account again has little room for variation. With the exception of "free persons of color" and their progeny, whom he views as hardworking, independent, and family-oriented, Sowell (1975, 35–44; 1978b, 8–23) sees African Americans as exposed to such a long series of deprivations that they became alienated from "mainstream" values. Yet, for the past several decades, not only have most African Americans not been poor, but most follow middle class norms and subscribe to what Kathryn Neckerman and her colleagues (1999) have labeled a "minority culture of mobility." This is not to say that Sowell's description has no applicability, but that it applies to a minority of the black population: the chronically impoverished. Indeed, the traits he emphasizes—impulsiveness, extravagance, fatalism, and so on—are the same traits that Oscar Lewis (1965) associated with the culture of poverty and that William Julius Wilson (1980) associated with the underclass. Lewis's ideas, which had become politically unpopular by the late 1960s, interpret these traits as the adaptations of very poor people of all races and ethnicities to a particular set of structural and psychological barriers. The multiethnic nature of the "culture of poverty" is clear from Lewis's (1965, 11) description of its composition in the United States: "This group would consist of very low-income Negroes, Mexicans, Puerto Ricans, American Indians and Southern poor whites."

Studies of underclass behavior likewise confirm that this adaptation is not limited to African Americans (Bourgois 1995; Moore and Pinder-hughes 1993).

The ideas of Paul DiMaggio (1994, 41), a sociologist of culture, pin-point other problems, such as the importance of "distinguishing be-haviors that are culturally driven from those that simply reflect ra-tional responses to circumstantial pressures." In other words, cultural explanations should not be reducible to class-based explanations. But Sowell's "negative story" is more about class than race. Indeed, the same can be said of his "positive story." Sowell describes African American culture as a culture of poverty (negative story), and he de-scribes West Indian culture as a culture of mobility (positive story).

Not surprisingly, chapter 5 scrutinizes not only Sowell's West Indian positive story but also his African American negative story. Among its discoveries, the chapter reveals that American slave owners did not universally distribute food rations to their dependents. On the Car-olina coast, slaves grew their own provisions. This heterogeneity im-plies that Sowell's negative story can be tested by contrasting the eco-nomic success of descendants of Carolina slaves with the economic success of those residing elsewhere. If Sowell is correct, the former should be more prosperous than the latter.

The Contemporary Caribbean:
All-Black Societies

The "all-black society" hypothesis offers a different cultural explana-tion for West Indian advantage. As already explained, it maintains that black workers reap advantages in places where there are few, if any, members of more highly ranked groups. In all-black societies, blacks aspire to and hold any position in the occupational hierarchy. Sowell is one of the advocates of this position, but he is concerned primarily with the pre-emancipation era. Others emphasize the consequences of immigrants having been socialized in all-black environments in the present and in person.

An all-black environment is associated with two quite different con-sequences. The first—which is technically demographic, not cultural—holds that blacks in the West Indies should be more skilled on average than African Americans (Ottley 1943; Reid 1939/1969; Ueda 1980).[1] This follows because in the West Indies most skilled workers, manual or nonmanual, are black, whereas in the United States most skilled workers are white. In fact, the differences between the two regions in black population proportions do not necessarily translate into blacks holding more skilled jobs in the West Indies than in the United States. The outcome also depends on the proportion of skilled jobs in the two places. If the American labor market generates more skilled jobs, relative to its population, than the West Indian one, it is conceivable that proportionately more African Americans hold skilled jobs than do residents of the West Indies, even if blacks hold all the prestigious jobs in the West Indies. This is an empirical question on which chapter 5 brings some data to bear.

However, most advocates of the "all-black society" hypothesis are not interested in whether the average African American is more or less skilled than the average West Indian. Theirs is rather a psychological formulation. As Milton Vickerman (1999, 40–41) explains in the case of black Jamaicans: "Their numerical preponderance has imparted a degree of self-confidence that has helped them to cope with persistent subjugation. Socialization in a society made up mainly of blacks has made having black role models seem normal. At the same time, there has always been an awareness that the various elites who have dominated the society have felt a certain nervousness at being surrounded by a large number of blacks."

In other words, growing up a member of the dominant race in a predominantly black society has different psychological consequences than growing up a member of a subordinate race in a mixed-race and racist society. The literature stresses two consequences. The first is that West Indian blacks are more ambitious than African Americans (Domingo 1925; Foner 1985; Glazer and Moynihan 1963; Osofsky 1963). A variety of stereotypes convey this impression, such as that West Indians make poor servants and that they make fine businesspeople (Reid 1939/1969). But more than stereotypes are involved. Colin Powell's biography conveys his strong conviction that hard work brings rewards (Means 1992). An immigrant from the Caribbean to Canada, where a small but long-established native black population also dwells, told an interviewer that compared to a black Canadian, a black West Indian is "not too ready to accept that he can't do something because he's seen blacks do it before" (McClain 1979, 49).

In addition to possessing perseverance and ambition, immigrants from the West Indies forcefully demand equal treatment. Arguing that African Americans accept their secondary citizenship too readily, W. A. Domingo (1925, 349) claimed: "The outstanding contribution of West Indians to American Negro life is the insistent assertion of their manhood in an environment that demands too much servility and unprotesting acquiescence from men of African blood. This unwillingness to conform and be standardized, to accept tamely an inferior status and abdicate their humanity, finds an open expression in the activities of the foreign-born Negro in America." Note that in this description the salient values have to do with fighting injustice. To be sure, the larger goal is economic prosperity. Nor is hard work ruled out. But the West Indian contribution is indignation rather than acquiescence, defiance not diligence.

Winston James (1998) uses similar logic to explain the overrepresentation of West Indians as leaders in the many organizations seeking to improve the position of black Americans after World War I. Although these groups differed in their goals and tactics, most were energized by West Indians who were outraged at the rebuffs they had received at the hands of white employers, landlords, and policemen. Their outrage, James argues, stemmed from their expectation that whites would treat them with civility and fairness, an expectation that only a foreign-born black would be naive enough to entertain. The immigrants responded with both individual complaint and collective action. Conversely, "black people from the South . . . who had come to New York during the Great Migration were . . . fully aware of the racial codes and, therefore, would not as readily have taken the risk of violating those codes" (James 1998, 85).[2]

More recently, Mary Waters (1993, 1997) has emphasized the significance of socialization in an all-black society. In her research in a large Manhattan food service firm, both white employers and West Indian workers told Waters that when West Indians perceive that racism is blocking their opportunities for advancement, they are more angry and militant than African Americans. Caribbean immigrants do "not put up with 'racist' nonsense when it does occur" (Waters 1997, 15). "In fact, the foreign born pride themselves in being more likely to stand up to whites when 'real situations' occur" (21). Waters links this greater militance to socialization in an all-black society, which increases individuals' confidence that confrontation is the appropriate response to abuse.

Indeed, in Waters's (1999) view, socialization in an all-black society enhances not only West Indians' willingness to confront racism but also their perception that racism can be overcome. This belief, in turn, has a healthy effect on West Indian–white relations. Because West Indians believe that they can overcome racism through their own efforts, they are less intimidated by whites, less angry at whites, and more comfortable with whites.

Waters labels this result "the comfort factor," a phrase she borrows from the journalist Jack Miles, who used it to distinguish his relationship to his Nigerian college roommate from his relationship with his African American classmates. To Waters, the phrase means that the relationship between West Indians and whites is cordial and pleasant; it is not marred by anger on the black side or guilt on the white. As a result, white gatekeepers treat West Indians more favorably than they treat African Americans, a point that receives further elaboration later in this chapter.

To sum up, many observers assert that immigrants from all-black societies have higher occupational aspirations and lower tolerance for discrimination than African Americans. These attitudes, in turn, motivate the immigrants to pursue advancement with more determination and to resist obstacles with more indignation. Some scholars go further, arguing that, partly because of their confidence that racism can be overcome, West Indians are less threatened by whites and are more comfortable with whites than African Americans. If correct, one or more of these responses would help West Indians to secure better job outcomes than African Americans.

Selectivity Theory

A second explanation that researchers have offered for West Indian economic advantage over African Americans is that the former are positively selected migrants. As used here, the term "selectivity" denotes a subset of individuals who systematically differ in some way from the larger population of which they are a part. Selection can be positive—the selected individuals have more education or are more ambitious than the average person at origin—or negative—the selected individuals have less education or are less ambitious. Note that these examples include two different types of characteristics: one is easily measured (education); the other is hard to measure (ambition). Most selectivity theorists ignore the distinction between traits that are easy to measure and traits that are not. They assume that positive selection means that movers are superior to stayers on both types of traits.

In the remaining chapters of this book, positive selection refers to selection on job-related characteristics that are hard to measure. That's because the previous chapter already showed that West Indians are advantaged on traits that are easy to measure like education and marital status. This is a fact, not a hypothesis. Attention now centers on whether West Indians also exhibit an advantage on hard-to-measure job-related characteristics such as intelligence, ambition, amicability, conscientiousness, and diligence.

Perhaps the first writer to associate positive selectivity with West Indian success was W. A. Domingo, though he did not use the term. "It must be remembered," he wrote, "that the foreign-born black men and women, more so even than other groups of immigrants, are the hardiest and most venturesome of their folk. They were dissatisfied at home, and it is to be expected that they would not be altogether satisfied with limitation of opportunity here when they have staked so much to gain enlargement of opportunity" (Domingo 1925, 347). Note that hardiness and venturesomeness are difficult-to-measure characteristics.

Note too that the interpretation that proponents of positive selectivity offer for West Indian advantage is similar to the interpretation that some culturalists offer: that Caribbean immigrants and their children have greater ambition and drive than African Americans do. Both perspectives agree that the relevant causal mechanisms are located within the personalities of the actors. But there is a critical difference. Selectivity theorists believe that only a subset of Caribbean-raised individuals have these desirable traits: those who choose to migrate. Those who choose to stay home are not exceptional. Culturalists, on the other hand, believe that all Caribbean-raised individuals, both movers and stayers, have these desirable traits. This conclusion follows from their assumption that socialization in the Caribbean environment, as opposed to the American South, is responsible for the immigrants' ambition and drive.

Everett Lee (1966) is the scholar responsible for popularizing the word "selectivity." Positing a link between the direction of selectivity and the motive for migration, he wrote: "Migrants responding primarily to plus factors at destination tend to be positively selected. . . . Migrants responding primarily to minus factors at origin tend to be negatively selected" (Lee 1966, 56). The most common plus factor at destination is a job that pays more than the potential mover currently earns; the most common minus factor is political repression.[3] In a similar vein, the economist Barry Chiswick (1978, 900–901) hypothesized: "Economic theory suggests that migration in response to economic incentives is generally more profitable for the more able and more highly motivated. This self-selection in migration implies that for the same schooling, age and other demographic characteristics immigrants to the United States have more innate ability or motivation relative to the labor market than native-born persons."

Chiswick was one of the first to subject this idea to an empirical test. In doing so, he reasoned that, as newcomers, most immigrants incur short-term deficits. Until they "learn the ropes," they cannot be expected to reap the benefits of their abilities. Therefore, he examined the trajectory of male immigrant earnings over time. Sure enough, he found that, some ten to fifteen years after their arrival in the United States, their earnings caught up with the earnings of nonmigrants with similar skills, family obligations, and residential locations; thereafter the immigrants out-earned natives. This pattern turned out to hold not only in the United States but also in Canada, England, and Israel. The only caveat Chiswick noted was that not all immigrants caught up with the earnings of their counterparts in the dominant group. Rather, they caught up with native-born individuals of similar ethnic or racial background. This, he felt, was not surprising since some native-born groups—African or Mexican Americans, for example—do not earn as much as native-born whites.

Additional studies found that men who migrated as children and the nonmigrant children of immigrants also show an edge over non-movers with similar job-related characteristics. But it is not as large. This observation led scholars to hypothesize that migrant parents transmit some portion of their greater motivation and talent to their offspring, though the mechanism responsible for this transfer has never been identified. Some studies showed that above-average achievement tends to disappear by the third generation, though a few groups—for instance, Asians and Russians—maintain an advantage into the third generation (Carliner 1980; Neidert and Farley 1985). Interestingly, the average educational achievement of third-generation Asians and Russians is also higher than that of natives. Yet, when these groups are made statistically "the same" on education and other job-related characteristics, Asians and Russians retain an edge.

Other factors besides generation and motive for migration also in-fluence selectivity—in particular, "migration costs" or "intervening obstacles." The higher the costs or the greater the obstacles to the move, the more positively selected the migrant. In his classic article, the obstacles Everett Lee mentions include geographic factors like distance, structural factors like immigration rules, family factors like the number of dependents, and individual factors like knowledge about conditions at destination. In recent years, scholars have paid a great deal of attention to the last of these. Early birds, or those who are among the first to leave a sending community, have little awareness of conditions at destination; they must forge their way on their own. That they relocate despite their ignorance is testimony to their positive selectivity. But as Lee (1966, 55) points out, "The overcoming of a set of intervening obstacles by early migrants lessens the difficulty of the passage for later migrants." Or, as Guillermina Jasso (2004, 262) writes: "The greater the obstacles to migration, the higher the quality of the immigrant; pioneer immigrants are, thus, of higher quality than the relatives who follow." More generally, the later a migrant relocates compared to others from the same sending community, the less positively selected he or she should be.

The distinction between primary and secondary (or "tied") movers is another phenomenon relevant to selectivity. In the case of economically motivated relocations, primary movers are those who expect to secure financial benefits as a result of the move. Secondary or tied movers are those who relocate because of their relationship to a primary mover. Such relations are usually based on marriage or kinship. The distinction is important because Lee's ideas about selectivity apply to primary movers, not to those who involuntarily accompany them. The implication of this distinction emerges in Chiswick's (1977) discovery that sons of foreign-born fathers and native-born mothers earn more than sons of native-born fathers and foreign-born mothers. His explanation is that foreign-born fathers are more positively selected on hard-to-measure job-related traits than foreign-born mothers because the former are more likely to have migrated for economic reasons, while the latter simply accompanied their husbands. To conclude, both Lee and Chiswick agree: the extent to which immigrants are positively selected depends on the motive for the move and the obstacles associated with it.

Hubs and Spokes   Recent research on West Indian migrants to New York and London brings an entirely new explanation for their employment advantage. Vilna Bashi's (2007) in-depth interviews with eighty-four West Indians revealed that those who moved not only elected to do so, but also were chosen. Most West Indian immigrants in this sample were invited to relocate by a previously arrived compatriot. At the same time, Bashi's research unearthed people in the Caribbean who were eager to move but had failed to find a sponsor. She concluded that sponsors were selective, choosing only those who would enhance their reputations with gatekeepers at destination and with coethnics at home.

A second finding was that most of the immigrants with whom she talked never sponsored the relocation of anyone else. Those who did, however, were responsible for the relocation of several compatriots. Furthermore, veterans not only "choose the individuals they will help to emigrate" but also "send undesirable immigrants back" (Bashi 2007, 89). Bashi labels this form of population movement the "hub and spoke" model. "One kind of migrant (the 'hub') is the central figure, who becomes an 'expert' at getting their compatriots into the country. . . . The 'spoke' is the beneficiary of the hub's assistance" (31).

The implication of this form of migration for labor market outcomes is clear. Those chosen must meet criteria set by the hub. Though the relevant characteristics vary from situation to situation, employability is certainly a key prerequisite because hubs frequently find jobs for spokes (Bashi 2007). Since no one likes to be embarrassed, hubs are not likely to recommend to employers spokes whose job skills or work ethic fall short; similarly, spokes are not likely to perform poorly on the job, because they do not wish to sully the reputations of their sponsors. Students of labor markets have found that employers are well aware that a web of personal obligations works to their advantage; that is why they prefer to hire people who come personally recommended (Stigler 1962). If, as many economists assume, industrious performance leads to more prestigious posts and higher pay, then—other things being the same—these handpicked West Indian immigrants will fare better than most anonymously hired applicants.

Of course, just what fraction of West Indian immigrants fit this mold is not clear. Bashi's findings are based on a small snowball sample; hence, at this point they are merely suggestive. Still, the mechanism she has uncovered, "sponsor selection," does an even better job of explaining West Indian success than does the traditional concept of "self-selection."

A Dissenting View

In the mid-1980s, the economist George Borjas challenged the claim that migrants' motives are the key to selectivity. Extending the ideas of A. D. Roy (1951), Borjas (1985, 1987, 1991, 1994) argues that economically motivated movers are positively selected when income inequality is greater in the receiving country than in the sending country and negatively selected when income inequality is greater in the sending country than in the receiving country. This expectation rests on the assumption that, within a given sending country, the individuals who leave are those who have the most to gain. When income inequality is greater at origin than at destination, individuals with low skills have the most to gain by moving. This follows because a low-skilled person fares better in an economy that gives moderate rewards to skill than in an economy that gives high rewards for skill. When income inequality is less at origin than at destination, individuals with relatively high skills have the most to gain by moving. Because income inequality in Latin America and the Caribbean is greater than in the United States, Borjas predicts that these immigrants are negatively selected. Obviously, if this argument is correct, then positive selection cannot be the reason for West Indians' labor market advantage over African Americans.

Like Everett Lee and Barry Chiswick, Borjas also acknowledges that selectivity is affected by "intervening obstacles," or "migration (mobility) costs." The higher the migration costs, the more positively selected the migrant. Borjas distinguishes two types of obstacles. One is the monetary and psychic cost associated with relocation. Among his examples are distance from the United States, length of time needed to find work, and culture shock. The second obstacle is immigration law. He writes: "There are statutory restrictions on the number of legal immigrants the United States will accept from any given country. Quotas play the important role of increasing migration costs of emigrants (if the numerical constraints are binding) since these individuals will presumably have to compete (and invest time and effort) to obtain the relatively scarce visas" (Borjas 1987, 535). As explained in chapter 2, both the 1924 Johnson-Reed Act and the 1952 McCarran-Walter Act placed firm limits on immigration from non-Western sending regions. According to Borjas, the time and effort that Caribbean movers had to expend to obtain a visa under these regimes was so great that only the cleverest and most determined succeeded. But the implementation of the Hart-Celler Act in 1967 greatly increased the number of persons eligible to immigrate from the Caribbean. The resulting drop in migration costs, coupled with the propensity of the less-skilled to benefit more from emigration than the skilled, meant that post-1967 arrivals from countries with high income inequality, like the West Indies, were negatively selected.

What is the empirical evidence that third-wave West Indians are negatively selected? As pointed out earlier, Chiswick's research showed the opposite: after a catchup period, male immigrants, irrespective of sending region, earned more than native-born men with similar skills and ethnic identities According to Borjas, however, Chiswick's methodology was flawed. By relying on a single cross-section (the 1970 census), Chiswick could not distinguish the effect of years since migration (YSM) from the effect of year of arrival (YOA).[4] While immigrants arriving before 1967 out-earned their coethnic counterparts after a decade or two, Borjas argues that low immigration quotas brought this about by making entry difficult, thereby enhancing the selectivity of movers from countries of high income inequality.

Over the next few years, Borjas (1985, 1987, 1991, 1994, 1995) used pooled samples of two, and later three decades of census data to study the earnings of immigrant males. His main finding was that, controlling for easily measured job-related characteristics, post-1967 arrivals from most non-Western locales incurred large deficits upon arrival, while newcomers from Europe and Canada fared as well or better than their pre-1967 counterparts. In terms of his statistical models, for a given number of years since migration, the effect of YOA on the earnings of post-1967 arrivals from countries with high income inequality was negative, while the effect of YOA on the earnings of post-1967 arrivals from countries with low income inequality was positive or insignificant. After a decade or so in the United States, Borjas predicted, the earnings of immigrants from Europe and Canada would overtake those of their native white counterparts, while the earnings of immigrants from the rest of the world would never surpass those of their native counterparts. In short, Europeans and Canadians were positively selected; most others were negatively selected.[5]

At first, as Borjas extended his research forward in time, he found that more recently arrived immigrants had ever greater initial deficits. Then, in 2000, an unexpected turnaround occurred: cohort decline ceased for men with less than ten years' residence in the United States, while men with less than five years' residence did about as well as their counterparts who had arrived twenty years earlier (Borjas and Friedberg 2006). Analysis revealed that only immigrants from six Asian countries and Mexico experienced this uptick. In the Asian case, Borjas and Friedberg credited new immigration legislation, which increased the number of H-1B visas. These are temporary visas for highly skilled immigrants, many of whom assume good jobs immediately upon arrival. As for the Mexicans, the researchers claimed that improvement was due to a decline in the wages of unskilled native-born workers rather than improvement in the wages of immigrants.

These countries aside, the trend has been for each year of arrival to be associated with lower earnings than the year before. Borjas's main explanation has been changes in the mix of sending countries. Because immigrants from countries with high income inequality make up an increasing proportion of immigrants coming to the United States, an increasing proportion are negatively selected. But this is only part of the story. Borjas also discovered that earnings deficits were growing over time among immigrants from the *same* third-world sending country. The changing mix of sending countries cannot account for changes occurring within a single sending country. But selectivity theory offers a reason for decline over time: a drop in migration costs. Selectivity predicts that latecomers will be less positively selected than early birds because the presence of previously arrived compatriots will ease their way. And the larger the number of previously arrived compatriots, the less positively selected the immigrant will be.

When writing about migration costs, neither Chiswick nor Borjas has stressed the effect of timing of migration; they have focused rather on the effects of distance between origin and destination, or on changes in immigration law. Yet the "early bird" hypothesis is wholly consonant with their perspective. In Borjas's parlance, the absence of previously arrived compatriots raises the psychic cost of resettlement. It may also raise the monetary cost, since the fewer the number of compatriots at destination, the longer the immigrant may need to search before finding work.

Some sense of the effect of previous migration on selectivity can be obtained from studies of rural Mexico by Douglas Massey and his collaborators (Massey et al. 1986; Massey, Goldring, and Durand 1994; Fussell and Massey 2004). They observed that early birds came primarily from the middle strata. Once these pioneers established beachheads in the United States, they sent home money and gifts. Soon migrant success stories, some exaggerated, some realistic, diffused through the sending community. These stories encouraged others to consider migrating, especially if they had relatives or friends who had already departed. After a period of time, a process set in that Massey calls "cumulative causation."

> Every new migrant reduces the cost of subsequent migration for a set of friends and relatives; with the lowered costs, some of these people are induced to migrate, which further expands the set of people with ties abroad and, in turn, reduces costs for a new set of people, causing some of them to migrate, and so on. . . . Once the number of network connections in an origin area reaches a critical level, migration becomes self-perpetuating because migration itself creates the social structure needed to sustain it. (Massey 1991, 28–29)

As a result, in the long run selectivity no longer operates, and the average migrant resembles the average town dweller.

Of course, at the same time that some towns have lost nearly all their able-bodied residents, other towns may have just begun losing inhabitants. At least, this was the pattern that Kerby Miller (1985) observed in Ireland. Emigration was associated with the commercialization of agriculture, which penetrated the country unevenly. Thus, by the early twentieth century, latecomers were departing from some parts of the country, while early birds were departing from others. For this reason, research that examines the selectivity of *all* persons arriving in a single year from a given nation (that is, research that does not distinguish residents of one sending community from another) may fail to capture the selectivity of migration. Evidence for this interpretation comes from Elizabeth Fussell's (2004) attempt to disentangle the effects of national origin and sending community. Using surveys drawn from communities in several countries in the Hispanic Caribbean, she compared the net effect of national characteristics and community characteristics on people's propensity to make a first trip to the United States. The only sending country for which a national effect obtained was Mexico, probably because its culture of migration is so entrenched. The decision to emigrate from Costa Rica, the Dominican Republic, Nicaragua, or Puerto Rico depended only on community characteristics. This discovery illustrates the difficulty of measuring selectivity accurately in the absence of detailed information on premigration residence.

To sum up, selectivity theorists disagree about whether or not movers from a third-world area like the West Indies should be positively or negatively selected on traits that are hard to measure. Both groups of scholars concur, however, that the greater the costs of moving, the more positively selected the mover. Unfortunately, some costs can be easily measured at the level of nations (for instance, distance or immigration law), but other costs (like acquaintance with previously settled compatriots) are best measured at the level of communities. For this reason, over the short run, immigrants from a particular nation are likely to exhibit a decline in selectivity, but as new sending and receiving communities enter the picture, the direction of selectivity may stabilize or improve.

White Favoritism

The third and final explanation for West Indian advantage is the "white favoritism" hypothesis. One of the first scholars to advance this proposition was Roy Bryce-Laporte (1972). On the one hand, he proposed, white landlords, shopkeepers, and employers view West Indians as superior to African Americans; on the other hand, he believed, the immigrants stress their exoticism and deliberately set themselves apart from native blacks, presumably in hopes of benefiting from the distinction. Soon other scholars began taking note of this state of affairs (Dominguez 1975; Forsythe 1983), but only a few have attempted to explain it.

The "white favoritism" hypothesis differs from explanations of West Indian advantage based on culture or selectivity in being other-directed rather than inner-directed. Only after West Indians and whites have interacted does white favoritism become a possibility. One way such interactions can produce white favoritism is through the mechanism of the comfort factor. As already pointed out, this phrase refers to Mary Waters's observation that whites feel more comfortable with West Indians than with African Americans. There are several behavioral differences responsible for this effect: West Indians are more relaxed with whites, they are not as angry, they do not necessarily feel that American society "owes them something," and they have less of a chip on their shoulders. In explaining these behavioral differences, Waters stresses the optimism of immigrants versus the pessimism of American blacks. In her view, the roots of immigrants' optimism lie in two previously mentioned conditions: socialization in an all-black society and the positive selectivity of migration. The immigrants believe "that opportunities exist in the U.S. and that their own black skin has not, and will not, prevent them from taking advantage of those opportunities. It is this belief that while racism might exist, it can surely be overcome with determination and hard work that propelled the immigrants to move from a majority black society to the U.S. in the first place" (Waters 1997, 19). Conversely, African Americans experience racism as a constant irritant in their lives, an irritant that has nothing to do with them personally and everything to do with them collectively. Believing that racism cannot be overcome with determination and hard work, some African Americans relate to whites in an oppositional manner (Ogbu 1978). As a result, whites experience greater comfort in their interactions with West Indians, a situation that motivates gatekeepers to favor the immigrants over African Americans. Thus, for Waters, socialization in an all-black society and the positive selectivity of migration together produce "the comfort factor," which, in turn, produces whites who favor West Indians over African Americans.

Other explanations for white favoritism assume that it is rooted in something other than true behavioral differences. Faye Arnold (1984) attributes it to American cultural legacies—in particular, an ideology that attaches a positive value to people and practices linked to Great Britain. Arnold describes New York's West Indian community in the following terms: "They were English subjects and self-identified as a distinctive 'Black English Culture' group. . . . The black immigrants' English ethnocentrism, speech patterns, cultural mannerisms, religious preferences (Anglican or Protestant Episcopal), dress and general lifestyle 'whitened' (that is, garnered advantages and opportunities typically denied blacks)" (Arnold 1984, 56).[6]

In elaborating on this point, Arnold finds it useful to contrast the position of West Indians in New York and London. In the latter, no advantage accrues for emigrating from a British colony or former colony. Indeed, "despite the intensity of their Anglophilia and regard for 'the mother country,' they are not perceived as 'black Englishmen' by most whites" (Arnold 1984, 57). Instead, Arnold maintains, West Indians are Britain's most stigmatized group, while another nonwhite colonized minority, South Asians, hold a more prestigious position.

Thus, Arnold assumes that every society ranks immigrants and minorities in a hierarchical fashion. In the United States, African Americans occupy the least desirable rung in this "hierarchy of discrimination." West Indians are ranked more favorably primarily because whites associate West Indians with the British, a background that has occupied the top rung in the hierarchy since the nation's founding. In Britain, obviously, being British is not a cause for celebration, and being a colonial or ex-colonial signifies conquest and dishonor. In such an environment, West Indians occupy a debased position. As nonwhites and ex-colonials, South Asians are likewise stigmatized, but they hold a more favorable position because their background is free from the taint of slavery and because their physical appearance more closely resembles that of whites.

The world systems theorist Ramón Grosfoguel (2003) proposes yet another causal nexus. At the bottom of a multi-tiered "racial/ethnic hierarchy" he places "colonial/racialized subjects." The groups fitting this description vary across destinations. In the United States, they are African Americans, Puerto Ricans, and other "oppressed groups that have been incorporated into the U.S. empire" (Grosfoguel 2003, 148). Higher on the ladder stand "colonial immigrants." These are migrants who come from regions colonized by a power other than the one in which they have settled, but who suffer from the low political and economic position of their homeland. British West Indians are "colonial immigrants" if they settle in the United States, but "colonial/racialized subjects" if they settle in Britain. Above "colonial immigrants" stand "immigrants." These movers usually come from places devoid of a colonial legacy; they face the fewest barriers to complete incorporation into the host society. For Grosfoguel, then, British West Indians in the United States rank above African Americans, Puerto Ricans, Mexicans, and Native Americans, though they are unlikely to encounter all these stigmatized groups in the same place.

The description of West Indians' position in Canada offered by the Ontario-bred writer Malcolm Gladwell matches Grosfoguel's prediction. Gladwell feels that West Indians occupy the lowest position in Canada's ethnic-racial hierarchy. As he put it: "In America, there is someone else to despise. In Canada, there is not" (Gladwell 1996, 81). Gladwell believes that the presence or absence of a significant native black population is the critical determinant of West Indian social standing, as does his fellow Canadian Cecil Foster (1996). Grosfoguel might explain this by claiming that the limited number of Canada's ventures into imperialism is responsible for the dearth of "colonial/racialized subjects" there. He would doubtless classify aboriginal populations like North American Indians or Inuits as "colonial/racialized subjects." But members of these groups rarely live in areas where West Indians have settled. Hence, Grosfoguel would not be surprised that British West Indians fall to the bottom of Canada's ethnic-racial hierarchy. But in fact, neither Grosfoguel nor Arnold have offered predictions about the standing of British West Indians in Canada.

To recapitulate, social scientists have offered three explanations for white favoritism. One is the "comfort factor": white Americans feel more comfortable with British West Indians than with African Americans. On the West Indian side, the bases for the comfort factor are socialization in an all-black society and the positive selectivity of immigration. On the African American side, the basis for the comfort factor is ongoing interpersonal and structural racism. These tensions motivate whites to favor West Indians. Another is Anglophilia: white Americans have a very positive image of things English; West Indians communicate their Englishness and profit from it. A third reason is the "coloniality of power" (Grosfoguel 2003). Even in a postcolonial age, group rankings are affected by the historical relationship between sending and receiving countries. From this perspective, English-speaking West Indians' position in America is low, but not as low as that of groups whose homelands were either incorporated into or directly controlled by the United States.

A Synthetic Vision

Perceptive readers may have noticed a problem with the argument so far. Presenting the three hypotheses sequentially eases the task of exposition but creates the impression that these explanations are mutually exclusive. There is no reason to believe that only one is correct. Indeed, there are reasons for believing that, if positive selectivity obtains, then white favoritism also holds. This interpretation follows because the selectivity of migration may enhance West Indian outcomes directly as well as indirectly. To see this, examine figure 3.1.

The figure is in the form of a path diagram, a scheme that uses arrows to convey causal relationships. Prior causes appear to the left of effects, and some effects are themselves secondary causes. There are five prior causes in the diagram: slave autonomy, English heritage, coloniality of power, all-black society, and selectivity. There are two secondary causes, or variables that function as both cause and effect: the comfort factor and white favoritism. These are secondary rather than prior causes because they are not part of the baggage that West Indians bring with them but rather part of the white American response to West Indians. The end of the causal chain is West Indian advantage; it is the ultimate effect that the figure is drawn to explain.

Another important terminological distinction is between direct and indirect effects. Paths going straight from any cause to the ultimate ef-

Figure 3.1   Explanations for West Indian Advantage

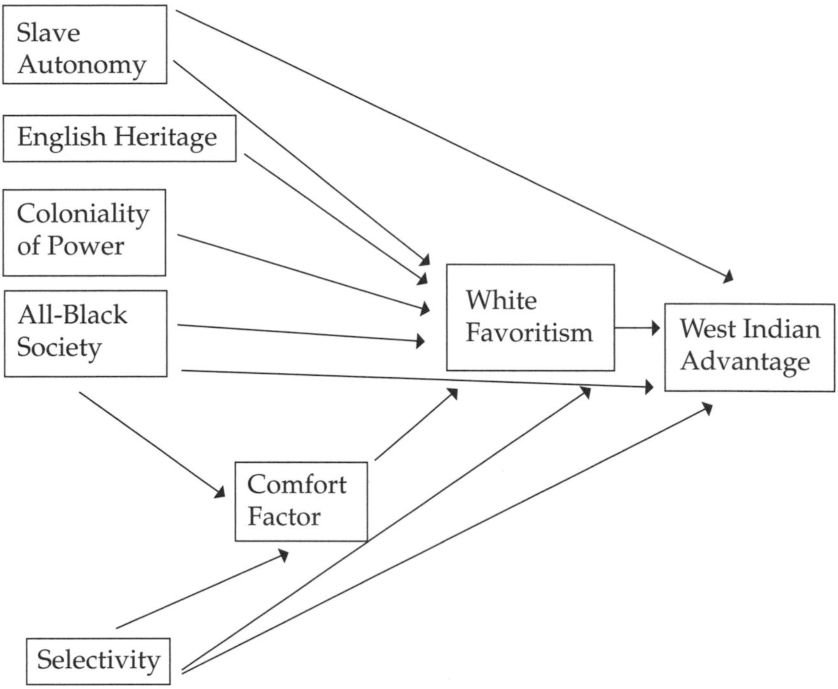

Source: Author's conception.

fect (at the extreme right of the diagram) are called direct effects. Thus, the arrow between slave autonomy and West Indian advantage conveys a direct effect. The path from white favoritism to West Indian advantage likewise conveys a direct effect. Conversely, paths from a prior cause to a secondary cause are called indirect effects. They operate by affecting an intermediate outcome, which, in turn, directly influences the ultimate effect. The arrow between English heritage and white favoritism captures an indirect effect.

The figure is thus a helpful tool in disentangling the causal implications of the hypotheses described in this chapter. To begin in the upper left-hand corner, the diagram shows an arrow going from the prior cause "slave autonomy" directly to "West Indian advantage." This path signifies that the Caribbean slave experience fostered traits (diligence, frugality) that directly enhance West Indian advantage. Note the absence of an indirect path between slave autonomy and white favoritism. Thomas Sowell is very explicit on this point: West Indian workers succeed not because white employers are impressed by their attitudes and behaviors, but because those attitudes and behaviors make West Indians more productive workers. Their work ethic is a sufficient cause of their success.

The second prior cause is English heritage. Admittedly, English heritage by itself is of no consequence. English heritage becomes causally linked to West Indian advantage only because of the Anglophilia of most American whites. As a Bahamian informant told Faye Arnold (1996, 22), "White Americans are wild about anything British." Thus, once Americans become aware of West Indians' English connection, they treat them better than they treat African Americans.

The third prior cause is coloniality of power. This term refers to the causal link that Grosfoguel posits between the colonial history of a sending region and the status of its emigrants at destination. Emigrants from colonies or ex-colonies will encounter more stigma in their mother countries than elsewhere. Thus, British West Indians "are frequently portrayed in New York's 'Euro-American imaginary' as 'hard working, educated, and entrepreneurial people,' while in London they are represented with the same racist stereotypes as are Puerto Ricans and African-Americans in New York" (Grosfoguel 2003, 159).

The fourth prior cause is an all-black society. The logic here is that socialization in an all-black society both raises the ambitions of West Indians and reduces their tolerance for racism—hence the direct arrow from socialization in an all-black society to West Indian advantage. Also emanating from the all-black society is an arrow to the comfort factor. This reflects Waters's claim that socialization in an all-black society is one reason why West Indians have more congenial relations with whites than African Americans do. West Indians' confidence that racism is not a hopeless impediment translates into a more cordial relationship with whites.

The last prior cause is positive selectivity. Unlike the previous four, positive selectivity applies to mover-stayer differences in general, rather than only to differences between West Indians and African Americans. The argument is that the average mover is more diligent and determined than the average stayer. Some formulations of this hypothesis also consider migrants more skilled—in the sense of having greater manual dexterity, intelligence, or other job-related talents—than nonmigrants. Whatever the precise packet of traits that migrants bring with them, they lead directly to better labor market outcomes—hence the arrow directly from selectivity to West Indian advantage. But there is also an indirect path from positive selectivity to the comfort factor. This reflects Waters's claim that the positive selectivity of migration is one reason why West Indians have more congenial relationships with whites than African Americans do. She emphasizes the optimism, ambition, and determination of immigrants. West Indians want to impress their supervisors; hence, they behave in ways that put their supervisors at ease. "Somebody is set over you and you do what you are told to do. It's not that you don't have any backbone or that you are subservient or anything, it's just that you are in the workplace and somebody has to be the boss. I think we accept that quicker than American blacks" (Waters 1999, 152). The indirect path from the comfort factor to white favoritism conveys the expectation that this acceptance will pay off.

Moving to the middle of the diagram, white favoritism differs from slave autonomy, English heritage, coloniality of power, an all-black society, and selectivity in two ways: First, it is a secondary cause or mediating variable; one or more of the five prior causes must initiate the causal chain that leads to white favoritism. Second, whatever its precursors, white favoritism imparts a comparative, not an absolute, advantage. White gatekeepers favor one group (West Indians) over another (African Americans). On the other hand, the causal impact of slave autonomy, an all-black society, and selectivity is absolute; an African American presence is not necessary for West Indians to reap whatever benefits these three causes bring. Waters proposes that African Americans and West Indians are equally productive workers but that West Indians are more amiable workers and, to the extent that an amicable relationship with authority is an important job-related characteristic, West Indians will have better economic outcomes than African Americans.

The remainder of this book is devoted to a more comprehensive examination of each hypothesis than has so far been published. Both historical and contemporary materials are consulted. The historical effort draws on published accounts of West Indian and United States history, supplemented by government statistics and figures from other authoritative sources. The contemporary effort likewise utilizes published accounts and authoritative figures, but it also includes considerable secondary data analysis. As it turns out, this diversity of strategies converges on the conclusion that positive selectivity explains West Indian advantage. Moreover, it operates as a direct cause; it does not operate indirectly through the comfort factor or through white favoritism. The only causal path the secondary data analysis supports is the direct path between selectivity and West Indian advantage.

• Chapter 4 •

Testing the Hypothesis of Selectivity

Tʜɪs is the first of three empirical chapters devoted to testing the three explanations for West Indian advantage. It focuses on selectivity because tests of selectivity show very clearly the utility of controlling for the number of years since an immigrant has migrated (YSM). To be sure, including this control is also useful in testing culture and favoritism, but this inclusion is easiest to understand in the case of selectivity. Hence, selectivity is considered first.

Each of these empirical chapters includes a review of the relevant literature. In the present instance, the review is brief because few studies have examined the selectivity of West Indian immigration. The chapter then presents several strategies that test the selectivity hypothesis. The first adds years since migration and then cohort of arrival (COA) to comparisons of the economic outcomes of West Indian immigrants and African Americans. The results indicate that immigrants do better the longer they have lived in the United States, but that this effect weakens as their cohort of arrival becomes more recent. The second strategy compares the economic outcomes of native-born West Indians and African Americans. It reveals that the economic outcomes of native-born West Indians are stronger than those of African Americans but weaker than those of foreign-born West Indians. The last strategy compares the economic outcomes of recently arrived West Indian immigrants with the outcomes of recently arrived African American internal migrants. Very few differences between the two groups of blacks are detected. All these results support the claim that the selectivity of migration is responsible for West Indian advantage, but the last is the most compelling.

Previous Research on Selectivity

In the migration literature, the term "selectivity" can refer to the distinction between movers and nonmovers on measurable job-related characteristics like education or on hard-to-measure job-related characteristics like ingenuity. Chapter 2 presents evidence that West Indian movers are stronger than West Indian stayers on many of the usual measurable job-related characteristics. But even if movers have more favorable measurable characteristics than stayers, they may not have more favorable hard-to-measure characteristics. George Borjas (1991, 38) writes: "Negative selection in unobserved characteristics (or ability) may be jointly occurring with positive selection in education, or vice versa. Simply because the United States attracts highly educated persons from some countries does not imply that these highly educated persons are the most productive highly educated persons in that particular country of origin." To see why this is so, consider that migration is expensive, especially international migration. Thus, movers may be more educated than stayers simply because more-educated people have higher incomes, and high income is needed to journey abroad. An entirely different approach is needed if a determination is to be made regarding a migrant group's selectivity on hard-to-measure traits.

How can it be shown that movers are more ambitious than stayers? Or smarter? To date, empirical evidence for selectivity on hard-to-measure characteristics has been based on a refinement of the residual method of causal attribution used in chapter 2.[1] Researchers testing for selectivity on hard-to-measure traits use a similar strategy, comparing the earnings of U.S. immigrants to the earnings of similarly qualified U.S. natives. But there is an inconsistency in the latter approach: it does not contrast migrants with those they left behind but with those they have joined at destination.

How can such a comparison illuminate the distinction between migrants at destination and nonmigrants at origin? The originator of the strategy, Barry Chiswick (1979, 369), defended it on these grounds: "If the distribution of innate ability and motivation is similar across countries, the average level of ability and motivation would be higher for the immigrants (particularly economic migrants) than for the native born in a population." In other words, diligence and creativity pay no heed to national or international boundaries. Even if residents in sending and receiving regions differ on measurable skills like work experience or education, both have equal amounts of human talent. Migrants stand out in both contexts because they are more gifted.

As pointed out in the previous chapter, because Chiswick (1979) believed that race and ethnicity have consequences for the native-born, he chose as a benchmark native-born persons of the same heritage as the foreign-born persons he was studying. For example, he compared black immigrants to African Americans, Chinese immigrants to Chinese Americans, and so on.[2] In an additional refinement, he introduced time into his calculations. Reasoning that immigrants' ability to reap the benefits of their unmeasured skills improves with acclimation to their environment, he noted how many years each immigrant had lived in the United States. When Chiswick compared the earnings of equally qualified foreign- and native-born coethnics, he found that time indeed mattered. For instance, black immigrants did not surpass their African American counterparts until eleven years after their arrival. Chiswick interpreted this outcome as evidence of positive selection on unmeasured characteristics; had the earnings difference consistently favored the native-born benchmark group, he would have interpreted it as evidence of negative selection.

Unfortunately, this causal attribution is problematic in the case of a West Indian–African American comparison. As pointed out in chapter 3, positive selectivity is but one of several phenomena potentially responsible for the advantage that West Indians display when they are made "the same" as African Americans on measurable job-related characteristics. Chiswick never considered the possibility that the culture of sending countries might be more conducive to job success than the culture of receiving countries. Nor did he expect that employers would favor immigrant workers by paying them more than comparably productive natives. But in the case of English-speaking West Indians, both these possibilities have been proposed.

Still, there are some insights to be gained from replicating Chiswick's strategy, as well as that of Borjas. First, it may be recalled that the results of the residual method presented in table 2.4 show West Indians with an advantage over African Americans on all economic outcomes except earnings. Chiswick's research suggests that the exception occurs because the average West Indian has not lived in the United States long enough to overcome the initial handicaps of relocating to a foreign land. Adding years since migration to the calculations may prove that, after a period of time, West Indians also secure an edge on this outcome. On the other hand, Borjas maintains that immigrants from nations of high income inequality like the West Indies will earn more than native-born persons only if they arrived before the implementation of the Hart-Celler Act in 1967. This prediction too deserves scrutiny, since it represents a serious challenge to any claim that today's West Indians are positively selected. To test this prediction requires adding year (or cohort) of arrival to the calculations, as well as YSM. Finally, once COA is included, it becomes possible to test the more general contention of scholars like Lee, Massey, and Jasso that early birds are more positively selected than latecomers.

The Empirical Effects of Time and Timing

Chiswick's idea that immigrants incur an initial disadvantage that gradually diminishes is appealing because longer residence should enhance immigrants' understanding of their new home. It is surprising that scholars do not routinely include years since migration in analyses of immigrant attainment. Comparisons that omit YSM reflect the immigrants' performance when their number of years since migration equals the average for the whole group. In contrast, when YSM is added to the calculations, the comparisons reflect the immigrants' performance during their first post-arrival year. It is also possible to use YSM to predict immigrants' earnings for whatever number of years since migration the investigator wants to examine.

Taking these considerations into account, table 4.1 presents ratios of foreign-born West Indian adjusted mean earnings to African American observed mean earnings during the immigrants' first post-arrival year. Asterisks convey statistical significance. In addition, the table reports the number of years, if any, after which West Indians will out-earn African Americans. Table 4.1 is limited to earnings because it has already been demonstrated (see table 2.4) that West Indians secure an advantage in labor force participation, unemployment, and occupational prestige.

Considering the men's ratios first, observe that newly arrived West Indians and African Americans had identical earnings in 1970 (ratio = 1.00), after which the ratio dropped to .91, climbing slowly to .95 by 2000.[3] The women's pattern is similar, except that the 1970 ratio was least favorable (.87) rather than most favorable. Regrettably, the 1970 results are less reliable than the others because of small sample size.[4] If 1980 is taken as the starting point instead, a clear pattern emerges: newly arrived West Indians earned more in recent censuses than in remote censuses.

How long will it take the immigrants covered in the post-1970 censuses to out-earn African Americans? Averaging the figures for the two sexes, about a dozen years in 1980, ten in 1990, and fifteen in 2000. Unexpectedly, the catchup time in 1990 was shorter than in 1980. This was probably the result of changes in African American rather than West Indian earnings. In 1980 the federal commitment to affirmative

Table 4.1   Ratios of Foreign-Born West Indian Adjusted Means to African American Observed Means on Logged Earnings and Years to Parity

	1970		1980		1990		2000	
	Men	Women	Men	Women	Men	Women	Men	Women
Ratio	1.00	0.87	0.91*	0.91*	0.92*	0.94*	0.95*	0.95*
Catchup time	0	0	12.6	11.1	11.0	7.57	17.3	13.1

Source: Author's calculations based on the 1 percent and 5 percent Integrated Public Use Microdata Series (IPUMS).
Note: These ratios adjust for years since migration. See the methodological appendix for a complete list of variables used in the adjustment.
* Statistically significant at the .05 level or better.

action was at its zenith, one consequence of which was the peaking of African Americans' earnings. Since table 4.1 captures differences between West Indians and African Americans, the results are sensitive to changes in the fortunes of either group. Nonetheless, adding YSM to the calculations offers a useful supplement to table 2.4 by showing that earnings do not constitute an exception to the generalization that West Indians have stronger labor market outcomes than African Americans. It just takes some time for an earnings advantage to emerge.

To what extent does adding cohort of arrival to the calculations change this conclusion? This innovation was introduced by George Borjas, who predicted that doing so would undercut the advantage associated with YSM because, in the absence of significant barriers to entry, immigrants from countries where income inequality is greater than in the United States—for example, the West Indies—are negatively selected. Between 1924 and 1967, such barriers were in place, and only a trickle of West Indians could legally enter the United States. With the liberalization that followed the implementation of the Hart-Celler Act of 1965, the number of visas available to residents of Western Hemisphere nations skyrocketed.[5]

To test Borjas's predictions, a new data set was created. Following the design that Borjas (1985) pioneered, it combined the four censuses analyzed previously and introduced indicators for census year and cohort of arrival. For every labor market outcome, testing Borjas's predictions requires calculating an adjusted mean for each cohort and dividing that mean by the actual African American mean. The approach used here differs from Borjas's in three ways. First, because selectivity is more applicable to primary movers than to people who move at the behest of others, immigrants who arrived when they were younger than age eighteen are excluded from the data set. Second, since Borjas's theory links selectivity on hard-to-measure skills with immigration law, one rationale for defining cohorts is to use periods when immigration law was similar. A second rationale is to measure the effect of time—that is, to determine whether, under similar immigration law, earlier cohorts outperformed later. There being insufficient numbers of pre-1924 arrivals, the following six cohorts of arrival were created: before 1953, 1953 to 1966, 1967 to 1976, 1977 to 1984, 1985 to 1991, and 1992 to 2000.[6] With the exception of the 1984–85 boundary, these dates coincide with the implementation (but not always the passage) of the McCarran-Walter Act, the Hart-Celler Act, the 1976 Immigration Act, and the 1990 Immigration Act. Though few West Indians profited from the last of these, Borjas and Friedberg (2006) find that men's earnings improved during the 1990s, a result they partially attribute to the 1990 act. In this analysis, to capture the effect of timing of arrival during an era when immigration law was essentially static, the 1977 to 1991 period is divided into two roughly equal components. Finally, the benchmark group is African Americans, not a choice Borjas would endorse. Note, however, that the effect of time is independent of benchmark. Were native whites the benchmark, the size of the ratios would change, but the temporal pattern of the ratios would be the same.

Table 4.2 conveys the results of the cohort analysis.[7] Since YSM is included in the calculations, the adjusted means describe West Indians' outcomes during their first year in the United States.[8] As before, including YSM makes it possible to estimate how many years must pass before a West Indian cohort does as well as similarly qualified African Americans. A zero catchup time means that, during their first year, West Indians fare as well as or better than their African American counterparts.

With the exception of earnings, most catchup times are zero. Several other noteworthy patterns appear. Consider Borjas's expectation that the generous quotas of the Hart-Celler Act would produce a decline in the "quality" of West Indian immigrants. If this is so, members of the 1953 to 1966 COA should have stronger ratios than members of the 1967 to 1976 COA. Of the eight comparisons that test this expectation, only four display the expected decline: men's labor force participation, women's unemployment, and the occupational prestige of both sexes. On earnings, Borjas's preferred outcome, both sexes register improvement. This is hardly a ringing endorsement for negative selection. Yet these results make sense because relatively few members of this cohort were joining previously arrived kin. As explained in chapter 2, the

Hart-Celler Act required labor certification for the great majority of Western Hemisphere residents. So many members of the 1967 to 1976 COA were more like early birds than latecomers.

The 1976 Immigration Act marked a major change: Western Hemisphere residents were now eligible for visas on the basis of kinship with previously arrived family members. And a substantial number had previously arrived. As selectivity theorists would predict, the large increase in kinship-based visas depressed the "quality" of the newcomers. On seven of the eight comparisons between the 1967 to 1976 cohort and the 1977 to 1984 cohort, the more recently arrived performed less well. Moving forward in time, the next set of comparisons, the 1977 to 1984 COA versus the 1985 to 1991 COA, produced five instances of cohort decline and three instances of cohort stability. Since there were few changes in the legal context, these dips probably reflect the lower "costs" associated with immigrating at the later date. As for the most recently arrived cohort, the West Indian results parallel those of Borjas and Friedberg (2006) in showing an occasional uptick. The 1992 to 2000 cohort fares poorer than its predecessor on three outcomes, equally well on three others, and better on men's unemployment and men's earnings.

This improvement may be related to the 1990 immigration law, but not in the way that Borjas and Friedberg suggest. They attribute some of the earnings improvement to H-1B visas, which often mean no wait for jobs. More relevant to the West Indian case, calculations based on published INS figures show that, after 1991, the proportion of quota-immigrants entering on the basis of job skills increased and the proportion entering on the basis of kinship declined. These trends were especially marked among arrivals from Barbados and Trinidad (U.S. Immigration and Naturalization Service, *Statistical Yearbook*, 1987, 1998, 1999, 2000). If, as Borjas and Friedberg imply, persons entering on the basis of their own skills are more "independent" than persons entering on the basis of family ties, the former should have stronger labor market outcomes than the latter, even after education and other characteristics are controlled.[9]

Unfortunately, the INS data on which the above conclusion is based do not distinguish male from female visa holders, but table 4.2 indicates that only men register a post-1991 uptick in prestige and earnings. Furthermore, attention to gender reveals that cohort decline is substantially greater among women than men. Women experience a near-linear decline in labor force participation and unemployment. In fact, the most recently arrived are as vulnerable to unemployment as African American women are (the ratio is 1.00). On occupational prestige and earnings, the pattern is curvilinear, with very early birds and

Table 4.2   Ratios of Foreign-Born West Indian Adjusted Means to African American Observed Means by Cohort of Arrival on Four Economic Indicators and Years to Parity

Cohort of Arrival	Labor Force Participation		Unemployment		Occupational Prestige		Log of Hourly Earnings	
	Men	Women	Men	Women	Men	Women	Men	Women
Before 1953								
Ratio	1.20*	1.32*	0.60	.56*	1.01	0.98	0.89*	0.91*
Catchup time	0	0	0	0	0	0	26.8	21.6
1953 to 1966								
Ratio	1.13*	1.24*	0.88	.56*	1.07*	1.07*	0.92*	0.95*
Catchup time	0	0	0	0	0	0	14.4	10.7
1967 to 1976								
Ratio	1.10*	1.27*	0.88	0.61*	1.05*	1.05*	0.94*	0.96*
Catchup time	0	0	0	0	0	0	10.6	7.85

1977 to 1984								
Ratio	1.06*	1.16*	0.76*	0.73*	1.33*	1.01*	0.92*	0.95*
Catchup time	0	0	0	0	0	0	14.4	11.1
1985 to 1991								
Ratio	1.06*	1.09*	0.82*	0.82	1.03*	0.98*	0.92*	0.94*
Catchup time	0	0	0	0	0	6.19	16.3	14.0
1992 to 2000								
Ratio	1.06*	1.03*	0.73*	1.00	1.02*	0.98*	0.94*	0.94*
Catchup time	0	0	0	0	0	8.34	12.0	14.6

Source: Author's calculations based on the 1 percent and 5 percent Integrated Public Use Microdata Series (IPUMS).
Note: Adjustment involves making West Indians the same as African Americans on human capital, family relationships, and geography. See the methodological appendix for a list of variables used in this adjustment.
* Statistically significant at the .05 level or better.

very recent arrivals doing less well than those entering in the 1960s and 1970s.

On the one hand, the ratios for women's occupational prestige (.98*) and earnings (.94*) remained the same from 1992 to 2000 as from 1985 to 1991. On the other hand, catchup time shows decline. For instance, on earnings, women arriving between 1985 and 1991 will catch up with African Americans after 14.0 years, and women arriving between 1992 and 2000 will catch up after 14.6 years. The 0.6-year discrepancy reflects differences beyond the second decimal place, differences that are not obvious in the three significant figures used to report the ratios but nevertheless are real.[10]

Why do West Indian women experience greater cohort decline than West Indian men? The most plausible explanation is that West Indian women are more often "primary movers" than men. As already explained, primary movers are individuals who expect to reap direct financial benefits from migration. In contrast, "secondary movers," or "tied movers," relocate in order to be in physical proximity with a primary mover. Theorists usually have primary movers in mind when formulating principles governing the selectivity of migration. For this reason, the selectivity of primary movers should be more sensitive to the costs of migration than the selectivity of secondary movers. Similarly, the economic outcomes of primary movers should be more closely linked to COA than the economic outcomes of secondary movers.

There are good reasons to suspect that West Indian women are more likely to be primary movers than West Indian men. For one, female immigrants from the English-speaking West Indies have slightly outnumbered males for about fifty years. For another, the literature on migration often describes post-1966 West Indian female migrants as primary movers (Clarke and Riviere 1989; Colen 1995). Add to this that, in the Caribbean, the proportion of families headed by women has long been high, as has the proportion of women in the labor force (Barrow 1996). A 1990 study of nurses in Trinidad revealed that 42 percent of respondents "exercised full financial responsibility in the care of their families" (Phillips 1996, 123). The study, which was undertaken during a time of extensive recruitment efforts by hospitals in the United States, also found that 85 percent of respondents expressed the intention to migrate.[11] Though the hypothesis that West Indian women are more often primary movers than West Indian men remains speculative, it meshes well with the discovery that cohort decline is more marked among women than men.

A final point about table 4.2. Borjas predicts that the earnings of post-1967 immigrants from countries of high income inequality will never catch up with the earnings of native-born whites or native-born Americans more generally. The analysis in chapter 2 implies that this is true of West Indian males but not females. The benchmark in the present chapter, however, is African Americans. Using this standard, the results in table 4.2 show that any deficits incurred by post-1967 arrivals will be made up in less than seventeen years. This is not an unduly long period of time; indeed, it is quite similar to the catchup times reported in the cross-sectional (single-year) tests of selectivity presented in table 4.1. In other words, for West Indians, the traditional method pioneered by Chiswick and the revisionist method pioneered by Borjas yield similar results.

Yet it would be premature to conclude that these two analyses prove that West Indians are positively selected. As noted earlier, there is a problem with the residual method of causal attribution. Explanations are inferred rather than demonstrated.[12] While some readers might be persuaded that West Indians overtake African Americans on all economic outcomes owing to positive selectivity, others might conclude that culture or white favoritism are equally plausible explanations.

One finding did emerge in this section that is uniquely consonant with selectivity: the declining advantage of those more recently arrived. Neither culture nor white favoritism anticipates a diminution of West Indian advantage by cohort of arrival. To be sure, some scholars might anticipate a diminution in white favoritism on the grounds that the larger a minority group, the more discrimination against it. As West Indian numbers increased, perhaps they engendered more hostility. For this objection to be convincing, all West Indians would have to face increasing barriers with the passage of time. But this is not the trend that the findings convey. Rather, other things being equal, those arriving in the 1990s do less well than those arriving in the 1970s. Admittedly, this is more true of women than men. Yet the gender interaction coincides with the way West Indian migration is organized. Indeed, this complication renders more tenable the assertion that selectivity contributes to cohort decline.[13]

Generational Effects

According to selection theorists, the advantages accruing to voluntary immigrants do not disappear with the demise of the immigrant generation. Their legacy lives on through their children, though with diminished intensity. Several scholars have found that the adult children of white immigrants (the second generation) have stronger economic outcomes than the adult children of native-born whites of native-born parents (the third generation) (Carliner 1980; Chiswick 1977; Featherman and Hauser 1978). The theory is that the first generation passes on to their offspring some of the talent, motivation, and ambition that originally impelled them to settle in a new land. Certainly, ethnographies have described the high expectations that West Indian immigrants have for their children, as well as the sense of obligation that second-generation West Indians feel toward parents who claim to have made sacrifices to give their offspring a better life (Butterfield 2006; Lopez 2003). With these considerations in mind, it is appropriate to ascertain whether second-generation West Indians have stronger economic outcomes than African Americans.

Before implementing this step, however, a technical difficulty must be recognized: after 1970, the U.S. Census replaced its question about parents' birthplace with an open-ended question about ancestry.[14] This means that "native-born West Indians" in the 1970 sample were blacks with at least one West Indian–born parent, whereas "native-born West Indians" in the post-1970 samples were second- and later-generation blacks who acknowledged some West Indian ancestry. If the selectivity of migration disappears by the third generation, then tests based on these later censuses are underestimates of the selectivity of the second generation. Complicating matters further, an unknown percentage of native-born West Indians described their ancestry as African American or black American rather than West Indian (Waters 1999). In short, because of changes in the census questionnaire after 1970, it is not possible exactly to replicate the strategy of previous researchers.

Table 4.3 contains the ratios of adjusted native-born West Indian means to observed African American means for all four census years. The pattern in the table is consonant with expectations. In 1970 the second generation significantly outpaced African Americans on five of eight outcomes, including both men's and women's earnings. In the next census, the native-born advantage extended to seven outcomes (1980), then it dropped to six (1990), and finally it dropped to four (2000).[15] Not unexpectedly, there are no outcomes on which native-born West Indians fare significantly less well than African Americans, though one value stands out as anomalous. In 1970 the ratio of native-born West Indian to African American women's unemployment was very unfavorable to the West Indians (1.43), though this result is not statistically significant.

In sum, native-born West Indians have economic outcomes that are often stronger than those of their African American counterparts, though not as often as the outcomes of longer-resident, foreign-born

Table 4.3   Ratios of Native-Born West Indian Adjusted Means to African American Observed Means on Four Economic Indicators

Year	Labor Force Participation		Unemployment		Occupational Prestige		Logged Earnings	
	Males	Females	Males	Females	Males	Females	Males	Females
1970	0.95	1.06*	0.87	1.43	1.11*	1.13*	1.08*	1.21*
1980	1.04*	1.08*	0.68*	0.79*	1.05*	1.07*	1.02*	0.99
1990	0.96	1.05*	0.76*	0.75*	1.02*	1.07*	1.00	1.05*
2000	1.13*	1.00	0.66*	0.83*	1.06*	1.04	0.98	1.03

Source: Author's calculations based on the 1 percent and 5 percent Integrated Public Use Microdata Series (IPUMS).
Note: See the methodological appendix for the variables used in the adjustment and for the restrictions placed on the analysis.
* Statistically significant at the .05 level or better.

West Indians. This patterns fits Chiswick's (1979, 370) expectation that "there is likely to be a regression toward the mean in the distribution of ability from one generation to the next . . . [but] . . . the earnings of the children of immigrants would exceed those of the children of native-born parents to the extent that their greater level of innate ability and motivation outweighs disadvantages from having parents with a foreign origin." Evidently, the children of immigrants reap some advantages from having talented parents, but there is also some dilution of talent across generations.

The discovery of a modest second-generation advantage fits selectivity theory but also has implications for the other two explanations for West Indian advantage: cultural superiority and white favoritism. As readers may recall, one implication of cultural superiority is that a strong work ethic is typical of all West Indians, not just of those who emigrate. The children of West Indian immigrants may fare slightly better than African Americans not because their parents were positively selected migrants but because their parents passed on to them some aspects of Caribbean culture. Thus, second-generation success is compatible with both the idea that migrants are positively selected and the idea that West Indian culture imparts a beneficial legacy. The results in table 4.3 provide no grounds for distinguishing between the two. At the same time, second-generation success is incompatible with the hypothesis of white favoritism. The reason is simple: the public cannot distinguish a native-born West Indian from an African American. Therefore, the public (employer, foreman, customer) cannot "favor" a West Indian over an African American. If favoritism operates at all, it must have sources other than stereotypes about different kinds of blacks. At minimum, these considerations imply that white favoritism alone cannot explain the success of West Indian immigrants. For if it were the only causal factor, second-generation West Indians would be economically indistinguishable from African Americans. That they fare measurably better means that positive selectivity, cultural superiority, or both must also be at work.

The Selectivity of African American Internal Migrants

The discussion turns now to the selectivity of African American internal migrants. If West Indian immigrants are more talented and diligent than those they leave behind, perhaps the same is true of African American movers. The first scholar to pursue this analogy was Kristin Butcher, who, in a 1994 article, evaluated the influence of relocation on earnings by comparing three groups of black men: African Americans residing in their state of birth, African Americans residing elsewhere than their state of birth, and black immigrants. She further separated the black immigrants into Jamaicans, "other Caribbeans," Africans, and a residual category. Butcher (1994, 281–82) concluded that the pattern

> for immigrants was very similar to the pattern among native-born black men who had moved out of their state of birth by the time of the Census. Indeed, on a variety of characteristics, including employment rates, marriage rates, average weeks of work, and average weekly earnings, Jamaican and other Caribbean immigrant black men were remarkably similar to native-born migrant black men. This pattern suggests that the distinction between "movers" and "stayers" is more fundamental than any inherent distinction between U.S.- and foreign-born black men.

This interpretation reflects quite a change in perceptions about African American migrants. For much of the twentieth century, southern black migrants to the North were viewed as culturally deficient, if not morally lax. Gunnar Myrdal's (1944, 976–77) classic World War II analysis is a good example of scholarly wisdom on this subject: "Social organization is generally at a low level among Southern Negroes but disorganization only reaches its extreme when Negroes migrate to cities and to the North. The controls of the rural community are removed; and the ignorant Negro does not know how to adjust to a radically new type of life. Like the European immigrant, he comes to the slums of the Northern cities and learns the criminal ways already widely practiced in such areas."

Twenty years later, Nathan Glazer and Daniel Patrick Moynihan published *Beyond the Melting Pot: The Negroes, Puerto Ricans, Jews, Italians, and Irish of New York City* (1963). Anticipating Sowell by a decade, they wrote glowingly about the economic success of West Indian blacks—contrasting them with black migrants from the South. "The West Indians' most striking difference from the Southern Negroes was their greater applicability to business, education, buying homes, and in general advancing themselves. . . . The ethos of the West Indian, in contrast to that of the Southern Negro, emphasized saving, hard work, investment, education" (Glazer and Moynihan 1963, 35). It is not clear whether this passage refers only to New York's southern blacks or includes those resident in the South, but it is clear that whoever southerners are, their values and behaviors are problematic.

A few years later, at a meeting convened to explore the causes and consequences of the increase in female-headed families among blacks, the eminent psychiatrist Robert Coles observed:

> The families I have seen seem to function quite well . . . in, say, Belle Glade, Florida or the Black Belt of Alabama. Then they go up to Boston or New York. The mother no longer is with her children working in the fields. She tries to get a job and probably does, as a maid. The children are left alone. The father, if there is one, goes on relief; or the whole family goes on relief. . . . What happens when they come into the cities . . . is that the families, I think, disintegrate. . . . I think the millions of people who have only in the last twenty or thirty years—one or two generations at most—come into the cities have not quite made the adaptation from rural living, with all the implications for family structure, to the urban situation. (American Academy of Arts and Sciences 1966, 302)

But the issue that concerned policymakers was not the rise in female-headed families per se; rather, it was growth in welfare recipiency, especially after Daniel Patrick Moynihan argued that blacks were moving north because welfare payments were more generous there (Farley and Allen 1987). In response to Moynihan's reasoning, the demographer Larry Long examined the correlates of welfare recipiency. After the publication of his findings, scholarly perceptions about southern migrants changed. Long (1974) found that southern-born black household heads who had lived at least five years in one of six northern metropolises were "less likely to be on welfare and less likely to be poor than the urban natives." In a later paper, Long and Lynn

Heltman (1975) reported that black men born in the South who had lived at least five years in the North had higher labor force participation rates and higher median incomes than northern-born nonmigrants. These results motivated Long (1974, 1975) to conclude that black migrants were a positively selected population. He inferred that the migrants were advantaged along social psychological dimensions that surveys did not capture—dimensions such as intelligence, ambition, optimism, and work ethic.[16] He went on to speculate that northern-born blacks might be more pessimistic about their prospects, that they might have a stronger sense of relative deprivation, and that they might have a higher reservation wage than the southern-born.[17]

Stewart Tolnay's (2003) research on a century of southern black migration has extended and qualified Long's conclusion. On the one hand, Tolnay found that southern black migrants were consistently more educated than southern black stayers; on the other hand, southern black migrants did not consistently secure better economic outcomes than equally qualified southern black stayers (Tolnay 2003).[18] Analyses undertaken with the data available to this study confirm this second conclusion. When the definition of a mover is broadened to include any African American living outside his or her state of birth, movers emerge as only slightly more economically advantaged than stayers (results not shown).[19]

One difficulty with comparisons of the economic outcomes of African American movers and stayers is that they rarely control for YSM. The reason is that few questionnaires ask internal migrants their date of arrival. Yet the economic outcomes of internal migrants, just like those of international migrants, are likely to be sensitive to YSM. The U.S. census routinely includes information on respondents' current place of residence as well as their residence five years prior to enumeration. This information renders another strategy feasible: comparing West Indian immigrants and African America internal migrants when both resided elsewhere five years prior to the decennial census. For African Americans, "elsewhere" is a different state; for West Indians, "elsewhere" is a different country. If the selectivity of migration is responsible for West Indian immigrants' advantage over African Americans, then their advantage should greatly diminish when both groups of blacks are migrants of roughly equal recency.

To explore this possibility, ratios of adjusted to observed means were estimated when the sample was limited to West Indians and African Americans who had relocated within the past five years. The results appear in table 4.4. They are impressive. In twenty-five of the thirty-two comparisons (78 percent), there are no significant differences between African Americans and West Indian immigrants. Of the

Table 4.4   Ratios of Adjusted Means of Recently Arrived Foreign-Born West Indian Immigrants and Observed Means of Recently Migrated African Americans on Four Economic Indicators

Year	Labor Force Participation		Unemployment		Occupational Prestige		Log of Hourly Earnings	
	Men	Women	Men	Women	Men	Women	Men	Women
1970	1.27*	1.16*	0.22*	0.63	1.12*	1.03	1.08	0.92
1980	0.94	1.05	1.01	0.98	1.00	0.98	0.93*	0.95
1990	1.00	0.98	1.39	0.58*	0.97	0.98	0.96	1.00
2000	0.96	0.96	0.70	1.08	0.97	0.98	0.99	0.96*

Source: Author's calculations based on the 1 percent and 5 percent Integrated Public Use Microdata Series (IPUMS).
Note: Adjustment involves making West Indians the same as African Americans on human capital, family relationships, and geography. See the methodological appendix for a list of variables used in this adjustment.
* Statistically significant at the .05 level or better.

seven contrasts that attain significance, five favor West Indians. Not unexpectedly, the two significant differences that favor African Americans pertain to earnings. This is the outcome on which previous analyses have already shown recently arrived West Indians to be vulnerable. Perhaps the more surprising result is the converse: that in six of the eight earnings comparisons West Indians are indistinguishable from African Americans.

As for the five significant contrasts that favor West Indians, four occurred in 1970. Given that no immigrant in the sample had resided in the United States longer than five years, these immigrants arrived between 1965 and 1970. Doubtless, most were beneficiaries of the newly implemented Hart-Celler Act. As pointed out earlier, having few previously arrived friends and relatives to ease their way, this group is likely to have been more positively selected than immigrants who left the Caribbean later, hence their strong showing. This exceptional circumstance aside, the message of the table is that economic differences largely disappear when both West Indians and African Americans are movers with the same YSM. This is very strong evidence that the selectivity of migration is responsible for the economic advantages of West Indian immigrants relative to African Americans.

To recapitulate, replication of models pioneered by economists show that the outcomes of West Indian immigrants improve as years since migration increase and that second-generation West Indians exhibit a small but perceptible advantage over African Americans. But these findings are logically compatible with explanations other than selectivity. The discovery that West Indian advantage declines with recency of arrival (COA) and that recently arrived West Indians and African Americans have statistically similar outcomes are logically compatible only with selectivity.

• Chapter 5 •

Testing Cultural Hypotheses

Oᴺᴇ of the central messages of chapter 3 is that there may be more than one explanation for the advantage that remains when West Indians and African Americans are made "the same" on measured job-related characteristics. Thus, empirical evidence that the selectivity of migration is one explanation does not mean there are no others. This chapter seeks empirical evidence for two cultural benefits that have traditionally been associated with West Indian birth: Sowell's claim about the positive effects of Caribbean slave autonomy and the popular belief that socialization in an all-black society is advantageous.[1]

In both cases, devising a test-strategy is facilitated by variations in the pervasiveness of the critical condition. In Sowell's case, neither in the Caribbean nor in the United States was slavery the homogenous, undifferentiated institution he imagines. In the case of racial composition, diversity also arises: neither the Caribbean nor sub-Saharan Africa consists entirely of all-black societies. These disparities make possible tests of the idea that Caribbean immigrants reap a cultural advantage over African Americans.

The Historical Arguments of Thomas Sowell

Sowell proposes three ways in which the historical experience of blacks within the Caribbean basin differed from the experience of blacks in the United States. Caribbean slaves had more opportunity to escape and rebel, they had more opportunity for economic independence, and, both pre- and post-emancipation, blacks had more opportunity to learn a skill. All of these ideas draw on the demographic fact that whites were a greater proportion of the population in the United States than in the Caribbean. But the first two ideas also draw on geography and economics, while the last—that Caribbean pre- and post-emancipation blacks had more opportunity to learn a skill—draws only on demography. This chapter assesses all three visions, first historically and then statistically. It turns out that Sowell's reading of the historical record is by and large accurate. Yet the statistical analysis does not support the message he takes from that reading because there are Caribbean immigrants whose history is quite similar to that of African Americans but who nonetheless outperform African Americans.

Escape and Rebellion

As Sowell presents the case, West Indian blacks waged a far more effective "war of resistance" against slavery than their American counterparts. The forms of resistance that interest him most are escapes, fugitive colonies, and insurrections.[2] Escape was difficult and required planning. Few runaways could succeed without help, and even then geographic and climactic conditions were crucial. Sowell (1975, 1978a, 1978b) believes that there was a higher rate of escape in the Caribbean than in the United States because

> the tropical climate made exposure less of a hazard to the escapee, and tropical vegetation made food more readily available in the wild, as well as providing cover in the largely unexplored interior of the island. The chance that an escaped slave would encounter even isolated white men . . . was very small, as compared to the chance that an escaped plantation slave would run into white patrols, white workmen, or white rural settlements in the South. (Sowell 1975, 99)

However, Sowell would be wrong to conclude that escapees were equally likely to survive. In the English-speaking world, islands like Barbados, which were flat and fully cultivated, offered no place to hide. In the Dutch Antilles, Aruba afforded very little "cover." On the other hand, several places offered good possibilities for fugitives to disappear into the interior, especially Trinidad, Jamaica, Belize, and all three Guianas: British, French, and Dutch (de Groot, Christen, and Knight 1997). Still, in only two Caribbean areas did Maroons, as escaped slaves were called, establish viable communities: Jamaica and Dutch Guiana (now Surinam).[3]

Unfortunately, information on the size of Maroon communities is sketchy. Informal observers reported 200 Maroons in a Guadeloupean community in 1726, 6,000 in three communities in Dutch Guiana in 1738, and 1,000 in two Jamaican communities in 1739. By the second decade of the nineteenth century, fewer than 1 percent of blacks living in the British Caribbean were counted as Maroons, almost all of them living in the mountainous interior of Jamaica (de Groot, Christen, and Knight 1997). In 1830, Stanley Engerman and Barry Higman (1997) estimate, 842,748 blacks dwelled in the British Caribbean; this implies a Maroon population of something under 8,500.

Surprisingly, the number of American escapees and their descendants appears to have been larger.[4] Over the years, a variety of opportunities for running away presented themselves, the first being service in the Revolutionary War. The British were short of men and offered freedom to slaves willing to serve in the army. Many ran off, served honorably, and obtained their liberty (Schama 2006). After the war, northern states slowly outlawed slavery, increasing the attraction of reaching these states. When Congress passed the Fugitive Slave Act of 1850, legislation that criminalized assisting runaways, foreign turf became especially attractive (Philip Foner 1983). Since slavery had been illegal in Canada since 1833, when Britain abolished it in the Empire, Canada was a prime destination for fugitives, particularly those resident in the North who feared forced repatriation to the South (Thomson 1979). In 1860 there were 60,000 blacks in Canada, three-fourths of them fugitives. In the lower South, a safe haven was harder to find.

If American slaves were more likely than Caribbean slaves to escape, "slaves rebelled much more frequently in the Caribbean than in the United States. The largest slave rebellion in the United States involved fewer than 500 slaves, and no rebellion seriously threatened white supremacy. In the Caribbean, hundreds or even thousands of slaves joined in widespread violence on dozens of occasions, destroying plantations and killing their owners" (Rogozinski 1992, 157). The reasons for this difference include the greater tendency for the African-born than the Creole to rebel and the greater freedom from supervision in the Caribbean (Craton 1997; Mullin 1992). Yet even here exceptions obtained. The island of Barbados witnessed relatively few uprisings, and none between 1701 and 1816 (Beckles 1984; Craton 1982). In fact, Barbadians were known for their "more cautious and less frontal mode of struggle" (James 1998, 116). Among the factors responsible for the difference, Winston James cites the island's relatively high proportion of whites, the flat terrain, and the imposing white military presence.[5] Though there were such exceptions, in general the Caribbean environment fostered more slave revolts, but not escapes, than did the American environment.

Provision Grounds

When Sowell writes about Caribbean slaves' economic independence, he is referring first and foremost to the practice of requiring slaves to produce their own food. In the West Indies, "provision grounds" could be up to two acres in size. They were often some distance from where slaves lived and worked; in Grenada, the distance was sometimes as far as ten miles (Marshall 1993). If slaves produced more than they could consume, they were permitted to sell the surplus and retain the proceeds. In Sowell's view, ex-slaves given these opportunities were better prepared to participate in a capitalist economy than ex-slaves who received all their provisions from their masters. "Thus, even under slavery, West Indian Negroes had direct personal responsibility for an important part of their own well being, and also acquired experience in economic activity on their own, since they cultivated their individual plots without supervision and were usually allowed to sell any surplus in the market" (Sowell 1975, 98).

But, like rebellion, self-provisioning was not universal in the Caribbean. It depended on the availability of peripheral land and the cost of importing food. On islands where sugar could be cultivated nearly everywhere, such as Barbados, Antigua, and St. Kitts, slaves depended on rations provided by the master. On most of the remaining islands and on the South American coast, slaves maintained provision grounds on peripheral land unsuitable for cash crops, though in some places owners also provided basic food rations (Beckles 1989; Marshall 1993; Mintz and Hall 1991; Sheridan 1996; Tomich 1993).

Relevant to the current inquiry is the discovery that, in some sections of the American South, slave owners encouraged independent production just as owners did in the West Indies. The region with the most highly developed tradition of slave self-provisioning was the Carolina Low Country, which, in its prime, extended from Cape Fear, North Carolina, to the St. John River area of Florida (Berlin 1998). One reason for the uniqueness of this area is that, in the 1670s and 1680s, contingents of Barbadians arrived on the South Carolina coast, along with their slaves. Disappointed with the development of their island and the subsequent contraction of opportunities, these settlers imported the Caribbean way of life to a new American colony (Greene 1987; Jordan 1968). A second reason the Low Country developed differently is that its main crop was rice. Growing rice was a

Figure 5.1   The Carolina Low Country

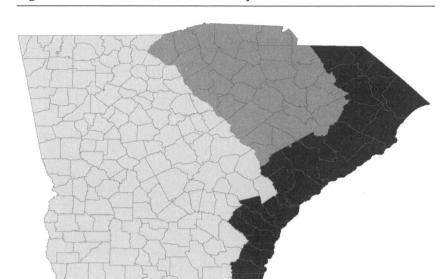

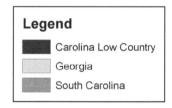

Source: Author's compilation from U.S. Geological Survey and the South Carolina Office of Research & Statistics.

more individualized undertaking than growing cotton or sugar; rice growers usually relied on a form of labor organization called the "task system." Each slave was assigned a set of tasks; after completing these, the slave's time was discretionary. This situation facilitated the establishment of provision grounds, where slaves grew crops for their own consumption as well as for cash or barter. In the Low Country, slaves familiar with their duties sometimes finished their tasks as early as one or two o'clock in the afternoon, after which they would cultivate their own plots (Morgan 1983, 1998). Jack Greene (1987, 207) writes that South Carolina slaves were able "to grow their own produce and raise their own animals for sale to whites in a domestic marketing system that in its extent and economic importance probably approached that of Jamaica." Self-provisioning likewise developed on the sugar plantations of Louisiana (McDonald 1993a, 1993b). Here too emigration may have played a role, since after the Haitian rebellion some sugar planters relocated to the Mississippi delta (Berlin 1974). Louisiana slaves produced not only vegetables for their own use but corn, hay, and other items for sale. Ira Berlin and Philip Morgan (1993) conclude that the Sunday markets of the Low Country rice ports and the Louisiana sugar country approximated those of the Caribbean.

In the rest of the South, slaves were less able to provide for themselves. When new cotton lands opened up in Alabama and Mississippi after 1815, planters were quick to limit the land that their newly acquired slaves could appropriate for their own use (Miller 1993). For cotton, the gang system rather than the task system was the more efficient form of labor organization. Slaves were controlled by a driver, who set the pace and determined starting and stopping times. Usually gangs worked from sunup to sundown, occasionally longer (Reidy 1993). There was little time left for the cultivation of individual plots; at best, slaves could do a little basket-making, fishing, or gardening on Sundays.[6]

Some scholars have drawn the same inferences about the cultural consequences of self-provisioning in the South as Sowell has drawn for the Caribbean. "Whatever time was left after the completion of a task belonged to the slave . . . thus giving slaves the chance to carry out self-directed economic activities for themselves and their families. . . . According to this argument, coastal freedmen's prior participation in the market . . . instilled in them a broad range of entrepreneurial experiences and choices that were denied to their inland counterparts laboring under the gang system" (Hargis and Horan 1997, 29–30). As a result, in the post-emancipation era, ex-slaves in the Low Country might have adapted more successfully to a competitive, capitalist economy than their more dependent, proletarianized counterparts in the cotton South.

The essential point is that independent slave production was neither wholly present in the Caribbean nor wholly absent from the mainland. Rather, the space that planters and slaves negotiated for economic autonomy varied from a little in places like Mississippi and Barbados to a lot in places like the Low Country and Jamaica. Even though, on average, a higher proportion of West Indian blacks had access to these opportunities and the scale of their activities was greater than in North America, the existence of alternatives in both regions paves the way for evaluating the contemporary relevance of each legacy (Berlin and Morgan 1993).

Occupational Opportunities

The Caribbean   A third reason why Sowell expects West Indians to outperform African Americans is that the former's demographic advantage imparts an occupational advantage. He writes: "The absence of a white working class meant that 'free persons of color,' and later the whole free black population could not be restricted to the most menial occupations or the more skilled and more responsible positions would have gone unfilled" (Sowell 1978b, 46).

So little data are available on free blacks in the Caribbean that Sowell may have based his conclusion on common sense. Written commentaries are contradictory. Some describe free blacks as landowners or skilled tradesmen, and some describe free blacks as dreadfully poor (Campbell 1976; Cox 1984; Handler and Sio 1972; Heuman 1981). If the object of analysis shifts to slaves, some reliable data can be assembled, but only in the case of urban slaves. An assessment of the occupations of rural slaves is hampered by conflicting information on the U.S. side.[7] The best-known source of data on urban American slaves is Claudia Goldin's (1976) tabulations based on the 1848 census of Charleston. Her calculations show that 16.6 percent held skilled jobs. For the British West Indies, Barry Higman (1984) presents figures that show that 25 to 33 percent of the slaves in three British West Indian cities did skilled work. Clearly, this contrast supports Sowell's expectation that the Caribbean offered better occupational opportunities.

Of equal interest to this study are arguments linking economic pursuits before emancipation and after. Writing about Jamaica, Sidney Mintz and Douglas Hall (1991, 332) remark: "The freedman needed to have skills and knowledge which would enable him to live independently. In this he had been prepared for independence by certain conditions of slavery, notably the initial insistence or concession that he provide his own food." More specifically, according to Mintz (1985, 135), "it was as slaves that these Caribbean peoples learned to budget their own time, to judge soil quality, to select seed, to cultivate and harvest, to prepare foods for sale, and otherwise to make the proto-peasant sector successful. They managed their family labor, learned to store and conserve seed, saved their earnings, acquired new habits of consumption, raised animals for sale and food." Mullin (1992) goes further, suggesting that, in the post-emancipation era, even Caribbean ex-slaves who could not hold on to their provision grounds profited from once

Figure 5.2   Jamaica

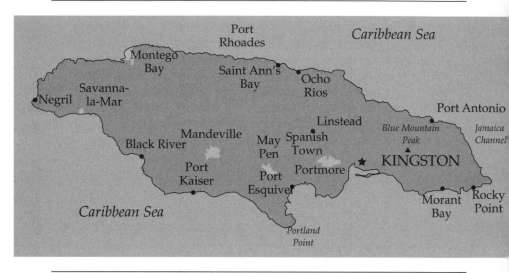

Source: CIA Factbook.

having had access to such land because they retained the confidence to bargain effectively about employment relations.

The largest number of ex-slave independent peasants emerged in post-emancipation Jamaica, where two-thirds had moved to free villages within a decade after emancipation. Similar trends occurred in other regions: in Trinidad, nearly half of the plantation labor force absconded by 1847 (Rogozinski 1992); in Guyana, thousands of ex-slaves pooled their resources, purchasing land communally (Adamson 1972). To be sure, ex-slaves faced their share of obstacles, such as outrageously large "minimum plot sizes" and outlandish interest rates (Adamson 1972; Bryan 1991). Yet few West Indians became sharecroppers in the sense of a tenant paying the landlord in kind rather than in cash (Moore 1987).[8] At worst, they paid their rent with their labor (Bryan 1991). Initially, subsistence production predominated, but eventually peasants produced cash crops like bananas, coffee, and cocoa. Most peasants did not work enough productive land to meet all their needs, so they supplemented their income with seasonal labor where they could find it. Still, Caribbean ex-slaves who stayed on the land were able "to carve out an autonomous realm beyond the boundaries of the plantation economy" (Lichtenstein 1998, 135).

Difficulties accessing land reached their nadir in Barbados. In a successful attempt to increase dependency among the black population,

Figure 5.3   Barbados

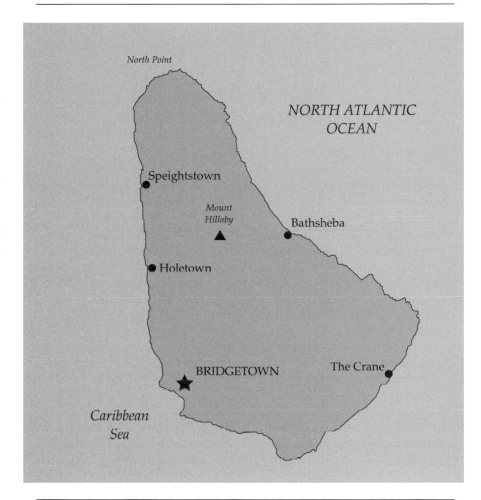

North Point

NORTH ATLANTIC
OCEAN

Speightstown

Mount
Hillaby

Bathsheba

Holetown

BRIDGETOWN

The Crane

Caribbean
Sea

Source: CIA Factbook.

the post-emancipation government shifted any land suitable for sugar to that purpose, thereby raising people's need for wages to buy provisions (Rogozinski 1992). In addition, a variety of legal statutes were enacted to bind workers to estates; for instance, the infamous Contract Law of 1838 stipulated that any laborer who worked for a planter for five days running was assumed to be under contract to that planter for a full year. Moreover, the facilities the ex-slaves had previously utilized at no cost, such as kitchen gardens and modest homes, were no longer free. A police magistrate described Barbadian land arrangements as follows: "The labourer received a house from his employer, of which he is to be tenant without rent as long as he gives his continuous service to the employer; but if he be absent without reasonable cause from his work, a rent is charged for that day, and in most cases an exorbitant rent, so as to compel his constant service" (Beckles 1990, 111). Philip Mason (1970, 283) writes: "It was virtually impossible for a former slave to break away from work on the sugar estate except by emigration."

Indeed, many sought emigration. As early as 1841, 2,500 had departed; by the end of the nineteenth century, 14.5 percent of Barbadians had spent at least some time working abroad (Beckles 2004). As pointed out in chapter 2, it was on Barbados that the Isthmian Canal Commission established a recruiting station in 1905. By the time black Barbadians could easily acquire land, it had lost most of its agricultural potential.

The Postbellum American South   Though emancipated slaves in the United States were as eager to become independent peasants as their Caribbean counterparts, in most places the white planter class maintained control over the land. In the Black Belt of Louisiana, Mississippi, Alabama, Georgia, and South Carolina, planters "used every social connection and legal stratagem to forestall foreclosure for bankruptcy or seizure for nonpayment of taxes" (Wright 1986, 84).

The simplest economic arrangement, wage labor, was possible only in those areas where landowners had the resources to meet payrolls on a "work as you go" basis. A credit crunch, particularly for cotton producers, made wage labor most likely in areas where rice, sugar, or tobacco were produced (Eric Foner 1983; Wright 1986). Cotton farmers, many of whom had to borrow to initiate the season, looked for an arrangement whereby they would meet their financial obligations at the end of the season. Various share arrangements "took shape as exslaves resisted the factory-like discipline of gang labor sought by planters, while the planters successfully denied freedpeople the unfettered access to productive resources they desired (and that many of their Caribbean counterparts had wrested from the planter class)" (Lichtenstein 1998, 134). The most disturbing consequence of the new share arrangements was that strapped tenants turned to landlords and merchants for loans or for provisions, the advance to be repaid with interest when the crop went to market. Scholars have calculated that the interest rates charged on such loans ranged from 21 to 71 percent, depending on the item involved (Mandle 1992). Most southern states passed laws giving creditors a lien on crops; so, once in debt, croppers' first responsibility was to their creditors.

Much has been written about the causes and consequences of debt peonage. Creditors' preference for cotton so impoverished people that some were malnourished (Steckel 1995). Yet there was considerable short-distance mobility among black croppers and tenants, indicating that at the end of the year some did accrue sufficient funds to pay their obligations (Cohen 1991; Mandle 1992; Wright 1986). Herbert Klein and Stanley Engerman (1985, 267) observe that "blacks' incomes increased throughout the post emancipation period." There was also substantial regional variation in farming arrangements from place to place (Coclanis 2000).

The most significant deviation from sharecropping occurred in the rice-growing region of South Carolina. It was one of the few areas in the postbellum South where freed blacks established independent farms. Before emancipation, its slaves were well known for their self-provisioning skills (Morgan 1983). Many factors were responsible for blacks' postbellum independence: the destruction of rice fields during the Civil War, the development of more efficient rice fields in and around Louisiana, and the political leverage blacks enjoyed in Reconstruction South Carolina. Yet the black masses' contribution also deserves emphasis, especially the strikes they initiated in 1876. In describing these events, Eric Foner (1983, 93) stresses that the participants were disproportionately "day laborers, whose small plots of land off the plantations gave them a degree of economic autonomy." Unlike many other black strikers in the American South, whose activities were brutally suppressed, these militants achieved some of their objectives. By 1890 few of the great plantations survived, and Foner estimates that ex-slaves owned about three-quarters of the farms in the region, thanks to continuing black influence on local politics. Like their Jamaican counterparts, Low Country landholders eked a bare subsistence from their acreage and met additional cash needs by occasional wage labor. So, in both regions, ex-slaves fulfilled their long-held desire for autonomy.[9]

This excursion into nineteenth-century history confirms some of Sowell's generalizations about the black experience in the West Indies and the American South. Compared to the United States, slave rebellions were more significant, provision grounds were more common, and occupational opportunities were more attractive in the Caribbean. But some of Sowell's ideas fall short. Escapes were more common in the United States. And both the Caribbean and the South were more heterogeneous than he supposes. Conditions in Barbados were closer to those in the United States; conditions in the Carolina Low Country were closer to those in the Caribbean. On the other hand, Jamaica exemplified the characteristics Sowell associates with the Caribbean: a viable community of escaped slaves (Maroons), extensive provision grounds, urban occupational diversity, and later a reconstituted peasantry of significant size. At the same time, much of the Black Belt (with the important exception of southern Louisiana) displayed the characteristics Sowell associates with the South: a low rate of rebellion, few provision grounds, urban occupational homogeneity, and high rates of debt peonage. In terms of structural arrangements conducive to creating the character traits that bode well for economic success (such as autonomy, diligence, and frugality), conditions in the rural West Indies (excluding Barbados) and in the Carolina Low Country were the most favorable. This interpretation follows from Sowell's view of landownership (or at least uncontested access to land) as central to developing "achievement motivation." Less valuable was residence in the mainstream American South, since landownership eluded a larger proportion of American than Caribbean ex-slaves.[10] But, following Sowell's logic, residence in Barbados must have been least conducive of all, since the only options open to blacks there were to till the white man's soil or leave.

Empirical Tests

West Indian Immigrants   These insights provide the basis for a strategy that tests Sowell's contention that historical differences between the two regions explain the contemporary differences between migrants from the two regions. If Sowell is correct, then emigrants from Jamaica should be more economically successful than emigrants from Barbados, while migrants from the Carolina Low Country should be more successful than migrants from elsewhere in the Southeast.

The first test requires a comparison of two sets of late-twentieth-century immigrants: Jamaicans and Barbadians. The comparison begins with the 1980 census because the 1970 census does not distinguish Barbados from other West Indian sending countries. The analysis follows the logic of previous comparisons. Jamaicans are expected to have more favorable outcomes than Barbadians. Thus, the means Jamaicans obtain on the four economic outcomes of interest are first adjusted to take into account any measurable advantages they may have (for instance, on education or location) over Barbadians. Then each Jamaican adjusted mean is divided by the analogous Barbadian observed mean. The resulting ratios appear in table 5.1.

Of the twenty-four ratios, ten favor Barbadians, ten favor Jamaicans, and four favor neither sending country, being equal to one. Only one of the twenty-four ratios attains statistical significance: in 2000 Jamaican-

Table 5.1   Ratios of Foreign-Born Jamaican Adjusted Means to Foreign-Born Barbadian Observed Means on Four Economic Indicators

Year	Labor Force Participation		Unemployment		Occupational Prestige		Logged Earnings	
	Males	Females	Males	Females	Males	Females	Males	Females
1980	1.03	0.99	0.86	0.92	0.97	0.98	0.99	0.98
1990	98.1	1.01	1.23	1.18	1.01	1.00	1.00	1.01
2000	98.9	1.00	97.5	90.7	1.00	1.03*	99.5	1.01

Source: Author's calculations based on the 1 percent and 5 percent Integrated Public Use Microdata Series (IPUMS).
Note: See the methodological appendix for the variables used in the adjustment and for the restrictions placed on the analysis.
* Statistically significant at the .05 level or better.

born women had significantly higher occupational status than their Barbadian counterparts. The remaining contrasts are indistinguishable from zero. Therefore, the findings offer no support for Sowell's contention that the presence of provision grounds or viable Maroon communities has any consequence for the economic outcome of Caribbean immigrants today.

African American Internal Migrants   Since African Americans also varied in their exposure to autonomy during and after slavery, the discussion turns now to testing Sowell's hypothesis in the U.S. context. The first task, of course, is to identify blacks born in the Low Country. The Low Country is usually defined as a set of sixteen coastal counties in Georgia and seven coastal counties in South Carolina (Coclanis 1989; Hargis and Horan 1997).[11] Unfortunately, no U.S. census reports county of birth; hence, Low Country natives cannot be identified. A proxy, however, can be constructed by exploiting the fact that, in 1980, the U.S. census reported both county of current residence and county of residence in 1975. Blacks born in the Low Country are here defined as those born in South Carolina or Georgia who resided in a Low Country county in 1975. The contrast category is blacks born in South Carolina or Georgia who resided outside the Low Country in 1975—that is, in inland South Carolina or Georgia counties.

Yet Sowell's hypothesis is about movers, not stayers. Thus, testing his ideas requires comparing members of these two groups who moved between 1975 and 1980, not those who stayed. More specifically, the analysis compares the economic attainment of Low Country natives (as defined here) who had moved anywhere in the United States outside the Low Country by 1980 with the attainment of South Carolinians or Georgians born in other counties (as defined here) who had moved anywhere in the United States by 1980. If Sowell is correct, those migrating out of the Low Country should have more favorable economic outcomes than those migrating out of inland counties because of the former's cultivation of provision grounds during slavery and cultivation of their own holdings thereafter.

The results of this comparison appear in table 5.2. The ratios represent adjusted Low Country means relative to observed inland county means. Since the expectation is that migrants from the Low Country have stronger outcomes, ratios greater than one are expected for all outcomes except unemployment. Note, however, that not a single ratio fits this expectation; rather, all comparisons favor residents of inland counties. Two ratios are quite large: the labor force participation of black female migrants from the Low Country is only 90.5 percent of the labor force participation of their counterparts from inland counties, and black males migrating out of the Low Country have an unemployment rate that is 31 percent higher than that of non–Low Country migrants. But neither these large ratios nor any of the small ones attain statistical significance. In sum, just as in the Barbados-Jamaica comparison, the comparison between Low Country and non–Low Country detects no statistical difference. Evidently, by 1980 recent black migrants whose forebears worked their own provision grounds during slavery and who owned their own land during emancipation fared no better than recent migrants whose forebears were not exposed to these "advantages."

This section began with Sowell's claim that Caribbean slaves had more opportunity for autonomy and self-sufficiency than slaves in the United States. The history books support this assessment with some important exceptions: Barbados and the Carolina Low Country. Of course, that these structural differences existed "once upon a time" does not mean that the persons living and laboring under these respective regimes developed the personality traits that Sowell, Mintz, Morgan, and others ascribe to them. Perhaps the presence of provision grounds and Maroon communities did make Jamaicans more independent and entrepreneurial than Barbadians. Perhaps not. Perhaps working under the task system made Low Country slaves more adept at budgeting their time than their counterparts trapped in the gang system. Perhaps not. What is known is that, in the long run, the conditions that might have produced these mind-sets changed. In the early twentieth century, inland counties became more prosperous than Low Country counties (Graham 1971); by the late twentieth century, Barbados had become more prosperous than Jamaica. Since the conditions

Table 5.2   Ratios of Low Country Adjusted Means to Observed Means for Neighboring Southern Blacks on Four Economic Indicators in 1980

Labor Force Participation		Unemployment		Occupational Prestige		Logged Earnings	
Males	Females	Males	Females	Males	Females	Males	Females
98.3	90.5	1.31	96.3	98.3	96.9	98.1	89.2

Source: Author's calculations based on the 1 percent and 5 percent 1980 Integrated Public Use Microdata Series (IPUMS).
Note: See the methodological appendix for the variables used in the adjustment and for the restrictions placed on the analysis. Migrants born in South Carolina and Georgia and residing in Low Country counties five years prior to migration are compared to migrants born in South Carolina and Georgia and residing in non–Low Country counties five years prior to migration.

that might have produced the above-mentioned character traits changed, it is hard to see why these mind-sets would not eventually fade. Thus, whether or not Sowell's vision had some merit in the past, it has no merit in the present.

The All-Black Society Hypothesis

Happily for the researcher, just as the organization of slavery differed within the Caribbean, so too does racial-ethnic composition differ within the Caribbean and within Africa. Some locations are more "all-black" than others. This demographic variation provides a basis for testing the all-black society hypothesis; persons emigrating from sending regions with differing proportions of blacks can be compared. If the all-black society hypothesis is correct, then the greater the proportion of blacks in the sending country, the more successful are its black emigrants in the receiving country. This idea is tested first on a sample of Caribbean immigrants and then on a sample of sub-Saharan African immigrants. It holds up in neither context. Before moving to these tests, however, the history of black demographic variation in the Caribbean and in Africa is worth recounting.

The History of Caribbean Racial Diversity

The British colonies officially freed their slaves in 1833, the French in 1848, the Dutch in 1862, and the Spanish in 1880 (Knight 1997). The long-term result of emancipation was a labor shortage. The cause was as much planters' desire to restrict the movement of freed blacks as freed blacks' desire to move when they pleased. In some regions, the modus vivendi became a black peasantry who worked part-time for white planters. In others, this arrangement left too much land fallow. In such regions, the solution was to import more labor.

Planters tapped a variety of sources. In time, India became the favored supplier, with over half a million persons arriving in less than a century. The subcontinent offered several advantages. India was a British colony, hence diplomatic barriers were at a minimum. Indeed, British imperialism was a major stimulant to emigration because it promoted landlessness and debt peonage (Mazumdar 1984). Other factors that encouraged emigration included a series of famines, population growth, and soil exhaustion (Vertovec 1992).

From the point of view of white planters in the Caribbean, these were indeed fortunate events. The pool of potential Indian migrants was enormous, and the population was accustomed to physical labor under tropical conditions. Soon those colonies in search of labor had recruitment offices in major ports. As might be expected, strong young males were preferred, but in the interests of extending their sojourn, planters also welcomed women—who ultimately made up about one-third of migrants.

Still, the introduction of Asians would not have met with long-term success had not Caribbean legislatures introduced an indenture system that tied migrant laborers to their employers. Employers offered free transport to the Caribbean in exchange for seven to nine hours of work a day, five or six days a week, over a five-year period. Planters also promised a modest wage (often tied to the task completed rather than the time worked), medical care, and housing. After five years, laborers could pay their own fare home, indenture themselves for an additional period, or remain in the colony as independent workers. A total of ten years qualified a laborer for a "free" ticket home.

The indenture of Indians was, of course, a scheme designed by the British for the British. Its goal was to supply one set of British colonies with labor from another. But Indian labor was so plentiful and so cheap that eventually the French and Dutch colonies asked Britain if they too could draw from this source. In this way, Indians came to constitute a significant part of the population wherever the recruitment of indentured labor loomed large (Richardson 1989; Schmidt 1989). In Surinam, dissatisfaction with dependence on Britain motivated planters to supplement Indian labor with recruits from Java, an island in the Dutch East Indies. In toto, some thirty thousand Indians and thirty thousand Javanese entered Surinam as indentured labor. The great majority of Indians—or Hindustanis, as they are called in Surinam—arrived before the turn of the century, though immigration from the subcontinent did not cease until 1917. The great majority of Javanese arrived thereafter, with recruitment ending in 1932.

Statistics indicate that, before indenture was outlawed, about one-fifth (22 percent) of the Indians who arrived in Trinidad, slightly over one-quarter (28 percent) of those indentured in British Guiana, and one-third (33 percent) of those introduced into Dutch Guiana returned to India (Hoefte 1998; Ramesar 1994).[12] From the perspective of the planter class, these numbers were high. The planters were eager to retain their experienced workers, at least during the labor-intensive cane-cutting season. Moreover, planters wanted to eliminate spending money on return passage. The simplest solution would have been reindenture, but this option appealed to few Indians. Hence, planters had to find another alternative. The most successful was to sell or rent land to workers whose contracts had expired. "Thus, by a curious irony, the sugar planter who . . . after emancipation, tried to prevent the purchase of land by former slaves, found himself obliged in the nineteenth century to grant land to the indentured immigrant in order to reduce the expense of immigrant labour. Indian immigration, designed to compete with the Negro landowners, ended in the establishment of a class of Indian landowners" (Williams 1962, 120).

Like black small landholders, "time-expired" Indian small landholders experimented with a variety of subsistence and market crops as well as the raising of goats and cattle for milk. But the Indians also introduced a unique staple to the region: "wet" rice. British and Dutch Guiana had land especially well suited for the cultivation of Asian rice—that is, rice that spends part of its life in water. Once government officials understood the potential of rice as a staple, some public funds were expended to support its cultivation. By 1901, British Guiana had begun exporting rice; some years later, Dutch Guiana also became a rice exporter, though Trinidad never did.[13] With these opportunities, most time-expired Indians were no longer at the mercy of planters, though many supplemented their earnings with seasonal work on large estates.

In the succeeding decades, Africans and Indians lived "segmented lives." Indians were overwhelmingly rural, while Africans inhabited both country and city. Those Indians who did not till the land worked in commerce or transport (Laurence 1994). Blacks farmed too, but the upwardly mobile sought urban jobs as civil servants and professionals. Since the two groups inhabited different worlds, ethnic conflict was muted.

In the 1950s, peaceful coexistence unraveled. The catalyst was the introduction of electoral politics, which quickly took on an ethnic cast. In all three colonies where Indians constituted a meaningful proportion (Trinidad, British Guiana, and Dutch Guiana), blacks captured the key political posts. One consequence of black political clout was the large share of patronage jobs that went to all three colonies' African-origin residents. Blacks usually controlled the civil service, the police, and national security. In Dutch Guiana, black power was sufficiently great that most Hindustanis and many Indonesians opposed the colony's efforts at independence. They did not trust Creole leaders (as the black population there is called) to respect the rights of other groups.[14] Nevertheless, the Netherlands granted its South American colony independence in 1975. Once Dutch Guiana became Surinam, "emigration to the Netherlands by all groups, but especially Hindustanis, rose precipitously" (Dew 1994, 7).

By the late 1970s, most of the English-speaking West Indies had also attained independence. But nowhere did independence bring prosperity. Instead, many Caribbean governments faced large budget deficits. The leading sources of loans—the World Bank, the International Monetary Fund (IMF), and the U.S. Department of the Treasury—were willing to help, provided borrowers initiated "structural adjustments." The adjustments they demanded were fiscal austerity, privatization and market liberalization (Stiglitz 2002).

Especially relevant to the present inquiry is that structural adjustment exacerbated inter-ethnic tensions. In Guyana (formerly British Guiana), where IMF demands were especially stringent,

> adjustment resulted in the marked . . . enhancement of the overall position of the majority East Indian racial group in the economy, substantially solidifying its historical dominance in business and agriculture in the modern period. This was the racial group that, in relative terms, emerged the biggest winners from the adjustment process. . . . Contrastingly, because of the locational characteristics of the second major race group, the African—their urban and public sector occupational locations in the main—adjustment effectively eclipsed this group in the new order of things. A dwindling public sector, reduced wage levels and depressed employment opportunities penalized the African section. (Ferguson 1995, 234)

In Trinidad, structural adjustment was in some ways less harsh. Although many public firms were privatized, persons directly employed by government faced pay cuts more often than staff reductions (*Economist Intelligence Unit* 2000). Moreover, because "Indians and non-Indians are represented in the public sector in proportion to their approximate status in the general population" (Ryan 1996, 253), the pay cuts affected both ethnic groups. On the other hand, policies that strengthened private enterprise differentially benefited Indians because "there are more Indian owned businesses than businesses belonging to any other group" (254). In addition, "Indo-Trinidadians have emerged as major stake holders in professions such as law, medicine, teaching, accounting, banking, pharmacy, dentistry and information technology" (xxv). Many employers, including some Afro-Trinidadians, believe that Indo-Trinidadians are more diligent and docile than Afro-Trinidadians (Center for Ethnic Studies 1993). Statistical support for the idea that Trinidad's employers hold such stereotypes comes from a multivariate analysis of earnings, which revealed "that although Indians have the lower level of monthly earnings in Trinidad and Tobago, Africans might be subjected to greater levels of discrimination via less favorable rates of remuneration" (Coppin and Olsen 1998, 134). In other words, measured job characteristics being the same, Indo-Trinidadians had begun out-earning Afro-Trinidadians.

Surinam has been least affected by structural adjustment because its leadership has not received IMF aid. Yet a careful reading of Surinamese history shows that, there too, stereotypes regarding work ethic came to favor Hindustanis over Creoles (van Niekerk 2000). A contemporary comparison of several groups in Paramaribo (the capital) on a "prosperity index" shows that blacks are more prosperous than Hindustanis, but again, the rumor surfaces that Hindustanis are disproportionately represented among Paramaribo's most prosperous businesspeople (de Bruijne 2001). While this claim cannot be verified, its truth may matter less than what the population believes about Hindustani wealth.

To conclude, in the latter part of the twentieth century, Indo-Caribbeans made substantial gains in Trinidad, Guyana, and Surinam. While initially handicapped by their rural residence, agricultural occupations, and low educational attainment, by the turn of the twenty-first century they competed with their African-origin compatriots for economic power. Moreover, though their birthrate has slowed, Indians constitute an increasing proportion in all three locales. Figures available in 2005 describe Indians as half the Guyanese population, 40 percent of the Trinidadian, and 37 percent of the Surinamese (U.S. Central Intelligence Agency 2005). Partly because of their numbers, their political influence has occasionally brought them presidencies and prime ministerships. All told, the position of African-origin peoples is less secure in Guyana, Trinidad, and Surinam than elsewhere in the West Indies.

Testing the Effect of Demographic Composition

If socialization in a nation where blacks have access to the entire range of occupational and political opportunities makes a difference (Glazer and Moynihan 1963; McClain 1979; Ottley and Weatherby 1967), then black emigrants from Jamaica, Barbados, and other overwhelmingly black societies should be more successful in the United States than black emigrants from Caribbean regions where an East Indian presence is significant. This expectation is tested first in the United States by comparing black immigrants from Trinidad and Guyana with English-speaking black West Indian immigrants from the rest of the region, and second in the Netherlands by comparing black immigrants from Surinam with black immigrants from the Netherlands Antilles, an all-black dependency.

The tests parallel the procedure used previously: each result is a ratio of the adjusted outcome of immigrants from mixed-race societies to the observed outcome of immigrants from all-black societies. Table 5.3 presents the results when immigrants from first Trinidad and then Guyana are compared to immigrants from the rest of the English-speaking Caribbean.

Because PUMS data for 1970 do not distinguish Guyana, it does not appear in the 1970 results. In addition, estimation problems undermine the reliability of the unemployment ratios in 1970.[15] These restrictions leave thirty ratios for the Trinidadian comparison and twenty-four for the Guyanese. When compared to Trinidadians, other West Indians fare significantly better in five comparisons and significantly worse in two. When compared to Guyanese, other West Indians never fare significantly better; in five, they fare significantly worse.

These results do not support the all-black society hypothesis. Admittedly, in three of four comparisons, female immigrants from all-black societies have significantly higher labor force participation than women from Trinidad. The reasons for this situation are not clear, but given the absence of this pattern among Trinidadian males or among Guyanese immigrants of either gender, the labor force participation shortfall is unlikely to be related to the demographic composition of Trinidad. Additional analyses (not shown) used the pooled sample of 1970 to 2000 censuses to determine whether residence in Guyana or Trinidad during the era of structural adjustment was associated with poorer labor market outcomes. It was not. In sum, there is no empirical support for the idea that the mixed-race environment of Trinidad or Guyana has a deleterious effect on black immigrants' economic

Table 5.3 Ratios of Foreign-Born Trinidadian and Guyanese Adjusted Means to Foreign-Born Other West Indian Observed Means on Four Economic Indicators

Year	Labor Force Participation		Unemployment		Occupational Prestige		Logged Earnings	
	Males	Females	Males	Females	Males	Females	Males	Females
1970								
Trinidad	1.04	1.11	n.a.	n.a.	0.95	1.07	1.00	0.97
1980								
Trinidad	.97*	.95*	1.01	1.43*	1.01	1.01	1.01	1.02
Guyana	1.02	.98	.98	1.13	1.00	1.03*	0.98	1.01
1990								
Trinidad	1.00	.97*	1.19	1.02	1.02*	1.00	1.00	.99
Guyana	1.00	.98	.80	.94	1.03*	1.03*	.98	.99
2000								
Trinidad	1.00	.95*	.94	1.12	1.01*	1.00	.99	.99
Guyana	.99	.99	.95	1.06	1.01	1.02*	.99	1.01

Source: Author's calculations based on the 1 percent and 5 percent Integrated Public Use Microdata Series (IPUMS).
Note: See the methodological appendix for the variables used in the adjustment and for the restrictions placed on the analysis.
* Statistically significant at the .05 level or better.

achievement. Moreover, this conclusion appears warranted irrespective of whether the exposure took place during or prior to structural adjustment.

The Netherlands provides another context for examining the difference between immigrants socialized in a mixed-race society versus an all-black society. This analysis compares Creole (black) immigrants from the multiracial society of Surinam to immigrants from the Netherlands Antilles, an overwhelmingly black society. The comparison must be done cautiously because Antilleans have unfettered access to the mother country, but Surinamese have needed a visa since 1980. Complicating matters further, between the mid-1970s and 1980, thousands of Surinamese emigrated to the Netherlands in anticipation of the implementation of barriers to entry upon independence. Once in place, such barriers should increase the selectivity of Surinamese immigrants relative to their Antillean counterparts because the latter can migrate at will. Yet obtaining a visa requires only that the applicant prove that he or she has close relatives in the Netherlands. In the early 1990s, three-quarters of the residents of Greater Paramaribo could make that claim (van Niekerk 2005).

The ratios in table 5.4 are the adjusted means of Surinamese divided by the observed means of Antilleans. The data come from three waves (1991, 1994, 1998) of the SPVA (Sociale Positie en Voorzieningengebruick Allochtonen), an ongoing survey of ethnic minorities in the Netherlands.[16] In order to reflect the history of Surinamese immigration, the analysis should distinguish three cohorts of departure: before 1970, during the 1970s, and after 1980. Unfortunately, the number of cases in the SPVA is not sufficient to support the calculation of separate adjusted means for these three groups. Based on an analysis of the total sample, table 5.4 contains only two statistically significant results. Creole women have higher labor force participation and lower unemployment than Antilleans. The all-black society hypothesis predicts the opposite: Antillean advantage. Moreover, six of the eight contrasts are insignificant. To conclude, black immigrants raised in multiethnic Surinam incur no disadvantage relative to black immigrants raised in the racially homogeneous environment of the Dutch Antilles.[17]

Africa

The second strategy used to test the all-black society hypothesis is to compare black immigrants from sub-Saharan Africa to African Americans. If socialization in an all-black environment is the key to West In-

Table 5.4   Ratios of Foreign-Born Creole Adjusted Means to Foreign-Born Antillean Observed Means on Four Economic Indicators

Labor Force Participation		Unemployment		Occupational Prestige		Logged Earnings	
Males	Females	Males	Females	Males	Females	Males	Females
1.02	1.24*	1.02	0.62*	1.00	1.01	1.01	1.01

Source: Author's calculations based on the 1991, 1994, and 1998 Sociale Positie en Voorzieningengebruick Allochtonen (SPVA).
Note: See the methodological appendix for the variables used in the adjustment and for the restrictions placed on the analysis.
* Statistically significant at the .05 level or better.

dian success, then sub-Saharan Africans also should have stronger labor market outcomes than African Americans. After all, black Africans, though colonized, were never slaves. For many decades, blacks have held most of the key economic and political positions in African countries. Therefore, black immigrants from sub-Saharan Africa should not perceive skin color as a barrier to achievement, a perception that should render them more ambitious than African Americans.

To compare the economic outcomes of the two groups of blacks, table 5.5 presents ratios of adjusted black African means to observed African American means. This analysis differs from others in this book by adjusting not only for differences between sub-Saharan Africans and African Americans on education, geography, and family but also

Table 5.5   Ratios of Adjusted Foreign-Born Sub-Saharan African Means to Observed African American Means on Four Economic Indicators

Year	Labor Force Participation		Unemployment		Occupational Prestige		Logged Earnings	
	Males	Females	Males	Females	Males	Females	Males	Females
1990	.96*	.78*	.78*	1.34*	1.02	.95*	.87*	.95*
2000	1.07	.91*	.66*	0.79	1.03	1.00	.92	.94*

Source: Author's calculations based on the 1 percent and 5 percent Integrated Public Use Microdata Series (IPUMS).
Note: See the methodological appendix for the variables used in the adjustment and for the restrictions placed on the analysis.
* Statistically significant at the .05 level or better.

on English ability. About 20 percent of Sub-Saharan Africans do not speak English very well. Another difference is that there are only enough cases to support calculating ratios in 1990 and 2000.

The results show that Sub-Saharan Africans generally do less well than African Americans. Others have come to a similar conclusion, though most of that work has focused on earnings (Corra and Kimuna, forthcoming; Dodoo 1997; Dodoo and Takyi 2002). Only on men's unemployment do Sub-Saharan Africans fare significantly better than African Americans. Of the remaining fourteen ratios, the immigrants do significantly less well on eight, and equally well on the remaining six.[18] To be sure, black Africans did make progress over the decade. The most likely explanation is their longer residency in the United States. In 1990 the average black African immigrant had lived in the United States only 8.6 years; in 2000 that figure had increased to 10.4 years. As demonstrated in chapter 5, the longer an immigrant resides in the host society, the better he or she performs in the labor market. Nevertheless, since West Indians fare significantly better than African Americans and sub-Saharan Africans fare less well than African Americans, socialization in an all-black society is unlikely to be the key to West Indian success.

Complications   Yet black Africans face several handicaps that might undermine the benefit associated with residence in all-black societies. For one thing, upon settlement in a Western society, they may experience more culture shock than the descendants of Caribbean slaves. For another, the darker skin tone of Africans may expose them to more discrimination than lighter-skinned Caribbean blacks encounter.[19] Another handicap for Africans is that their homelands are less economically affluent and politically stable than most Caribbean nations.[20] Studies suggest that political instability has played at least as large a role as poverty in motivating African out-migration (Gordon 1998). This is a problem because immigration scholars believe that economically motivated movers have stronger labor market outcomes than politically motivated movers (Borjas 1987; Chiswick 1979). Finally, a surprisingly high proportion of Africans express the desire eventually to return home (Apraku 1991; Arthur 2000). Again, scholars of immigration suppose that immigrants who perceive their relocation as permanent have stronger economic outcomes than those who perceive their relocation as temporary. These considerations may depress the attainment of immigrants from sub-Saharan Africa relative to immigrants from the Caribbean.

One way to circumvent these difficulties is to undertake an intra-Africa comparison. This is in any event a good idea because the history of Africa is as varied as the history of the Caribbean. At one end of the spectrum lies Ethiopia, which was politically subservient to the West only during the brief Italian occupation of 1936 to 1941. The rest of Africa was firmly under European control from the late-nineteenth to the mid-twentieth century. In some colonies, Europeans exerted their influence primarily through the civil service and the military; in others, Europeans forcibly took "ownership" of land and engaged in farming. European agriculture was concentrated in Kenya, Rhodesia, Namibia, and, of course, South Africa. No doubt, South African history is unique. While most African regions experienced less than a century of European hegemony, white domination of South Africa dates to 1652 (Furlong 2001). Most African regions achieved independence in the 1960s and 1970s, disgorging their nonblack population in the process. But South Africa's whites have yet to be dislodged. White political control persisted until 1994, when apartheid was officially dismantled through democratic elections. As recently as 1996, 17.3 percent of the prime-age male labor force was white, and the jobs they held were far more prestigious and lucrative than the jobs held by the black or mixed-race population (Powell and Buchman 2002).

In short, sub-Saharan African countries approximate all-black societies to different degrees. This demographic reality implies that comparing immigrants from South Africa with their counterparts from the rest of Africa is a better strategy for testing the all-black society hypothesis than comparing immigrants from sub-Saharan Africa to African Americans. Unfortunately, the number of South Africans in the data is small; to create a large enough sample, it is necessary to combine cases from the 1990 and 2000 censuses.[21] Table 5.6 presents the ratios of adjusted black South African immigrant means to other black

Table 5.6   Ratios of Foreign-Born Black South African Adjusted Means to Other Sub-Saharan Black African Observed Means on Four Economic Indicators

Labor Force Participation		Unemployment		Occupational Prestige		Logged Earnings	
Males	Females	Males	Females	Males	Females	Males	Females
.97	.85*	1.13	1.51	.95	1.09*	1.01	1.03

Source: Author's calculations based on the 1990 and 2000 Integrated Public Use Microdata Series (IPUMS) combined.
Note: See the methodological appendix for the variables used in the adjustment and for the restrictions placed on the analysis.
* Statistically significant at the .05 level or better.

sub-Saharan African immigrant observed means. There are few significant differences. South African females have lower labor force participation and higher occupational prestige; otherwise, the outcomes are statistically identical. The message is clear: relative to socialization in all-black sub-Saharan Africa, socialization in mixed-race South Africa neither helps nor hurts.

To sum up, within the African context, as within the Caribbean, the racial composition of the home country has no consistent effect on the economic performance of black immigrants. Black immigrants who share their homelands with South Asians (Trinidad, Guyana, Surinam) or with whites (South Africa) have the same labor market outcomes as their compatriots from more homogeneously black homelands.

Conclusions

This chapter tested two cultural arguments for West Indian advantage: one historical, one contemporary. The historical argument maintains that because West Indian slaves experienced more autonomy than American slaves did, the descendants of the former are today more enterprising than the descendants of the latter. But historical analysis shows that conditions on Barbados were not conducive to slave autonomy, while conditions in coastal South Carolina were. The statistical analysis contrasts West Indian immigrants from Barbados with those from Jamaica and black migrants from South Carolina with those from North Carolina. The comparisons detect no significant difference between migrants from Barbados versus Jamaica or between migrants from South versus North Carolina. Thus, slave autonomy cannot explain West Indian advantage.

A second potential source of cultural advantage is socialization in an all-black society. Because West Indian blacks are raised in locales where race is not systematically associated with class, they nurture higher ambitions and demand greater respect than African Americans do. Yet Trinidad, Guyana, and Surinam have large and successful Indian communities; in other Caribbean locales, the nonblack population is small. Statistical analysis shows that the job outcomes of West Indians from overwhelmingly black Caribbean locales are indistinguishable from the outcomes of those who share their nation with Indians. Additional comparisons were undertaken involving blacks from sub-Saharan Africa. The most interesting of these is the comparison between black immigrants from South Africa (a white-dominated nation) and immigrants from the rest of sub-Saharan Africa (a black-dominated region). There is no evidence that the racial composition of the sending country makes a difference in the job outcomes of black immigrants. These results impugn both the historical and contemporary versions of the cultural hypothesis.

Some readers may feel that, compared to the United States, even mixed-race sending countries endow their black residents with more achievement motivation than America does. But if all West Indian and African nations transmit the advantages associated with an all-black society equally well, then the effect of living in an all-black society cannot be measured. Since the assumption motivating this study is that all explanations for West Indian advantage are empirically verifiable, every effort is made to construct empirical tests. If it is not possible to find either West Indians or sub-Saharan Africans who have been denied the benefits of an all-black society, then the effect of those benefits cannot be proved empirically.

• Chapter 6 •

Testing the White Favoritism Hypothesis

A TTENTION now turns to the final explanation for West Indians' economic advantage over African Americans: white favoritism. More research relevant to this hypothesis has been published than is the case for either the culture or selectivity hypotheses. This chapter reviews the central findings of this literature, which encompasses several methodologies and includes several countries. The discussion then offers two tests of white favoritism. Both take advantage of a theoretical perspective known as queuing theory, which predicts that, if white employers rank West Indian immigrants more favorably than African Americans, then West Indian economic outcomes profit from increasing proportions of African Americans. One way to test this prediction is to compare the outcomes of West Indian immigrants in the United States with the outcomes of West Indian immigrants in nations devoid of a "native" black population. Without a native black population, or some substitute for it, West Indians should fare less well outside than inside the United States. A second way is to examine the relationship between the percentage of a United States labor market that is African American and the economic outcomes of its West Indian residents. If the advocates of white favoritism are correct, the larger the proportion of African Americans in a United States labor market, the more successful its West Indian residents will be.

As it turns out, both empirical strategies yield a similar conclusion: the size of the African American labor force has no relation to West Indian economic attainment. The immigrants perform as well in places devoid of native blacks as in places where African Americans constitute a high proportion. These results imply that white favoritism has little bearing on West Indian economic attainment, though this conclusion does not mean that white favoritism is a fiction. Some white Americans may feel more positively about West Indians than about African Americans. The calculations in the chapter do not test that assertion; they show only that such sentiments do not contribute to West Indians' labor market outcomes.

Previous Research Relevant to the White Favoritism Hypothesis

This section focuses on studies that have examined the ranking of West Indians relative to the ranking of other ethnic and racial groups. The review includes research conducted in the United States as well as in Britain, Canada, and the Netherlands. To enhance the reader's understanding of the latter three contexts, a very brief history of West Indian immigration to each country is offered first. The discussion then examines the status of West Indians as portrayed in ethnographies, surveys, and field experiments. Within each research method, American studies are considered first, then studies undertaken in other West Indian destinations are described. The few secondary data analyses that have been published are presented in the next section, along with the secondary data analyses devised for this volume.

The British Context

In the immediate post–World War II era, because of the McCarran-Walter Act (1952), few British West Indians could settle in the United States. Canada also limited arrivals from the Caribbean until 1962 (Plaza 2001–2002). There was, however, another alternative. "Under the British Nationality Act of 1948, residents of the newly independent Commonwealth nations could claim citizenship in the United Kingdom and Colonies. Among other things, this status . . .guaranteed free entry into Britain and the full exercise of citizenship right once there" (Freeman 1987, 186). Encouraged by this new law, 492 Jamaicans arrived in Liverpool in 1948 aboard the SS *Empire Windrush*. This event marked the beginning of migration from the British West Indies to the mother country. By the 1951 U.K. census, over 17,000 West Indian blacks were living there (Peach 1996).

Yet, this open-door policy was short-lived. In the late 1950s, job opportunities diminished, housing shortages surfaced, and race riots erupted. After months of discussion, in 1962 the British government introduced its first immigration rule: employment vouchers would henceforth be required of entrants planning to work. Because dependents could still gain admission without prearranged employment, in the years that followed women and children composed the overwhelming majority of arrivals (National Planning Agency 1969). Almost all settled in England, just over half in London, the rest in other metropolitan areas. Finally, in 1968, the government ceased granting residents of colonies or ex-colonies the right to settle or work in Britain at all; entry was limited to direct descendants of British citizens. In 1971 the number of Caribbean-born persons in Britain peaked; it has been declining ever since.[1]

Of course, West Indians were not the only colonials and ex-colonials to enter Britain in the postwar era. Large numbers from the Indian subcontinent and smaller numbers from Africa and Asia entered too. However, West Indians were probably the most disappointed. Perceiving themselves as British subjects returning to the "mother country," they were dismayed to find that most whites viewed them as both outsiders and inferiors.

The Canadian Context

Like the United States, Canada had closed its doors to nonwhites in the 1920s, but like Britain, Canada experienced labor shortages after World War II. When admission policies favoring Europeans failed to meet demand, Canada looked further. In 1962 birthplace was abolished as a criterion for entry. Applicants were admitted either because they were close kin of Canadian residents or because of their occupational skills. In 1967 Canada shifted to a system that assigned points on the basis of assets such as age, linguistic ability, education, and occupation, as well as on the basis of Canadian demand for those skills and assets. The presence in Canada of an assisting relative also brought points, as did the immigration officer's personal evaluation of the applicant (Boyd 1976; Kelley and Trebilcock 1998). With minor modifications, this policy remains in effect today.

Since the mid-1960s, Canada has received significant numbers of English-speaking Caribbeans. By 2001, nearly 300,000 had arrived in Canada (Statistics Canada 2001). Of course, West Indians are neither Canada's only blacks nor its only immigrants. Slavery was legal in Canada until the early 1800s; free blacks dwelt there too, some having received land as compensation for supporting Britain against America, some having arrived on the Underground Railroad. But this native black population, which was concentrated in the Maritimes, grew very slowly until West Indians arrived. With them, of course, came other nonwhite groups, especially East Asians and South Asians. By 2001, approximately 18 percent of the Canadian population was foreign-born, the great majority nonwhite, and many lived in Toronto, especially if they were West Indian.

The Dutch Context

The Netherlands is another former imperial power that attracts residents of its ex-colonies and dependencies. In its heyday, Holland controlled Surinam, on the north coast of South America, and it still controls several islands off that coast (for example, Aruba and the Dutch Antilles). Beginning in the 1960s, Surinamese, who are of African (Creole), Indian (Hindustani), Javanese, and Chinese origin, as well as Antilleans, who are primarily of African origin, began moving to the Netherlands. In the mid-1970s, impending independence motivated thousands of Surinamese to flee. They lost their right to unrestricted entry in 1980, five years after Surinam received its independence. Still, such a large number have relatives in the mother country that obtaining a visa on the grounds of "family reunification" is not difficult. Antilleans, on the other hand, can still enter at will. As a result, there is a great deal of circulation between Holland and the Antilles. Within the Netherlands, Antilleans are quite geographically dispersed, whereas the majority of Creoles live in Amsterdam, and Hindustanis prefer The Hague.

Immigrants from the Americas are not the only ethnic minorities in the Netherlands. The nation houses Indonesians, who arrived in the 1950s and are now quite well integrated, as well as Turks and Moroccans, who are less well integrated. Members of these last two groups were recruited as manual laborers in the 1960s. When the need for their skills declined, Dutch authorities banned labor migration and hoped the workers would return home. Instead, Turks and Moroccans took advantage of policies that permitted family reunification and sent for their wives and children. With about 9 percent of the Dutch population reporting a non-Western ancestry, racial and ethnic tensions in the Netherlands run high (Statistics Netherlands).

Ethnography

The United States Ethnography is the method that first exposed the perception that whites prefer West Indians to African Americans. Consider, for instance, Nancy Foner's (1985) interviews with New York Jamaicans. One of the standard questions she asked was whether Jamaicans in New York were treated *the same as white American people*. Instead of answering the question, 40 percent of Foner's respondents elaborated on their perception that white Americans treated Jamaicans and other West Indians better than they treated African Americans. Of course, on first meeting, this preference might not be obvious, since whites rarely could distinguish West Indians from African Americans on sight. But "once you say something and they recognize you're not from this country, they treat you a little different" (Foner 1985, 718). In the same vein, a Belizean-born Los Angeles teacher told Faye Arnold (1996, 16): "West Indians are treated the best. I have had—to be truthful—I have spoken to a few people and they told me that they had dealings with Whites—you know people working with white people— and they feel that foreign Blacks are treated a little more considerate than American." Similarly, a West Indian from the Bay Area told Percy Hintzen (2001, 154), "Once whites understand that you are foreign, that acknowledgment lends itself toward you as a matter of fact to be viewed differently. If as a West Indian, you adopt the American accent and American cultural norms, you definitely will be viewed as a black American."

Some second-generation West Indians confess to making special efforts to communicate their heritage because, without an accent, conversation is insufficient to identify them. Mary Waters (1996, 182–83) describes the strategies of some young U.S.-born West Indian New Yorkers: "One girl carried a Guyanese map as part of her key chain so that when people looked at her keys they would ask her about it and she could tell them that her parents were from Guyana. One young woman described having her mother teach her an accent so that she [could] use it when she applied for a job or a place to live. Others just try to work it into conversation when they meet someone." In the same vein, Arnold (1996, 19) recounts that accentless West Indian women communicate their origins "by doing such things as bringing West Indian dishes to potlucks; reggae, calypso , and other recordings by West Indian artists to employee socials; and inviting coworkers to West Indian cricket matches, weddings, dances, and the like."

Not all West Indians concur that whites treat them more favorably. Because he was told his accent was a liability to an entertainment career, Sidney Poitier (1980) spent months losing his; similarly, a West Indian in northern California told Hintzen (2001, 143) that he thought whites did not respect his accent: "They make fun of anybody who . . . speaks in an accent or a different language." Others see class as an intervening variable. Waters (1996, 1999) noted that poor inner-city youth were unaware that white Americans view West Indians more favorably, whereas middle class suburban youth expressed this idea. Milton Vickerman's (1994, 1999) interviews with Jamaica-born adult men yielded the opposite conclusion. The longer his informants had lived in the United States and the higher their social class, the less they believed that whites favored West Indians over African Americans. Vickerman attributes the change to experiencing racism: "The longer they live in this country, the more such episodes they encounter and the more they tend to identify with African Americans" (1994, 99).

Still, far more interviewees assert white favoritism than challenge it. Interestingly, most of those interviewed have been West Indian; few researchers have solicited the opinions of whites. However, Mary Waters conducted interviews with black and white personnel in a large New York City catering firm that relies on foreign-born black labor. White managers there had no hesitation in communicating that West Indians were the more desirable workers. "If I had one position open and if it was a West Indian versus an American black, I'd go with the West Indian," reported a forty-two-year-old white male manager. When asked why, he replied, "Their reliability, their willingness to do the job . . . they have a different drive than American blacks" (Waters 1993, 11). Yet, on inquiring about the origins of this opinion, she found that

> all of the whites stated that before working in this worksite they were very unaware of differences between foreign-born and American-born blacks and that they were surprised when they first encountered the differences. The most common way in which the whites learn about the differences between foreign-born and American-born blacks is by talking with their employees about it. The tensions and distance between Americans and the foreign born are talked about by the immigrant workers and signal to the whites the differences between the groups. . . . While the whites report that they only recently became aware of differences between foreign-born and American-born blacks, they now describe what they perceive as different values and behaviors between the groups. (Waters 1993, 11–12)

Some West Indians admit to attempting to mold white opinion in their favor. They have told interviewers that, when meeting whites, they take steps to communicate not only their heritage but the meaning of that heritage. A respondent told Faye Arnold (1996, 25): "I always go to school the first week. I volunteer. I join the PTA, the Parents Council, you name it. I let those teachers know that we are not to be trifled with, not when it comes to our kids' education. I tell them that we come from Trinidad and Tobago so our culture is different. We expect our kids to be, well, students and will do what is needed to see that they do." West Indians interviewed in New York and Washington, D.C., likewise report that emphasizing their distinctiveness from African Americans gets them better treatment (Foner 1998; Mortimer 1976). This strategy is consonant with the etiology attributed to white managers' awareness of West Indian–African American differences, as well as with the survey results presented here.

Great Britain   Of course, the number of native blacks in Great Britain is few. But there are several nonwhite groups in that country. Are West Indians the least favored among them, as Faye Arnold supposed?

Only a small amount of ethnographic work in Britain speaks to this issue, but the findings are consonant with Arnold's supposition. A Birmingham man involved in a training program for minority youth remarked: "West Indians did not present themselves in ways that would make them acceptable . . . [they] have a chip on their shoulder" (Lee and Wrench 1983, 30).[2] Another observed that West Indians were "aggressive, militant and volatile" and "don't take much pride in their work." Of course, participants in training programs may be disproportionately disgruntled. Nevertheless, a theme across this literature is that South Asians (Indians, Pakistanis, Bangladeshis) are the better workers. A boss in a food manufacturing plant described West Indians as "lazy, arrogant and undisciplined," but Asians as "hard working, diligent and conscientious" (Jewson et al. 1990, 18). Similarly, in his interviews with West Midlands managers, Richard Jenkins (1986) found that most preferred Asians to West Indians.

Survey Research

The United States   Surveys are another way of measuring the position of minorities. Because ethnographic studies have paid little attention to whites' attitudes toward West Indians, opinion polls are the primary source of information about whites' views. Surprisingly, surveys offer little support for the claim that whites in the United States favor West Indians over African Americans.

Probably the oldest questionnaire designed to tap prejudice is the Bogardus Social Distance Scale (Schaefer 1998, 48–49). Initially fielded in 1926, the scale contains a list of thirty minorities and asks respondents to answer seven questions about each one, ranging from how they feel about intermarriage with the minority to how they feel about permitting the minority to immigrate to the United States. Answers range from 1 ("very positive") to 7 ("very negative"). The average of these numbers across respondents constitutes a group's "social distance score." Using a national sample of college students in social science classes, the original study was fielded five times: 1926, 1946, 1956, 1966, and 1977.

As might be expected, West Indians were not included on Bogardus's original list of minorities. However, in 2001, Vincent Parrillo and his colleagues fielded a new version of the scale (Parrillo and Donoghue 2005). Observing that the complexion of America had changed since Bogardus selected his thirty groups, Parrillo made a number of substitutions. Of relevance to this study, Parrillo included three groups of black immigrants: Jamaicans, Haitians, and Africans. Keeping in mind that high numbers mean stronger prejudice, compare the social distance scores of the black groups: African Americans 1.33, Africans 1.43, Jamaicans 1.49, and Haitians 1.63. Because the authors do not provide standard deviations, it is not possible to determine whether the differences between groups are statistically significant. However, the number of cases is so large (2,916) that it is highly likely that the differences between African Americans and all three foreign-born black groups are significant.

Only one other nationally representative survey has inquired about the relative position of West Indians. In 1990 the University of Chicago's General Social Survey (GSS) featured a special module on attitudes toward "new" immigrant groups (Smith 1991). The questionnaire asked respondents to rank groups in terms of their "social standing" on a scale ranging from 1 ("low") to 9 ("high"). Among the included black groups, respondents accorded "Negroes" the highest standing, at 4.17; "African Blacks" were next at 3.58, followed by "West Indian Blacks," whose standing averaged 3.56. The term "Negroes" was used to produce comparability with previous versions of the survey. Despite the questionnaire's use of this dated label, "Negroes" received a higher average score than West Indians did. In sum, survey research indicates that the American public views African Americans more positively than it views blacks from any other country.

Psychologists too often study the responses of college students. Kay Deaux (2006) reports a study in which New York City college students were asked to evaluate how people in general rate several racial-ethnic groups. White respondents ranked West Indians below Europeans and equal to Hispanics, but "West Indian respondents believed that people in general held very positive view of West Indian immigrants, virtually indistinguishable from those toward Western European immigrants and decidedly more positive than those toward Eastern European and Latino immigrant groups" (Deaux 2006, 177). This inquiry shows that West Indians have an inflated perception of their standing in the larger society. However, this study sheds no light on the rankings of West Indians relative to African Americans because no questions about the latter were included.[3]

Teceta Thomas's inquiry (reported by Deaux 2006) at two West Coast colleges was more explicit. White Americans, black Americans, and black immigrants were asked to list stereotypes about all three groups. Black Americans elicited more negative than positive traits, and black immigrants elicited about the same number of positive and negative traits. However, "white participants in particular were often vague about the latter target group, and more than one-third of them listed no attributes at all" (Deaux 2006, 175). In other words, these West Coast whites had little conception of who black immigrants were; hence, they could not define the immigrants' characteristics, real or imagined.[4]

The 1999 Immigrant Second Generation in Metropolitan New York Study illustrates yet another strategy. It asked 3,424 persons between the ages of eighteen and thirty-two if they had experienced prejudice looking for work (Kasinitz, Mollenkopf, and Waters 2003). Respondents were native-born whites, African Americans, Puerto Ricans, and members of several "new Immigrant groups," including West Indians. All respondents either arrived before the age of twelve or were American-born. One-third of African Americans answered that they had experienced prejudice looking for work, compared to 26 percent of West Indians, 22 percent of Puerto Ricans, 20 percent of Dominicans, and 6 percent of whites. The African American–West Indian difference, while not large (7 percent), is in the direction expected by the white favoritism hypothesis.

How can the contradiction between the national survey results and the New York survey results be explained? Why does the "average American" view African Americans more positively than black immigrants, while New York's black immigrants report less job discrimination than African Americans? One possibility is that white favoritism is more prevalent in New York than elsewhere in the country. Being the center of West Indian America, New York is the setting where whites are most familiar with West Indians and where whites should be most aware of the differences between the two groups of blacks. A second possibility is that group rankings based on self-report are different from group rankings based on others' perceptions. Especially since the civil rights movement, whites have been reluctant to talk openly about their sentiments toward blacks (Sniderman and Carmines 1997). A third possibility is that a group's rank "in general" and its rank in the labor market are not necessarily the same. After all, in most surveys of the public at large African Americans rank toward the middle of the racial-ethnic hierarchy, but in studies of employer opinion African Americans rank near the bottom (Lim 2001; Moss and Tilly 2001).

These possibilities suggest that the best measures of group rankings in the eyes of employers come from studies that focus explicitly on work rather than on social distance or social standing. Moreover, the findings of a study conducted in one geographic area (such as New York) may not generalize to another.

Canada   Canadian leaders like to describe their nation as an "ethnic mosaic," by which they mean a society that respects ethnic boundaries and treats all groups equally. But research by John Porter (1965) found this description to be more rhetoric than reality. He used the term "vertical mosaic" to describe the propensity for some backgrounds to enjoy higher prestige than others. Though West Indians do not enjoy a higher standing in Canada than European ethnics, neither have three decades of survey research found them at the bottom of the social hierarchy. Contrary to Malcolm Gladwell (1996) and Cecil Foster's (1996) expectations, ordinary Canadians consistently rank West Indians above South Asians (Berry and Kalin 1995; Berry, Kalin, and Taylor 1977; Bibby 1995; Breton et al. 1990). However, none of these surveys adequately distinguishes Muslims from non-Muslims. This failure is a problem because whites may hold non-Muslim South Asians in substantially higher regard than Muslim South Asians.[5]

Equally important, Canada's visible minorities have a different view of their country's ethnic hierarchy. The 1978 study "Ethnic Pluralism in an Urban Setting" showed that 22 percent of Toronto's West Indians admitted "experiencing discrimination when trying to find a job"; the next highest figure was for Toronto's Chinese, at 17 percent (Breton at al. 1990). In early 1992, the *Toronto Star* asked similar questions of a sample of the city's ethnic minorities, three of which were nonwhite (Dion and Kawakami 1996). Forty-one percent of West Indians reported that they had experienced discrimination finding work, compared to 29 percent of South Asians and 22 percent of Chinese. With respect to questions about promotions and wages, the proportions reporting discrimination were lower, but West Indians remained the most dissatisfied.[6] Finally, Statistics Canada sponsored the Ethnic Diversity Survey in 2002. It asked: "In the past 5 years, do you feel that you have experienced discrimination or been treated unfairly by others in Canada because of your ethnicity, race, skin colour, language, accent or religion?" Thirty-two percent of blacks answered "sometimes" or "often," and another 17 percent answered "rarely"; the comparable figures for the next closest group, South Asians, were 21 percent and 13 percent, respectively (Statistics Canada 2003). Those respondents who reported having experienced discrimination were asked to identify the contexts. Two-thirds stated that they had experienced discrimination at work or when applying for a job or promotion.

In sum, Canadian survey results resemble American survey results in showing that rankings change with the race-ethnicity of the rater. In Canada, African-origin respondents perceive themselves more often as victims of discrimination than do members of other minority groups, yet most Canadians rank West Indians more favorably than they rank South Asians.

Great Britain   Britons are widely assumed to be less tolerant than Canadians, although Jeffrey Reitz (1988) concludes that this perception a myth. Two studies that shed light on group standing in Britain are the annual British Social Attitudes Survey and the Fourth National Survey of Ethnic Minorities. Both uncover a mild tendency for the public to stigmatize South Asians (Indians, Pakistanis, Bangladeshis) more than Caribbean blacks (Jowell et al. 1992; Modood et al. 1997). For instance, the 1994 Fourth National Survey asked white respondents the open-ended question: "Of all the racial, ethnic and religious groups in Britain, against which do you think there is the most prejudice?" Thirty-nine percent replied "Asian," 17 percent "Muslims," 12 percent "Caribbeans," and 10 percent "Pakistanis."[7] The meaning of the label "Asian," of course, is unclear, but the relative position of West Indians is not.

In 1983, 1986, and 1991, Britons were asked whether they thought that "most whites would mind a little or a lot if a West Indian were their boss," as well as whether they themselves "would mind a little or a lot if a West Indian were their boss." Parallel questions were asked regarding Asians. It turned out that there was no difference in the proportion of respondents who "minded" whether the boss was West Indian or Asian. Less surprising, more respondents felt that "most whites" would mind (around 54 percent) than admitted that they themselves would mind (around 17 percent) (Jowell et al. 1992).

British perceptions were also included in a module of the 1988 Eurobarometer that investigated attitudes toward immigrants. Table 6.1 shows the results for Great Britain, the Netherlands, and France, the three European nations that house significant West Indian populations. Respondents were asked to rate how "favorably" they felt toward a group. The most favorable score was 100; the least favorable was 0. On this scale, British respondents ranked West Indians 59.4, about the same as black Africans (59.0) and slightly higher than South Asians (57.4).

When surveys solicit the experiences of ethnic minorities, however,

Table 6.1   Attitudes Toward Immigrants: Eurobarometer 1988

Group	Great Britain	Netherlands	France
Northern Europeans	72.8 (1.93) [945]	74.3 (1.58) [975]	76.2 (1.98) [966]
Southern Europeans	68.4 (1.80) [953]	70.9 (1.57) [991]	73.5 (1.91) [993]
Jews	67.6 (2.01) [944]	73.9 (1.66) [985]	67.0 (2.35) [983]
West Indians	59.4 (2.15) [945]	68.9 (1.71) [976]	69.8 (2.20) [983]
Surinamese		67.3 (1.80) [985]	
South Asians	57.4 (2.19) [943]	65.8 (1.66) [974]	58.5 (2.33) [969]
Southeast Asians	58.8 (2.04) [921]	66.4 (1.64) [970]	61.6 (2.38) [983]
North Africans	58.1 (2.00) [929]	63.9 (1.70) [992]	54.1(2.57) [990]
Black Africans	59.0 (2.10) [935]	65.3 (1.73) [977]	60.0 (2.35) [986]
Turks	57.3 (2.00) [896]	63.0 (1.90) [993]	53.2 (2.51) [972]

Source: Reif and Melich (1991).
Note: The question was "Now I would like to get your feelings about the groups on this list. I would like you to rate them on a scale that runs from 0 to 100. Ratings between 51 and 100 mean that you feel favorable toward that group. Ratings between 0 and 49 mean that you don't feel too favorable toward that group. A rating of 50 means that you don't feel particularly favorable or unfavorable toward that group." Groups were described in the following way: Southern Europeans as "Greeks, Italians, Spaniards, and Portuguese"; West Indians as "West Indies, Caribbean"; South Asians as "Indians, Pakistanis"; and Southeast Asians as "Cambodians, Laotians, and Vietnamese." The figures reported are the weighted mean, the weighted standard deviation (in parentheses), and the unweighted number of cases (in brackets).

the results are quite different. The 1982 National Survey of Ethnic Minorities asked: "Have you yourself ever been refused a job for reasons which you think have to do with race or colour?" Twenty-four percent of West Indians answered yes, compared to 9 percent of Asians. On related questions, of which there were six in the survey, West Indians consistently perceived the workplace as more discriminatory than Asians did (Brown 1984). Fourteen years later, the same survey asked: "Have you ever been refused a job for reasons you think were to do with your race or colour or religious or cultural background?" Twenty-eight percent of black Caribbeans answered yes, as did 15 percent of Asian Indians, 11 percent of Pakistanis, and 3 percent of Bangladeshis. Calculations for London produced nearly identical results. When the responses to other, similar questions were examined, the propensity of West Indians to report the highest levels of job discrimination persisted. For instance, to the question "Do you feel that there are real equal opportunities for everyone regardless of race, color, or religious or cultural background where you work?" West Indians were the most likely (59 percent) to answer no, followed by Asian Indians (37 percent), Pakistanis (36 percent), and, finally, Bangladeshis (23 percent) (Modood et al. 1997).

The Netherlands   Regrettably, most of the research on immigrants and minorities in the Netherlands identifies groups on the basis of birth-place rather than race-ethnicity. As a result, despite their ethnic diversity, the Surinamese are usually treated as a single group. Though it is hard to know exactly what the term "Surinamese" means to the Dutch public, respondents generally do not rank this group at the bottom of the social ladder. For instance, in two studies the social distance scores of Surinamese were significantly lower (more favorable) than the scores of Turks or Moroccans (Hagendoorn 2001; Hagendoorn and Hraba 1987). Similarly, on the 1988 Eurobarometer the Dutch public gave Surinamese a favorability score of 67.3 (see table 6.1). This figure is slightly below the score of West Indians (68.9) but significantly above the scores of North Africans (63.9) and Turks (63.0). In other words, survey research uncovers a Dutch ethnic hierarchy in which Antilleans and Surinamese are viewed more favorably than Moroccans and Turks.

As noted earlier, in the United States, Britain, and Canada, there is a disjuncture between public perceptions of the ethnic hierarchy and minority perceptions of that hierarchy. In these three countries, African-origin residents report that they experience more discrimination than other ethnic minorities report. At the same time, surveys of the American, British, and Canadian public do not invariably place African-origin persons at the bottom. In a break with this pattern, Holland's blacks are *less* likely to report discrimination than members of other ethnic groups. This can be seen in responses to questions on the Sociale Positie en Voorzieningengebruick Allochtonen (SPVA), an ongoing survey of ethnic minorities and the only data source that distinguishes the Surinamese by ethnicity. Participants in the 1991 wave were asked: "Do you think you have equal chances in acquiring a better job to native Dutch employees?" About one-quarter of respondents of Antillean and Creole heritage disagreed, while 34 percent of Hindustanis, 46 percent of Moroccans, and 52 percent of Turks disagreed. Another SPVA question, this one directed only to the unemployed, asked for "the most likely reason you don't have work at the moment" and offered a myriad of choices. Among those selecting the option "discrimination" were 4.8 percent of Antilleans, 6.85 percent of Moroccans, 7.3 percent of Creoles, and 15 percent of Hindustanis and Turks.[8] These responses yield slightly different rankings than the "equal chances" question described earlier. On the first question, Moroccans rank below both Antilleans and Creoles, and on the second they rank about the same as Creoles and slightly below Antilleans. In short, the SPVA results do not convey a consistent position for Moroccans, but Turks and Hindustanis perceive more employment barriers than either group of blacks.[9]

Field Experiments

Field experiments compare the ability of members of dominant and minority groups to find identical jobs or identical housing. The usual approach is to generate bogus credentials that describe all applicants similarly save for their names or pictures, which are designed to convey the critical distinction. When the telephone is used, accents can also serve as a means of conveying group membership. Though this technique has its critics (Heckman 1998; Riach and Rich 2002), it is a more reliable indicator of discrimination than social surveys or ethnographic accounts.

Unfortunately, in the United States no field experiment has included West Indians, though in her book *To Be an Immigrant*, Deaux (2006) describes a "video" field experiment that she designed with Jennifer Eberhardt (Eberhardt and Deaux 2000). Viewers see the same black man apply twice for a job, once using a Caribbean accent and once using an American accent. They are then asked to rate his performance and predict his future success. Deaux reports that viewers rank the man with the West Indian accent more favorably than the man with the American accent. Unfortunately, she does not provide details about the viewers, such as their number, age, and geographic or racial characteristics. Moreover, a video experiment is not the same as a field test. Hence, generalizing from these results would be premature.

In a 1985 field experiment in Toronto, members of several groups responded to want ads by telephone. Employers were most likely to reject South Asians (44 percent), followed by black Caribbeans (36 percent) and applicants with Italian or Slavic accents (31 percent). White Canadians were least likely to be rejected (13 percent) (Henry and Ginzberg 1985). Indo-Pakistani applicants had to make nineteen or twenty telephone calls to secure a job interview, while black West Indians needed to make only fifteen or sixteen. This difference, however, was not statistically significant.

In 1973–74, 1977–79, and 1984–85, British scholars devised experiments in which native whites, southern Europeans, West Indians, and South Asians applied for identical jobs in several major cities. In all three trials, only 10 percent of the Greek and Italian applicants experienced discrimination, but one out of three West Indians and South Asians were turned away (Brown and Gay 1994). The most recent British experiment took place in northern England and Scotland in 1996. The participants were young school-leavers. Whites were three times more likely than equally qualified Asians and five times more likely than equally qualified African-Caribbeans to secure a job interview. This is the first time that a significant difference between blacks and Asians has been reported in Britain (Commission for Racial Equality 1996). Though the report does not comment upon nativity, the timing of the study and the young age of the participants suggest that the participants in this most recent trial were the children of black immigrants rather than immigrants themselves.

Finally, the Dutch study of Frank Bovenkerk, Mitzi J. I. Gras, and D. Ramsoedh (1995) is one of the most sophisticated yet to be fielded. The strategy began with a telephone inquiry and, if this went well, moved on to a personal interview. The groups of interest included Dutch whites, Surinamese, and Moroccans, who varied on both gender and education. The central finding was that, controlling for education and gender, Surinamese and Moroccans both experienced discrimination, but their respective rates of discrimination were the same (Gras and Bovenkerk 1999).[10]

Taken together, these studies indicate that West Indian immigrants have more difficulty securing work than native whites, but no more difficulty than do other foreign-born nonwhites.[11] When both West Indians and another minority were included (South Asians in Canada and Britain, Moroccans in Holland), the differences in the ability of the two groups to obtain jobs were statistically identical.

To recapitulate, the strongest support for white favoritism comes from ethnography. West Indian Americans in particular strongly subscribe to it. In addition, the results of one survey were consonant with the hypothesis: more young African American New Yorkers than young West Indian New Yorkers reported experiencing job discrimination. Yet when the American public is polled, no black immigrant group ranks above African Americans. As for the expectation that West Indians fall to the bottom of the ladder outside the United States, this is the perception of West Indians in Britain and Canada but not in the Netherlands. Finally, in field experiments involving more than one non-Western group, West Indian immigrants fare as well (or as poorly) as the other minority. In the absence of similar studies in the United States, the discussion turns next to tests of the white favoritism hypothesis that use secondary data.

A Research Strategy

Proponents of white favoritism make two slightly different arguments, though they do not acknowledge the distinction. The first affirms that

West Indians and African Americans actually exhibit behaviors that motivate employers, coworkers, and customers to rate the former more favorably than the latter (Waters 1999). These behaviors, which have their roots in West Indian culture or in the selection of migration, give West Indians a good reputation. As a result, their superiors reward them more readily than African Americans.

The second argument asserts that there are no actual behavioral differences between the two groups of blacks. According to Arnold (1984), American whites rank West Indians more favorably than African Americans because they associate the former, but not the latter, with England. West Indians in England have the same traits as those in the United States, but West Indians cannot profit from their "English connection" in England. Grosfoguel (2003) proposes a different causal mechanism. Whites in the United States perceive British West Indians more favorably than African Americans because the United States never directly controlled British West Indians in the way that it controlled African Americans. Likewise, he supposes that whites in the United States perceive British West Indians more favorably than Puerto Ricans, Mexicans, and Native Americans. Though the history of these three groups differs, their respective homelands have been subjugated by the United States government. Colonial and quasi-colonial domination, Grosfoguel argues, requires a stronger ideological justification than other kinds of hegemony. Moreover, such ideologies do not disappear simply because the formal colonial tie no longer exists.

Because of the type of data available to this study, it is not possible to distinguish between the causes of white favoritism. Secondary data analysis only supports tests of its consequences. Social scientists call the testable portion of the causal linkage an "indirect effect." In figure 3.1, it is represented by the arrow from white favoritism to Caribbean advantage. As the figure makes clear, discrediting this causal linkage has no bearing on the viability of white favoritism as a real phenomenon. Whites may indeed favor West Indians; the two strategies below test only whether that favoritism has an economic impact.

Both strategies draw on an important corollary of white favoritism: the larger the local African American population, the better the economic outcomes of the local West Indian population. This corollary is an example of a more general principle: the larger a low-ranked group, the better off are members of higher-ranked groups. Queuing theorists do a good job of explaining this principle. They use the metaphor of a queue or line to convey how applicants are arranged in the eyes of employers. In the case of minorities, queuing theorists perceive workers lined up such that members of the most desirable minority stand at the head, members of the second most desirable stand next, and so on down the line. Members of the least desirable minority stand at the tail. To be sure, most employers are concerned about characteristics other than ethnicity and race—qualifications, for instance. But in many instances qualified applicants can be found within each minority. In this situation, queuing theorists expect employers to give first preference to members of the group they esteem most and to move down the line only as the supply of more favored groups declines. Qualifications being the same, employers will hire or promote members of the least desirable background only when the supply of more favorably ranked groups is exhausted. By the same logic, when the workforce must be reduced, members of the least desirable minority are the first to be made redundant (Hodge 1973; Lieberson 1980).

These dynamics mean that, in a single labor market, the larger the proportion of the labor force ranked below a given group (or the smaller the proportion above), the more successful that group will be. Extending this principle to two or more labor markets, a group will be most successful where the proportion of more stigmatized groups is largest. For instance, W. Parker Frisbie and Lisa Neidert (1977) found that, across southwestern cities, the larger the proportion of African Americans, the higher the occupational status of Mexican Americans. They explain this by hypothesizing that employers rank Mexicans above African Americans, who rank at the bottom. Similarly, proponents of white favoritism hypothesize that employers rank West Indians above African Americans, who rank at the bottom. Therefore, empirical research should show that the larger the proportion of African Americans, the higher the occupational status of West Indians.

Extending this logic to other economic outcomes, a general strategy for testing white favoritism would be to vary the proportion of African Americans with whom West Indians compete and observe the result. If whites rank West Indians above African Americans, then the higher the proportion of African Americans in a labor market, the stronger should be the outcomes for West Indians in that labor market. This strategy is pursued here in two ways, cross-nationally and domestically. The cross-national strategy compares the economic outcomes of West Indian immigrants in New York with the outcomes of their counterparts in Toronto, London, and Amsterdam. Clearly, the latter three cities contain very few native blacks, though these three cities might contain other minorities that employers rank below West Indians. If they are numerous enough, these other minorities could play the same "upgrading" role for West Indians that African Americans supposedly play in the United States. As will become clear, this situation holds only in Amsterdam, and there only among men. Still, this result illustrates why knowledge of non-U.S. ethnic hierarchies is critical for interpreting the results of any cross-national test of white favoritism.

The domestic strategy explores the effect on West Indian outcomes of variations in African American proportions across U.S. metropolitan areas.[12] If white employers favor West Indians over African Americans, then the larger the proportion of African Americans in a metropolitan area, the better will be the economic outcomes of its West Indians.

The Cross-National Test

Selected to represent the American side of the cross-national comparison are residents of the New York metropolitan area. New York is home to more West Indians than any other American city, and it is also where most of the research on the white favoritism hypothesis has taken place. New York is where white employers told Mary Waters that they prefer West Indian immigrants to African Americans and where more young African Americans than West Indians said they'd experienced prejudice when looking for work. London, Toronto, and Amsterdam serve as contrasts. Paris, also a major West Indian destination, is excluded for two reasons. One is the absence of information about the relative ranking of French West Indians in the eyes of French employers. Without knowledge on this score, it is impossible to predict whether West Indians should do better in Paris or in New York. Another is that French West Indians have unfettered access to France. As a result, these migrants may be less positively selected than their New York counterparts. The same difficulty may hold for migrants from the Netherlands Antilles to Amsterdam: no border impedes travel from the islands to the metropole. As a result, the Dutch comparison is limited to those Surinamese Creoles who were required to obtain entry visas—that is, those who arrived after 1979.

The cross-national test draws on the 1990 U.S., 1991 U.K., and 1991 Canadian censuses and on three waves of the Dutch SPVA (1991, 1994, and 1998). A first task is to determine whether London, Toronto, or Amsterdam contains minority groups ranked below West Indians and, if they do, to estimate the respective size of such groups in the 1990s. Of central concern is how the respective proportions compare to the proportion of African Americans in New York's labor force in 1990, when African Americans accounted for 8.6 percent of the male labor force and 9.8 percent of the female labor force. If the advocates of white favoritism are correct, the presence in London, Toronto, or Amsterdam of a group both ranked below West Indians and equal in labor market share to New York's African Americans would ensure equal outcomes for West Indians in and outside the United States. If the group ranked below West Indians in the contrast city is larger than African Americans, then West Indians in New York would be relatively less successful; if the group ranked below West Indians in the contrast city is smaller than African Americans, then West Indians in New York would be relatively more successful.

The research described in the previous section explored group rankings in the three cities. British research has focused entirely on the relative position of South Asians and West Indians. Some studies rank South Asians higher, some rank them lower, and some rank them equivalent to West Indians. Given these findings, a very conservative assumption is that London's South Asians rank below West Indians. Yet, even under this assumption, New York's West Indians should fare better than London's because South Asians were a smaller proportion of London's 1991 labor force (5.9 percent of men and 4.5 percent of women) than the African American proportion of New York's 1990 labor force. More likely, the two groups are ranked about the same, in which case a New York advantage is even more probable. An assessment of the Toronto labor market yields the identical conclusion. Again, South Asians are West Indians' closest contender, and researchers find them above, below, and equal in standing to West Indians. South Asians were an even smaller proportion of Toronto's 1991 labor force (3.8 percent of men and 2.6 percent of women) than of London's. Consequently, even under the very conservative assumption that Toronto's employers prefer West Indians to South Asians, the former will be more successful in New York than in Toronto.

To predict the Dutch outcome supportive of white favoritism is more difficult. The ethnic minorities of interest are Turks, Moroccans, and Hindustanis. All three rank below Creoles in one or more studies. As before, the most judicious response is to assume that Turks, Moroccans, and Hindustanis all hold lower status than Creoles. Surprisingly, this assumption produces different expectations by gender. About 9.3 percent of Amsterdam's male labor force consists of Turks, Moroccans, and Hindustanis, while only 4.0 percent of Amsterdam's female labor force comes from these groups. The reason for the gender difference is the low labor force participation rates of Muslim immigrant women in Amsterdam. Under these circumstances, white favoritism predicts that Creole men should do about as well as New York's West Indian men, but that Creole women should do less well than New York's West Indian women.

Table 6.2 displays the results. Interpreting the table requires recognizing the differences between a cross-national test strategy and a single-nation test strategy. One difference concerns the choice of a benchmark: African Americans cannot serve as a benchmark in cross-national comparisons because African Americans do not live in Toronto, London, or Amsterdam. Hence, in table 6.2 native-born whites

Table 6.2   Ratio of Adjusted Foreign-Born West Indian Means to Observed Native-Born White Means: New York, London, Toronto, and Amsterdam

City, Year	Labor Force Participation		Unemployment		Occupational Prestige		Log Earnings	
	Men	Women	Men	Women	Men	Women	Men	Women
United Kingdom								
London, 1991	1.00	1.06	1.50	1.83	0.92	0.94	n.a.	n.a.
New York, 1990	1.01	1.15	1.81	1.90	0.94	0.96		
Canada								
Toronto, 1991	0.96	1.04*	2.27	3.30	0.87	0.90	0.93*	0.96
New York, 1990	1.01	1.36	2.10	1.99	0.90	0.91	0.91	1.00
Netherlands								
Amsterdam, 1991, 1994, 1998	0.93	1.19	2.54	1.58	0.92	0.95	0.94*	0.97*
New York, 1990	0.99	1.35	1.99	1.96	0.91	0.91	0.82	0.91

Source: Author's calculation based on the UK Sample of Anonymised Records (SARs), the Candian Public Use Microdata Files on Individuals (PUMFI), the Dutch Sociale Positie en Voorzieningengebruick Allochtonen (SPVA), and the U.S. Integrated Public Use Microdata Series (IPUMS).

Note: Shading conveys intercity contrasts that are consistent with the predictions of white favoritism.

* Statistically significant difference between New York and the contrast city (p < .05).

are the benchmark. A second difference concerns the parameter of interest. In single-nation studies, the parameter of interest is the ratio of an adjusted mean to an observed mean, usually the ratio of a West Indian adjusted mean to an African American observed mean. But each cross-national comparison generates two such ratios: the ratio of a West Indian adjusted mean to a native white observed mean in New York and the ratio of a West Indian adjusted mean to an observed native white mean in the contrast city. Interest centers on the difference between them. Do West Indians do relatively better in New York, in the contrast city, or does location make no difference? To facilitate interpretation, asterisks appear in table 6.2 when a statistically significant difference obtains between the New York ratio and the ratio for a contrast city.[13]

A statistically significant difference between New York and a contrast city is not always support for white favoritism. It is when Toronto or London are contrasts, provided New York is preeminent. In the Amsterdam contrast, white favoritism predicts no significant difference for men and New York's preeminence for women. In table 6.2, shaded cells convey results consonant with white favoritism.

The London–New York results appear in the top panel of the table. Three of the six London–New York differences are consonant with white favoritism—that is, New York's West Indians do a little better. Yet none of these are shaded because none attain statistical significance. Still, this conclusion may be hasty because the British census provides no information about year of arrival. If the calculations could be adjusted for this variable, white favoritism might be supported. Because, on average, West Indians in London immigrated earlier than West Indians in New York, adjusting for differences in the two groups' years of arrival might strengthen New York outcomes relative to London outcomes. Indeed, some U.S.-U.K. comparisons that control for years since migration do show an advantage for the United States (Model 2005; Model and Ladipo 1996). On the other hand, in her national-level study, Melonie Heron (2001) found this to be true only for men.

The middle panel presents the New York–Toronto comparison.[14] Here most of the intercity differences are in the direction predicted by white favoritism, but only one—women's labor force participation—reaches statistical significance. Interestingly, there is another New York–Toronto comparison that reaches statistical significance, but it is in the wrong direction. Relative to native white men, Toronto's West Indians earn significantly *more* than New York's West Indians. For the result to be consonant with white favoritism, the New Yorkers would have had to earn more. Hence, this contrast is starred but not shaded.

Previous comparisons between black immigrants to Canada and the United States convey the same mixed pattern. Using the 1980 U.S. and 1981 Canadian censuses, Jeffrey Reitz and Raymond Breton (1994) found no difference in the earnings of recent black male immigrants to the two countries; recent black female immigrants, on the other hand, did a little better in the United States. Using the 1990 U.S. and 1991 Canadian censuses to study occupational status, Heron (2001) detected no difference between West Indian immigrant males in the United States and Canada; females, on the other hand, fared better in Canada. Using the same data to study earnings, Michael Baker and Dwayne Benjamin (1997) reported that the gap between black immigrant men in the United States and their native white counterparts was a little larger than the gap between Canadian black immigrant men and their white counterparts. A decade later, disaggregating by birthplace and age at migration, Monica Boyd (2005) observed that, relative to their white immigrant counterparts, blacks who immigrated as children earned more in the United States than Canada, but blacks who immigrated after age fourteen earned more in the United States only if they were females from Jamaica. In short, both the results in table 6.2 and those reported by others show a mixture of findings. Sometimes West Indians do better in the United States, sometimes in Canada. Such a pattern does not support white favoritism.

Turning finally to the Amsterdam results, three of the men's contrasts are shaded (labor force participation, unemployment, and occupational prestige); none of the women's contrasts are shaded. Recall, however, that in the Dutch case the result consonant with white favoritism varies by sex. In the case of men, a finding of no difference between Amsterdam and New York is consonant with white favoritism; in the case of women, a finding of a New York advantage is consonant with white favoritism. But the expected sex differences do not appear. Rather, the Amsterdam–New York comparison yields similar results for men and women. On all outcomes but earnings, there are no significant differences between Amsterdam's Creoles and New York's West Indians. On earnings, the contrasts are starred because there are significant intercity differences. Creoles in Amsterdam—both male and female—earn significantly more (relative to their native white compatriots) than West Indians in New York earn (relative to their native white compatriots). The straightforwardness of this pattern suggests that white favoritism, with its differential predictions for men and women, is not the most useful theoretical lens for interpreting the New York–Amsterdam comparison.[15]

A simple way of summarizing the results in table 6.2 is to ask: how many intercity differences are statistically significant? Of the twenty-two comparisons in the table, four are significant: one favors New York over Toronto (women's labor force participation), one favors Toronto over New York (men's earnings), and two favor Amsterdam over New York (men's and women's earnings). Clearly, there are few significant differences in the economic outcomes of West Indian immigrants, whether they settle in New York, London, Toronto, or Amsterdam. Contrary to the expectations of white favoritism, the presence or absence of an African American population has no bearing on the economic outcomes of West Indian immigrants.

But how can this be the case when so many West Indians believe whites treat them better? To illuminate this paradox, a study of Australian immigrants is informative. In an influential article, M. D. R. Evans and Jonathan Kelley (1991) examined both the results of an opinion poll describing the perceptions of Australians toward immigrants and the results of regression models predicting the earnings of immigrants. The poll included questions like: "If a native-born Australian and a migrant both were applying for a job and both were equally qualified, which one would you hire if you had the choice?" (Evans and Kelley 1991, 743). On this question, the authors paid particular attention to the answers offered by owners and high-level managers. About 30 percent of these people admitted that they would hire the native. Yet the coefficients in the regression models conveyed no significant earnings deficit. In other words, despite some Australian gatekeepers' admission to survey researchers that they were prone to discriminate, there was no evidence that immigrants in Australia were suffering from discrimination.

Evans and Kelley explain this by contrasting the small number of actors in this drama relative to the size of the Australian economy. Perhaps one-third of Australian gatekeepers discriminate; immigrants make up less than 30 percent of the Australian labor market. There is adequate space, the authors argue, for immigrants and nondiscriminatory native gatekeepers to find one another. The authors go on to distinguish two kinds of discrimination: exclusionary discrimination and economic discrimination. The former is social, the latter financial. Because enough employers do not discriminate, minorities can overcome economic discrimination. For this reason, economic discrimination is less consequential than exclusionary discrimination.

This insight may have some relevance to the West Indian case, though it must be applied cautiously because almost all the immigrant groups included in Evans and Kelley's study were white. Aboriginals, for instance, were not considered, but the evidence that Australian employers discriminate against them is overwhelming (Inglis and Model 2007). The issue for West Indians in the United States is not whether they are discriminated against but whether they suffer less discrimination than African Americans do. In the Immigrant Second Generation in New York Study cited earlier, the difference between the proportion of New York's African Americans and the proportion of New York's West Indians who reported experiencing prejudice in their search for work was a mere 7 percent. To be sure, the West Indian advantage might have been larger if all the West Indians had perceptible Caribbean accents. Yet it is obvious that not all New York employers distinguish West Indians from African Americans. Furthermore, regardless of how many New York employers favor West Indians, the proportion of the workforce that is African American, hence available to "upgrade" West Indians, is only 8.63 percent for men and 9.79 percent for women. Add to this that the two groups of blacks do not always compete for the same jobs, and the likelihood that white favoritism is responsible for the economic advantage of West Indians relative to African Americans decreases. Stated more generally, modest differences in group rankings are unlikely to contribute significantly to disparities in the economic outcomes of relatively small groups.

The Domestic Test

Attention focuses now on the final analysis of the book: an inquiry into the effect of African American proportions on the outcomes of West Indian immigrants in the United States. The analysis parallels the previous one in testing the idea that the larger the proportion of the labor force that is African American, the better the outcomes of West Indian immigrants. A large empirical literature has already demonstrated that the greater the proportion of African Americans in a given labor market, the better the outcomes of whites (Huffman and Cohen 2004; Semyonov, Hoyt, and Scott 1984; Tigges and Tootle 1993). Since whites profit from the presence of African Americans, if white employers prefer West Indians to African Americans, then West Indians should also profit from the presence of African Americans.

This hypothesis is pursued at the level of metropolitan areas because these are good approximations of labor markets. The expectation is that the larger the percentage of African Americans in a metropolitan area's labor force, the better the economic outcome of West Indians working in that area. The first step in testing this idea is to calculate the percentage of African Americans in the labor force of each metropolitan area, separately by census year and sex. Because the 1970 data available to this study do not identify all individuals' metropolitan areas, 1970 is excluded from the analysis. Next, the appropriate African

American percentage is added to each West Indian immigrant's record. For instance, in 1990 the female labor force of the Hartford metropolitan area was 9.13 percent African American. This figure was therefore added to the records of each of the five West Indian women in the 1990 sample living in that area. Next, the average proportion of African Americans across all West Indians' metropolitan areas was calculated, separately by census year and sex. In 1990 one-half of West Indian women lived in metropolitan areas where the labor force was at least 15.3 percent African American; the other half lived in metropolitan areas where the labor force was less than 15.3 percent African American. Each West Indian was then assigned to one of two groups, depending on whether the percentage of African Americans in his (her) metropolitan area was above or below the average for his (her) sex and census year. Then two West Indian adjusted means were calculated: one for West Indians residing in metropolitan areas where the percentage of African Americans in the labor force was "equal or above average," and the other for West Indians residing in metropolitan areas where the percentage of African Americans in the labor force was "below average."[16]

Table 6.3 conveys these results. Following the pattern used in the previous table, asterisks identify comparisons in which the percentage of African Americans in a metropolitan area has a statistically significant effect, positive or negative, on the economic outcome of West Indians residing in that area. Shading identifies the comparisons consonant with the white favoritism hypothesis, that is, comparisons in which a higher percentage of African Americans in the local labor market is associated with a statistically significant improvement in West Indians' economic outcomes.

Five of the twenty-four contrasts in the table attain statistical significance. Of these, three are in the direction predicted by the white favoritism hypothesis, and two describe situations in which smaller proportions of African Americans are associated with stronger economic outcomes for West Indians. Clearly, there is no relationship between the proportion of the local labor force that is African American and the attainment of its West Indian population.

In summary, to the extent that statistical analysis can illuminate the white favoritism hypothesis, it falls short. Why then have so many West Indians and not a few whites expressed the idea that West Indian–white relations are more cordial than African American–white relations? Again, Evans and Kelley's (1991, 748) conclusion is relevant: "Exclusionary discrimination does not necessarily imply economic discrimination." In the present context, a more appropriate formulation is: personal favoritism does not necessarily imply economic favoritism.

Table 6.3 Adjusted Foreign-Born West Indian Means on Four Economic Indicators by Sex, Year, and Percentage of Metropolitan Area Labor Force that Is African American

Year	Labor Force Participation		Unemployment		Occupational Prestige		Log Earnings	
	Men	Women	Men	Women	Men	Women	Men	Women
1980								
Below average	0.86	0.75	0.06*	0.06	39.0	41.1	2.41	2.15
Average or above average	0.86	0.76	0.08	0.07	38.7	41.5	2.40	2.22
1990								
Below average	0.77	0.79	0.06*	0.14*	40.3	44.1	2.36	2.24
Average or above average	0.83	0.75	0.13	0.07	40.2	43.6	2.30	2.31
2000								
Below average	0.79	0.75	0.08*	0.07	39.9	43.9	2.70*	2.63
Average or above average	0.82	0.77	0.06	0.07	41.5	45.0	2.72	2.62

Source: Author's calculations based on the 1 percent and 5 percent Integrated Public Use Microdata Series (IPUMS).
Note: Excludes West Indians who do not live in metropolitan areas or whose metropolitan area is not identified in the data. Shaded cells identify West Indian economic outcomes on which increasing African American proportions have a statistically significant, positive effect (p < .05).
* Percentage of African Americans has a statistically significant effect on West Indians' economic outcome (p < .05).

This same point was proposed as an interpretation of figure 3.1. In that figure, several factors are depicted as causes of white favoritism (Anglophilia, the coloniality of power, the comfort factor, and so on). White favoritism, in turn, is depicted as a cause of Caribbean economic advantage. The statistical results in this chapter dispute the linkage between white favoritism and Caribbean advantage. They do not dispute the first set of linkages because they have no bearing on those linkages. Ordinary white Americans may favor West Indians over African Americans. Discarding the hypothesis that white favoritism is a cause of West Indian economic advantage does not require abandoning the hypothesis that white favoritism is a real phenomenon.

· Chapter 7 ·

An *Immigrant* Success Story

THIS book began by asking: why do black immigrants have stronger labor market outcomes than African Americans? As it turns out, black immigrants from Africa or from the Hispanic Caribbean do not have stronger labor market outcomes than African Americans. And though West Indians display an immediate advantage on labor force participation, unemployment, and occupational prestige, they do not earn more than African Americans until a decade or more after their arrival. Additional scrutiny reveals that a portion of West Indians' advantage can be attributed to their higher educational achievement, more attractive geographic location, and so on. But controlling for these characteristics does not make their advantage disappear.

Three sets of hypotheses have been put forward to account for this fact. The first is that English-speaking West Indians have accumulated a cultural advantage over African Americans. Proponents of this view fall into two camps. One maintains that regional differences in the organization of slavery produced regional differences in attitudes toward work. The other maintains that socialization in an all-black society stimulates higher ambition and a greater willingness to confront racism than socialization in a society where whites hold all the desirable posts. The second hypothesis is that their immigrant status makes West Indians more talented and industrious than African Americans. This explanation draws on selectivity theory, a perspective that expects economically motivated migrants, irrespective of heritage, to be endowed with greater ability and drive than those who stay home. Proponents of the third hypothesis, white favoritism, credit West Indians' English accent or their purportedly more gracious demeanor as reasons for white favoritism.

Each of the three hypotheses was tested empirically. The explanation that the analysis supports is the positive selectivity of migration.

143

The analysis supports this idea in three ways: the larger the supply of previously arrived compatriots, the weaker are West Indian economic outcomes; on some outcomes, the children of West Indian immigrants are more successful than their African American counterparts; and during the first five years after relocation the economic outcomes of West Indian immigrants and African American internal migrants are statistically indistinguishable. Selectivity predicts all these patterns.

Methodological Quibbles

The first step to producing the results in this book is to convert the three explanations into testable hypotheses. This involves associating a causal mechanism with each explanation, finding a way to turn that cause "on" and "off" and observing the consequences. In the case of selectivity, this is relatively simple because selectivity is already a theory—perhaps only a theory of the "middle range," but a theory nonetheless (Merton 1957). If the selectivity of migration is the cause of West Indian advantage, then if the selectivity of migration can be applied to African Americans, the difference between the two groups should disappear. It does. This is the most compelling evidence in the book.

In the case of culture and favoritism, identifying the causal mechanism is more difficult because these explanations are informal. Supporters of white favoritism, for instance, have not specified precisely how it translates into West Indian economic advantage. The solution adopted here is to interpret white favoritism in terms of queuing theory. This interpretation yields the hypothesis that the larger the proportion of African Americans in a labor market, the more impressive West Indian success will be. If this operationalization of white favoritism is flawed, the test is not valid.

Cultural explanations are even more difficult to prove. The main problem is the inability to isolate causal mechanisms and identify individuals who have not been exposed to them. At first glance, identifying variation in the experiences that have been associated with West Indian culture seems easy. Not all West Indian slaves grew their own food; not all West Indian societies are all-black. But culture is so diffuse that it is impossible to turn it on and off. Irrespective of the means of provisioning, slavery in Barbados was more like slavery in Jamaica than like slavery in Alabama. Irrespective of the proportion black, socialization in Trinidad is more like socialization in Granada than like socialization in New Jersey. If there is no way around this problem, if the key causal mechanism does not exhibit variation, if *all* West Indians are "essentially" different from *all* African Americans, then social science cannot explain West Indian advantage. Obviously, this is not the position taken here. The analyses in this book are based on the assumption that variations in social arrangements do have cultural consequences. If this assumption is flawed, the culture tests are not valid.

Finally, even if the empirical tests of the three explanations are constructed correctly, the results are only as good as the means used to obtain them. Quantitative research is constantly being improved, but shortcomings in data and method remain. The shortcomings in data cited most often are that they do not represent the populations of interest, that they contain measurement error, and that they lack necessary information. Much of this book's methodological appendix is devoted to evaluating the representativeness of the samples and assessing the quality of the information they contain. The discussion there shows that these data sets are at least as reliable as any typically used in quantitative social research.

But there remains information that the data do not contain—"omitted variables" that, if present, would strengthen the conclusions of the analyses. For example, some observers believe that the public schools of former British colonies offer an education superior to the education available to African Americans in public schools in the United States. If this is true, then even when the two groups of blacks have spent the same amount of time in school or obtained the same degrees, West Indians have profited more from their educations.[1] Thus, some information about the quality of each individual's education would be a welcome addition. Another would be information about years of work experience. The analysis proceeds under the questionable assumption that calculations that control for age and education contain reliable controls for work experience. But employment continuity is strongly influenced by race and sex.[2]

A different set of problems arises with cross-national comparisons. The biggest difficulty is that their results may be confounded by differences that operate at the level of countries rather than individuals. To illustrate: England opened its doors to mass migration from the West Indies more than fifteen years earlier than North America. Might this not mean that its West Indians are more positively selected than those who later settled in the United States or Canada? Another illustration is undocumented West Indians, whose numbers are higher in New York than in any other city in the world. Perhaps the reason New York's West Indians have similar outcomes to those in non-U.S. cities is because New York's large undocumented population depresses the results from the United States. And so it goes. The methodological problem is that the number of differences between countries is greater than the number of countries used in the cross-national comparisons. "Statistically, this means that there are too few degrees of freedom, that models become 'overdetermined,' that intercorrelations among independent variables cannot be adequately dealt with and that results may not be robust. Substantively, it means that competing explanations of the dependent variable may not be open to any decisive evaluation" (Goldthorpe 1997, 5).[3]

Partly because of these concerns, each hypothesis in this book is subject to multiple tests, no one of which is considered definitive. For instance, most statistical tests are undertaken on four economic outcomes, on both genders, and on multiple years. In addition, all hypotheses are subject to at least two uniquely designed tests, often more. In this way, the answer to the research question depends on the results of several analyses rather than on the results of a single test.

Yet some readers may still feel uncomfortable because a statistical analysis "tells us rather little about just what is going on at the level of the social processes and action that underlie, as it were, the interplay of the variables that have been distinguished" (Goldthorpe 1997, 13). In other words, statistical results do not describe the actions of human beings or of human institutions; they convey the consequences of those actions. This is certainly the case with the results reported here. They support the assertion that selectivity on unmeasured characteristics is responsible for West Indians' economic advantage over African Americans, but that assertion is inferred; it is not observed.

Implications for African Americans

The primary motive for undertaking this study was to assess the claim that West Indian advantage provides "some clues as to how much of the situation of American Negroes in general can be attributed to color prejudice by whites and how much to cultural patterns among blacks" (Sowell 1981, 216). Since the analysis uncovered no linkage between West Indian culture, variously operationalized, and West Indian attainment, the admonition that African Americans would do better if they behaved like West Indians is nonsensical. A more precise but equally inappropriate exhortation would be that African Americans should behave like immigrants or the children of immigrants. But this prescription is not unique to African Americans. Behaving like immigrants or the children of immigrants would enhance the economic outcomes of many native-born Americans, regardless of their race, ethnicity, or national origin. Consider this quote from a Boston manager:

The Cape Verdean guys back there [in the kitchen] are my hardest workers. These guys are absolutely fantastic workers. . . . When I was younger . . . in all restaurants, you always had young, white, American boys washing dishes. Now, you know, I almost try to stay away from them in a way because they're so lazy at times. . . . I get Cape Verdean kids in here and they bust their butt. You know, I get these white kids in here, they're young, sixteen, seventeen, eighteen years old, and they think they're just going to hang out and just be lazy all day. (Moss and Tilly 2001, 362)[4]

Furthermore, employers' belief that immigrants are more hardworking and docile than natives is not limited to black immigrants (Aponte 1996).

A second implication relevant to African Americans is that white favoritism is not responsible for the economic advantage of West Indians over African Americans. To be sure, a few scholars believe that white favoritism already has been demonstrated.[5] African Americans are even more likely to believe it.[6] An African American told Mary Waters (1999, 131): "We have this attitude that, like, this guy's gonna take my job, my boss is gonna give him the job for less, and in some cases that's true. I've heard a guy I've worked for, he said if it was up to him, he wouldn't hire any Americans, and he'd hire foreigners. This was his words, and he was the boss." West Indians agree. A Belizean woman told Faye Arnold (1984, 152): "When I worked in the garment district . . . Jewish people that I worked with told me that they preferred to hire me rather than an American black and I said, 'What's the difference?' And they told me, 'You are different; you stay here long and you will see.'" A Jamaican told Milton Vickerman (1999, 143): "I see where West Indians have a chance of getting a job over the black American because . . . these employers—mostly the whites—see where we . . . are better workers. . . . If . . . both of us should go in for a job—one as a [sic] American and [the other] a West Indian . . . the West Indian will have a better chance over the American."

However, the fact that many people believe whites favor West Indians does not make it true. No scholar has systematically compared actual interchanges between white gatekeepers and West Indians with actual interchanges between white gatekeepers and African Americans. What scholars usually obtain are accounts of such interchanges. Most of these accounts come from West Indian employees or white employers of African Americans; very few come from African American employees or white employers of West Indians. Given the distortion associated with interracial exchanges, it is possible that these assessments are stereotypes, not realities. Alternatively, to the extent that they are realities, the differences between West Indian and African American workers are no greater than the differences between most immigrants and most natives. This is the interpretation that the analysis supports. West Indian immigrants do not get jobs because employers perceive them as having a stronger work ethic than African Americans; West Indian immigrants get jobs because employers perceive immigrants as having a stronger work ethic than natives.

How can this interpretation be reconciled with the belief that American whites like West Indians better? One possibility is that West Indian immigrants and African Americans do not compete as often as white favoritism advocates suppose. Indirect support for this comes from a census-based study of West Indian and African American industrial distributions in the New York metropolitan area (Model 2001). Of particular interest is whether the two groups of blacks gravitate to the same industries. Because gender segregation is considerable, men and women were examined separately. The results show meaningful numbers of the two groups of blacks in only a couple of industries— private hospitals and nursing homes and private households—and in fact the latter niche no longer attracts meaningful proportions of either group. This implies that, for the most part, West Indian immigrants and African Americans do not see each other at work. Of course, the industrial distribution represents the end-result of hiring decisions; thus, it obscures ethnic favoritism at the hiring stage. Yet the significance of social networks as conduits to employment is so great that it is likely that the industrial differences between African Americans and West Indians reflect differences in the distribution of job applications at least as much as they reflect real differences in employer preferences (Falcón and Melendez 2001). For instance, in the food service industry where Waters (1999) did fieldwork, almost all hiring was done on the basis of employee recommendation.

The perceptions of a few West Indian interviewees accord with this interpretation. One of Percy Hintzen's (2001, 159) Bay Area respondents put it this way: "I have experienced prejudice and hostility from black Americans who actually accuse me of taking their jobs, and I say, 'We're not even in the same field. What are you talking about?' 'Well, you come here and take jobs at a cheaper rate.' And that was directed at me because I was from the Caribbean." According to another, African Americans "perceive West Indians are here to take their jobs. And most West Indians, when they get to this country, they take the jobs that Americans don't want to do, that black Americans don't want to do. I don't know if I should say this, but to me, some black Americans would rather be on welfare than accept certain jobs that the West Indians take" (Hintzen 2001, 145). Thus, ordinary people, both black and white, confuse the perception that immigrants will work for less money than natives with the perception that immigrants are taking their jobs (Smith and Edmonston 1997). Because immigrants and natives usually compete for different jobs, white favoritism does not translate into West Indian advantage.

A second way to reconcile the belief in white favoritism with the reality is to judge white favoritism a relatively weak sentiment. This interpretation draws on the research of Evans and Kelley (1991, 747), who found both the Australian public and Australian gatekeepers expressing a willingness to discriminate against immigrants but found no evidence of discrimination in immigrants' earnings: "The venerable sociological image of a social distance ordering, with the closest groups facing little discrimination and the most distant groups facing a great deal, does not match Australian reality." Indeed, in the United States it is not clear that the public knows enough about racial and ethnic distinctions to make meaningful rankings. Their willingness to answer closed-ended survey questions about specific groups does not mean that they understand the characteristics of these groups. In the 1989 GSS, respondents were asked to rank the social standing of a large number of ethnicities, one of which was an artificial group, Wisians. Forty percent of respondents chose to answer the question; they ranked Wisians above thirteen groups, including West Indian blacks, Mexicans, Vietnamese, and Iranians (Smith 1991). In short, ordinary people know little about the distinctions among ethnic and racial minorities.

Nor is it clear that American employers know enough to construct the finely graded labor queue that scholars credit them with building. Most field studies find that members of the dominant group receive more favorable treatment than members of subordinate groups, but few find that one subordinate group receives more favorable treatment than another. This implies that employers act on the basis of broad stereotypes, such as immigrant versus native, or black versus white, or East Asian versus Caucasian. Native white employers' ability to distinguish a Mexican from a Puerto Rican or a Bangladeshi from an Indian is probably small. Yet, qualifications being the same, Mexicans have significantly poorer occupations than Puerto Ricans, and Bangladeshis have significantly poorer occupations than Indians (Model 1997; Model and Fisher 2007). Differential discrimination is unlikely to account for these differences.

The final implication of this research of relevance to African Americans is its consequences for affirmative action. Opponents of affirmative action have long maintained that West Indian economic achievement demonstrates that racism is no longer an obstacle in the United

States; therefore, affirmative action in employment is not necessary. The research in this book shows that West Indians are a positively selected population. It is hard to see how this conclusion has any relevance to affirmative action in employment for African Americans.

In the early twenty-first century, however, the affirmative action debate has focused almost entirely on higher education. The great debate, of course, has been over whether affirmative action in higher education is constitutional. West Indians have not figured prominently in the great debate. The policy having recently been found legal, West Indians and other non–African American blacks have generated a small debate. The small debate is over whether or not non–African American blacks should qualify for affirmative action in college admissions. And the reason some think they should not is that non–African American blacks are well represented both in colleges generally and in the more prestigious colleges specifically (Massey et al. 2003; Massey et al. 2007).

Support for the claim that West Indians are well represented in colleges can even be found in the 2000 PUMS. The following percentages of eighteen- to twenty-two-year-olds hold high school diplomas but not college degrees and were attending school on April 1, 2000: 75.0 percent of foreign-born black Africans, 68.8 percent of native-born West Indians, 57.5 percent of native-born whites, 57.2 percent of foreign-born West Indians, and 47.5 percent of African Americans.[7]

Support for the claim that West Indians are well represented in prestigious colleges was presented in chapter 1, which reported the uproar following dissemination of the results of Aisha Haynie's study of the ancestry of Harvard's black students. "Fourth and higher generation African Americans who represent nearly 90% of the American black population, accounted for only 45% of the black students" (*Harvard Magazine* 2004). Over one-fifth claimed some Caribbean heritage. The remainder mentioned some other non–African American background. Lee Bollinger, former University of Michigan president, defended this situation on the grounds that "it matters in American society whether you grow up black or white. It's that differential effect that really is the basis for affirmative action" (Rimer and Arenson 2004). Mary Waters criticized it, noting that if affirmative action "is about making up for 200 to 500 years of slavery in this country and its aftermath, then you're not doing well. And if it's about having diversity that includes African-Americans from the South or from inner city schools, then you're not doing well, either" (quoted in Rimer and Arenson 2004, A1).

In June 2003, the Supreme Court upheld those affirmative action programs that sought to enroll, not a fixed percentage, but a "critical mass" of underrepresented minorities (Harvard Civil Rights Project

2003). To achieve this goal, the Court endorsed a procedure called "a whole file review". But the Court did not give an opinion on what information the file should contain. Unfortunately, in the absence of information about candidates' ethnic backgrounds, none of the above-mentioned affirmative action strategies can alleviate the underrepresentation of African Americans in higher education.

Aisha Haynie (2002, 55) writes: "Because all black students applying to these [for example, elite] schools are in essence competing for the same limited number of places, black American students have become an ethnic minority relative to other ethnic groups at Harvard. The remedy for this situation is indeed simply to take ethnic heritage into account when making admissions decisions." But the "common application" currently used at Harvard and scores of other private colleges offers only one racial-ethnic option for African-origin students. It asks if the applicant is "African American, African, Black." Under these circumstances, it is unsurprising that admission officials do not "have a good idea of what they're getting" (Rimer and Arenson 2004, A1). But the same common application already permits Asians and Hispanics to list their "countries of family origin." Applicants can also identify as Mexican American, Puerto Rican, Native Hawaiian/Pacific Islander, and so on. Why are blacks treated differently? The University of Massachusetts uses an application of its own design. Its options include "Black, Non-Latino," and "Cape Verdean."[8]

In a fascinating analysis, Douglas Massey and his colleagues (2007) show that there are only a few differences between black college freshmen of African American and black immigrant background in terms of either socialization or academic preparation.[9] Yet, in the absence of an indicator distinguishing the two groups of applicants, admissions officials admit relatively more applicants with an immigrant background than applicants with a native background. And the more selective the college, the greater the overrepresentation. Massey and his colleagues (2007, 268) conclude that

> the fact that most indicators of socioeconomic status, social preparation, psychological readiness, and especially academic preparation are identical for immigrants and natives suggests that immigrant origins per se are not favored in the admissions process but, for whatever reason, children from immigrant families have come to exhibit the set of traits and characteristics valued by admissions committees, both those that are readily observable (grade point average, quality of high school, and advanced placement courses taken) and those that are more difficult to observe directly (self-esteem, self-efficacy, and social distance from whites).

As should be expected, affirmative action in higher education has exacerbated tensions between African Americans and other black groups. To alleviate these tensions, university administrators need to acknowledge the diversity of black America. Moreover, the Supreme Court has actually facilitated that recognition by mandating that admission decisions be based on a careful reading of each applicant's file. If these files contained adequate ethnic information, all black subgroups—African American, English-speaking West Indian, Cape Verdean, African, Haitian, and so on—would have a chance to become a distinct "critical mass." Alternatively, and perhaps more appropriately, affirmative action's primary objective should be to secure a "critical mass" of African Americans.

Implications for West Indians

It is quite clear that, irrespective of its empirical validity, many black immigrants are invested in a worldview that endows "West Indianness" with positive traits and "African Americanness" with negative traits. A Trinidadian informant gave Mary Waters a wonderful example of this tendency. She began by observing that in the Islands people do not work as hard or seem as driven as their compatriots in the United States. However, rather than use this "fact" as evidence that West Indian and African American cultures are similar, the informant believed that, once in the United States, West Indians "get more independent and more responsible" (Waters 1999, 88). For other immigrants, Waters finds that "the idea that people back home have it easy or don't work as hard as people in the United States is held at the same time that the immigrants believe it is some sort of inbred trait among West Indians to be superworkers. The immigrants generally do not recognize that it is because they are immigrants that they work in this driven way" (130). These West Indians are constructing a *cultural* explanation for traits that are rooted in the *selectivity* of migration.

Another example of an inconsistency associated with intra-black distancing is that the immigrants pride themselves on not putting up with "racist nonsense" at the very same time that they condemn African Americans for being "too quick to cry race" (Waters 1999, 147, 150). As one respondent told Hintzen (2001, 157): "I try to deal with each incident individually. As it happens, I deal with it. I do whatever is necessary. I make whatever complaints. I write letters at a flash. And get satisfaction, what satisfaction is available." Vickerman (1999, 100) sums it up: "West Indians are not shrinking violets. In fact, the opposite is true; in seeking their ambitions they are often quite assertive." At the same time, West Indians complain that African Americans "racialize" everything. A professional told Hintzen (2001, 151): "I think there's quite a bit of them that once they cannot achieve something that they want to achieve, or they've been set back in some specific area, they think it's racism." According to a Trinidadian: "We're not saying that there is no racism, we're not saying that there's not prejudices. . . . But you don't have to be negative all the time" (Waters 1999, 150). Here again, West Indians perceive their approach as more effective than African Americans' approach, even though the distinction between the two approaches may be more apparent than real.

Why do many West Indians accept whites' negative depictions of African Americans? First, Caribbean immigrants *need* to believe that their work ethic is unusual; they need to believe that theirs is the productive approach to racism. If immigrants cannot influence their destiny, their journey to the United States may have been for naught. Second, a West Indian identity may enhance academic achievement. In an experiment designed to detect the effects of academic self-confidence, Deaux and her colleagues found that West Indian college students who identified as West Indian scored higher on a portion of the GRE than West Indian students who identified as African American (cited in Deaux 2006). The investigators interpreted the results as evidence that, relative to a West Indian identity, an African American identity depresses academic achievement.[10] Third, there are emotional benefits to perceiving oneself as "superior." After exploring West Indians' and African Americans' experiences with discrimination, the social psychologist Carla Hunter (2005, 94–95) concluded: "Not perceiving racism may actually be a form of denial that enables West Indian Americans to persevere while living in a society that places them in a racial category rather than an ethnic category." West Indians may hold on to the notion that the white public views them favorably in order to stave off the anxiety, anger, and depression associated with being a victim of racism.

Theoretical Implications

Only a few theoretical perspectives include predictions that are relevant to black immigrants. The empirical findings described in this volume are usually at variance with those predictions.

Selectivity Theory

Contemporary selectivity theory dates to the late 1960s when Everett Lee (1966) proposed that economically motivated movers are more skilled than those they leave behind, and politically motivated movers are less so. He also acknowledged the significance of "intervening factors," or what economists call "the costs of migration." These include financial costs, like travel expenses or forgone earnings while unemployed; the temporal costs of surmounting barriers to immigration, such as waiting in line, obtaining forms, securing approvals, and so on; and the emotional costs of leaving loved ones to go to a strange land. Intervening obstacles are attenuated to the extent that movers have information about their destination or know individuals who can assist their departure and relocation. For this reason, early birds or those who leave a family or community first tend to be more positively selected than latecomers.

Some ten years later after Lee, the human capital theorist Barry Chiswick (1978, 901), unaware of Lee's ideas, claimed that positive selection was associated with the "conventional economic migration of workers for higher real earnings." Shortly thereafter, this optimistic vision was attacked by George Borjas (1985), who asserted that economic motivation was a necessary but not sufficient condition for positive selectivity. Economically motivated movers from countries like Jamaica, where income is more unequally distributed than in the United States, send negatively selected migrants; sending countries like Sweden, where income is less unequally distributed, send positively selected migrants. Borjas also acknowledged the effect of immigration costs, including immigration law. With the implementation of the Hart-Celler Act, he expected the earnings of immigrants from regions of high income inequality, like the West Indies, to decline to the point that they would never catch up with those of their native counterparts.

In terms of catchup time, the results in chapter 4 show that West Indian earnings catch up with African American earnings in less than two decades. This finding would not disturb Borjas (1995, 238), however, because he does not endorse the use of ethnically comparable natives as a benchmark:

> What would we conclude, for example, if the data revealed that the relative wage of Mexican immigrants converged to that of Mexican natives or that the relative wage of Asian immigrants converged to that of Asian natives? The fact remains that the wage of Mexicans is itself 17% below that of the typical U.S.-born worker, while the wage of Asian natives is 11% above. Intra-Mexican or intra-Asian convergence, therefore, is a less interesting phenomenon if we are concerned about the impact of immigration policy on the costs of welfare programs or on the contribution of immigrants to the economy's skill endowment.

This is a telling quote. It implies that the United States should not admit immigrants who belong to minorities whose native-born coethnics earn less than the typical U.S.-born worker. But if this is a goal, empirical calculations of catchup time are unnecessary. The earnings of native-born ethnic groups provide a simple criterion for determining which immigrants should be admitted and which should be turned away. In short, Borjas has set such a high standard for positive selectivity that most nonwhite applicants are disadvantaged at the outset.

Equally important, the choice of benchmark does not affect the conclusion that the economic outcomes of West Indian immigrants decline with recency of arrival. To be sure, the magnitude of the shortfall varies by benchmark—it is larger if native whites are used, and smaller if African Americans are used. But the propensity for economic well being to decline with arrival date does not change. To be sure, Borjas detected cohort decline among immigrants within a variety of sending regions. But he explained it entirely in terms of immigration law. Rather than impugn his result on the grounds of methodological weakness, as some writers have done (LaLonde and Topel 1991; Yuengert 1994), the argument here is that Borjas's work suffers from theoretical weakness. While he acknowledges that the costs of migration matter, he considers them only in the most rudimentary fashion. As a result, he is right for the wrong reason: more recent cohorts of West Indians are not as positively selected as their predecessors, not because of immigration law, but because their predecessors cushioned their arrival.

Segmented Assimilation Theory

Segmented assimilation is a relatively new perspective on immigrant attainment; it argues that the children of modestly skilled, nonwhite, non-entrepreneurial immigrants are at risk of incorporating the "oppositional" values of the most disadvantaged segment of the African American community. Since West Indian blacks are physically indistinguishable from African Americans, and since they are native English speakers, since they often live in African American neighborhoods and attend ghetto schools, they would seem ideal candidates for assimilation into the underclass.

Chapter 2 describes an empirical effort to evaluate the applicability of segmented assimilation to West Indian American young adults. The results do not support the idea that they are taking on the behaviors of the African American underclass. Chapter 4 presents a comparison of African Americans and native-born West Indians on four economic outcomes. Its conclusion is that native-born West Indians fare a little better than African Americans. The results of the Immigrant Second Generation in Metropolitan New York Study concur. On a wide range of outcomes including schooling, employment, and incarceration, "black immigrants, largely from the Anglophone Caribbean, are doing even better than native blacks" (Mollenkopf 2005, 116).

Perhaps one reason segmentationists have predicted a negative trajectory for second-generation blacks is that they have overlooked the intergenerational transmission of the positive selectivity of migration. This is precisely the point of Massey's critique of Mollenkopf's paper. In an effort to explain why West Indians outperform native blacks, Massey (2005, 122) writes: "The tabulations presented in the paper do not control for the selectivity of the original migration . . . black Caribbean immigrants were generally selected from the lower professional and middle classes." This quote, of course, refers to positive selectivity on easy-to-measure traits like occupation and education. But the analysis in this book shows that West Indian immigrants are also positively selected on hard-to-measure traits like diligence and ambition. As a Harvard student told Aisha Haynie (2002, 47): "There's nothing particular about Jamaica; it's more the whole immigrant philosophy . . . now you have black immigrants who, who want to succeed in the country, and that idea gets transferred to their kids, that they have to succeed, and one of the major ways, of course, is through education."

World Systems Theory

Lastly, the results of the analysis have implications for the ethnic-racial hierarchy put forth by the world systems analyst Ramón Grosfoguel (Grosfoguel 2003, 2004; Grosfoguel and Georas 2000). How are positions in his hierarchy determined? They are the consequence of the "coloniality of power," an idea proposed by the Peruvian sociologist Anibal Quijano, whose starting point is that the racial-ethnic hierarchy that European imperialism brought to the Americas is as influential today as it was in the past. Therefore, in their respective mother countries, immigrants from colonies and former colonies stand at the bottom of the racial-ethnic hierarchy. Grosfoguel labels these people "colonial/racialized subjects," by which he means that they are targets of the pernicious stereotypes that were originally used to justify imperial power. In the United States, imperialism was more subtle and indirect. Still, Grosfoguel (2003, 148) asserts that "oppressed groups that have been incorporated into the U.S. empire including those within the nations' borders throughout a long history of colonialism are best understood as 'colonial/racialized subjects.'" These include the groups that Robert Blauner (1972) characterized as "internal colonials," for example, African Americans, Mexican Americans, Puerto Ricans, and Native Americans.

Slightly higher on the scale stand "colonial immigrants." These are persons who left a colony or former colony and sought refuge in a host society other than their own mother country. "The absence of a colonial history within a particular empire makes an important difference in terms of how the identities of migrants are constructed and, thus, perceived" (Grosfoguel 2003, 158). To illustrate, Grosfoguel cites West Indians in New York, where they are perceived positively, and West Indians in London, where they are perceived negatively. Higher still stand "immigrants" whose homeland has escaped the stigma of colonialism or who, for other reasons, are sufficiently free of tarnish to make economic progress. They and their offspring display rapid socioeconomic integration into their host society.

Theoretically, this is a very appealing scheme; however, it does not stand up to empirical scrutiny. This conclusion follows whether the focus is on actual outcomes like those that Grosfoguel includes in the appendix to his book (for example, unemployment or occupation) or on more experiential measures of discrimination like field experiments. The Netherlands provides an appropriate context for evaluating Grosfoguel's expectations because it houses both "colonial immigrants" (Moroccans) and "colonialized/racialized subjects" (Antilleans and Surinamese). Grosfoguel would expect the former to outdistance the latter. According to the 1994 Dutch Labor Force Survey, 54 percent of prime-age Moroccan men were in the labor force, and those in the labor force had a 32.4 percent unemployment rate. The labor force participation rate of Dutch Antillean men was 72 percent, and their unemployment rate was 21.4 percent. Like most published data on immigrants to the Netherlands, these figures show that Moroccans fare poorly relative to Antilleans or Surinamese (Muus 1995). This, of course, is precisely the opposite of what Grosfoguel's hierarchy predicts.

Field experiments yield results that are slightly different, but still incompatible with Grosfoguel's predictions. They show that levels of discrimination against Moroccan and Surinamese Creole job applicants are the same. Moreover, the discussion so far has omitted reference to Turks, whom Grosfoguel characterizes as "colonial immigrants" even though Turkey was never colonized by any imperial power. On most outcomes, Dutch Turks are much more like Moroccans than like Surinamese or Antilleans (Cross 1994; Martens 1999; Muus 1995).[11]

Just as Turks do not, strictly speaking, meet the criterion for "colonial immigrants," so do other classifications in Grosfoguel's schema take on an ad hoc character. For instance, despite their colonial legacy, Cubans are classified as "immigrants" because the U.S. government accorded them special treatment as part of its anticommunist agenda.

Dominicans became "colonial/racialized" subjects partly because whites had difficulty distinguishing them from Puerto Ricans and partly because they tended to live near Puerto Ricans and assume jobs typical of Puerto Ricans. Second-generation West Indians are "African-Americanized" because, without an accent, they are indistinguishable from African Americans.

The discovery that white favoritism is not causally linked to West Indians' economic advantage over African Americans challenges the notion that employers are sensitive to the fine-grained hierarchies that scholars construct. Doubtless, when Dominicans were first coming into New York, few white employers knew the difference between a Puerto Rican and a Dominican. Doubtless, most people cannot distinguish a second-generation West Indian from an African American. The Cuban situation represents a different type of exception. As an entrepreneurial group, Cubans who encounter discrimination from native whites can go to work for fellow Cubans. Thus, Cubans' economic attainment may be at odds with their ranking in the minds of white gatekeepers or social researchers.[12] In sum, Grosfoguel would do better simply to argue that the political and economic standing of sending nations affects the political and economic standing of emigrants. Efforts to make predictions about precise rankings on the basis of this fact are theoretically appealing but empirically inaccurate.

Implications for Further Research

Two directions for further research are worth recommending: new studies about perceptions of black ethnic diversity in the United States and better studies about trends in "cohort quality" among immigrants to this country. The first would profit from in-depth interviews, ethnography, or field experiments, and the second involves primarily survey research and secondary data analysis.

White Perceptions of Black Diversity

West Indians   Few readers can fail to ask: if white favoritism does not bring West Indians an economic advantage over African Americans, then do white Americans actually favor West Indians? The available research on the subject does not answer the question. One way to begin is to undertake in-depth interviews with a sample of whites selected for variations in their knowledge about and contact with West Indian blacks. The most likely characteristic that would affect knowledge and contact is geography (Tormala and Deaux 2006). Several matters deserve exploration. Do respondents believe that there are differences between West Indians and African Americans? If so, what are these differences, and from where do they come? Do respondents acquire the idea of intra-black differences only after contact with, if not "consciousness-raising" by, West Indians? Or are these differences communicated in other ways, such as through personal contacts or the media?[13] Are these differences caused by Anglophilia, as Arnold (1984) supposes?

An equally informative alternative would be ethnographic study or participant-observation of the interactions of all three groups: whites, African Americans, and West Indians. This method, which is best undertaken in a workplace setting, would allow the researcher to make his or her own judgments regarding the relationships between the three groups. These observations might profitably be contrasted to the actors' own accounts of their interrelationships. In short, evaluating the prevalence of white favoritism requires supplementing approaches that center on a West Indian perspective with approaches that incorporate a white American perspective.

Black Africans   The economic disadvantage suffered by black African immigrants is one of the least acknowledged facts of the American immigrant experience. Consider the following remark by a black immigrant from Zimbabwe: "It is an ironic fact of life . . . that the more foreign Africans appear, the better their chances of success. . . . If two people, an African American and an African immigrant, apply for the same job, chances are the African immigrant will get it" (Carson 2003).

Yet black Africans have similar economic outcomes to equally qualified African Americans. That is to say, while black Africans have a large gross advantage on most economic indicators, this is entirely due to their stronger credentials. Controlling for education and other personal characteristics, there is little difference between African Americans and black Africans (Corra and Kimuna, forthcoming; Dodoo 1997; Dodoo and Takyi 2002). Furthermore, West Indians fare substantially better than black Africans. Recently, scholars have also found that the children of black African immigrants in the United States have lower educational attainment than the children of similarly qualified West Indians (Rong and Brown 2001).

Why do West Indians have stronger economic outcomes than black Africans? The analysis presented in this book suggests that the selectivity of migration might be a factor. First, though most Africans are not officially "refugees," many have political rather than economic motives to relocate (Gordon 1998). Traditional selection theorists consider the politically motivated mover as less positively selected than the economically motivated mover (Chiswick 1978, 1999).[14] Second, a large percentage of immigrants from Africa express the intention of returning home.[15] Traditional selection theory likewise posits that temporary movers will be less positively selected than permanent movers (Chiswick 1999; Duleep and Regets 1999).

Yet there is another possible explanation for the relatively weak labor market outcomes of black Africans. It is color. As mentioned in the last chapter, research has shown that darker skin color is consistently associated with poorer economic outcomes (Keith and Herring 1991). Nor is this finding limited to the United States. A black African seeking accommodation in London reports the following dialogue:

> The price seemed reasonable, location
> Indifferent. The landlady swore she lived
> Off premises. Nothing remained
> But self-confession. "Madam," I warned,
> I hate a wasted journey—I am an African.
> Silence. Silence transmission of
> Pressurized good-breeding. Voice, when it came
> Lipstick coated, long gold-rolled
> Cigarette-holder pipped. Caught I was, foully.
> "HOW DARK?" . . . I had not misheard . . . "ARE YOU LIGHT OR
> VERY DARK?"
> —From Wole Soyinka, "Telephone Conversation," 1984, cited in Daley (1996, 61)

Since the skin tone of black Africans does not vary as much as the skin tone of West Indians or African Americans, it is difficult to see how secondary data analysis can evaluate the contribution that skin tone makes to black African outcomes in the labor market or the housing market. The field experiment would be a far more informative strategy. What would be revealed by field experiments in which blacks of varying hues, surnames, and accents sought identical employment or identical lodgings?

Such field experiments could not only measure the contribution of skin tone to black African disadvantage but also gauge the sensitivity of nonblack gatekeepers to black ethnic diversity. Do rental agents treat "equally dark" African Americans and black Africans similarly? Do employment officials prefer West Indian accents to black African accents? Most field experiments do not detect significant differences in the treatment of visibly different minorities. Yet several American scholars argue that Asians and Hispanics are undergoing a process of "whitening"—that is, the boundaries between Hispanics and whites and between Asians and whites are blurring (Bean and Stevens 2003; Gans 1999; Yancey 2003). If this is so, might not the growing ethnic diversity within black America blur the boundary between blacks and whites? One possibility is that whites perceive blacks as monolithic and treat them accordingly; all African-origin peoples are "the same." Another possibility is that whites perceive blacks as diverse; some African-origin peoples are different from others. This second possibility might contribute to breaking down the color line. Alternatively, greater recognition of black diversity might magnify the distinction between good blacks ("foreigners") and bad blacks ("natives"). Field experiments are an excellent way to explore these issues.

Trends in "Cohort Quality" Among Immigrants

Borjas was the first to uncover the phenomenon of cohort decline, which he associated with the increase in visas following passage of the Hart-Celler Act. The West Indian pattern, however, is not related to immigration law. One phenomenon it is clearly related to is gender: West Indian women exhibit greater cohort decline than West Indian men. In a previous chapter, a tentative interpretation of this interaction was proffered: compared to West Indian men, women may more often be primary movers. Selectivity theory expects the outcomes of primary movers to respond more strongly to the "costs of migration" than the outcomes of secondary or tied movers. While theoretically appealing, concrete evidence is needed before this interpretation could be accepted.

The difficulty in accounting for the West Indian results underscores the large number of factors potentially responsible for cohort change. In addition to the migrant's status as a primary or secondary mover, the kind of visa he or she holds might matter (Jasso 2004; Jasso, Rosenzweig, and Smith 2000). Kin-based relocation, for example, should show more decline than employment-based relocation. Even within employment-based relocation, variance could be expected. Some holders of employment-related visas depart because of the assistance they expect to receive from family and friends. This description is less likely to apply to professional and entrepreneurial migrants, some of whom depart solely because of the opportunities that their personal skills or financial capital can provide (Portes and Rumbaut 1996).[16] For these individualistic movers, friends and relatives play a relatively minor role in the decision to move.

Two empirical obstacles to documenting cohort decline have loomed large. The first is the increase in earnings inequality in the United States. Over the past two decades, deindustrialization, deunionization, and minimum wage stagnation have eroded the ability of low-skilled workers to earn a living. Some scholars say that these changes, rather than declining "cohort quality," underlie the decrease in earnings experienced by the more recently arrived (LaLonde and Topel 1991; Lindstrom and Massey 1994). One way around this problem is to examine economic outcomes other than earnings: labor force participation, for instance. After all, selectivity is an individual trait, and labor force participation is the economic outcome over which the individual has the most discretion. Scholars interested in selectivity should put more weight on labor force participation.

A second problem has to do with the data used to define the cohort of arrival. Some scholars have argued that U.S. census data are inappropriate for this purpose (Jasso 2004; Jasso, Rosenzweig, and Smith 2000; Lindstrom and Massey 1994).The census contains many who are not immigrants—for instance, foreign students and foreign nationals employed temporarily in the United States. More worrisome, the quality of the key variable, the year of arrival, is in doubt because significant numbers of immigrants "arrive" more than once. In an effort to provide better-quality data, several government agencies have jointly funded an ongoing longitudinal study of legal immigrants, the New Immigrant Survey (NIS).[17] A paper drawing on this source compares responses to a carefully crafted date-of-arrival question to responses to the standard date-of-arrival question in the U.S. census. It demonstrates that the census response underestimates time spent in the United States (Redstone and Massey 2004). In defense of the census question, an analysis by Dowell Myers (2004) indicates that inaccuracies in the date-of-arrival question arise primarily in the Mexican case. He claims that, for most other groups, the response is a good approximation of reality. Then, too, the New Immigrant Survey has flaws. It neglects undocumented immigrants, a group that is partially picked up by the U.S. census. If understanding selectivity is the goal, the exclusion of illegal immigrants is a shortcoming; if understanding visa effects is the goal, the New Immigrant Survey is ideal.

These debates will not be resolved anytime soon. Even if the New Immigrant Survey is a more reliable source of information about date of arrival than the U.S. census, its first wave was initiated only in 2003. Many years must pass before it will contain enough cohorts to support the study of selectivity. There are, however, some empirical refinements that could improve the analysis of cohort change sooner. To begin, it is useful to conceptualize each migrant as leaving one *community* and entering another, not leaving one *country* and entering another, because most movers secure the resources they need from their communities, not from their countries.

This implies that scholars would do well to measure cohort of arrival at the smallest available unit of analysis—communities before states, states before countries, and countries before continents. In this book, region was used because West Indian advantage was conceptualized at the level of a region (the West Indies). However, if the research goal is to understand cohort change, then analysis should proceed at a finer level of analysis. In the same vein, Cynthia Feliciano (2006, 60) recommends that research on selectivity take "into account the regional origins of immigrants *within* sending countries" (emphasis added). Unfortunately, secondary data analysts rarely have information about the community of departure; they usually have information only on the country of departure. Similarly, they have information only on the community of current residence and, in the case of the U.S. census, on the community of residence five years earlier. It is therefore not surprising that there is much about the effects of cohort of arrival that secondary data analysts do not understand.

Conclusion

Socioeconomic inequality is one of the most common motives for social science research. The advantage of whites over blacks generates scores of studies annually, as does the advantage of natives over immigrants. Of course, nearly 13 percent of the United States population is black, and over 11 percent is foreign-born. Thus, these inequalities have obvious consequences. The inequality that motivates this book, however, affects only 0.37 percent of the United States population.[18] Why devote so much attention to such a small segment of American society?

The main reason is Americans' long hope that an understanding of West Indian achievement would suggest a solution to the nation's gravest domestic problem: inequality between blacks and whites. As "successful" blacks, West Indians represent the exception that proves the rule. Perhaps they could point the way to solving "the American dilemma"?[19] One policy analyst who has studied West Indians with this goal in mind is Thomas Sowell. Drawing selectively on history, he concludes that West Indians' past imbued them with personal qualities that African Americans lack. Thus, personality traits—ambition, diligence, self-sacrifice—rather than the presence of racism or deprivation lie at the heart of African American disadvantage.

Today this interpretation is still heard. To reiterate a quote from chapter 1, according to Harvard professor Henry Lewis Gates, "we need to learn what the immigrants' kids have so we can bottle it and sell it, because many members of the African-American community, particularly among the chronically poor, have lost that sense of purpose and values which produced our generation" (Rimer and Arenson 2004). Gates, the son of a West Virginia paper-mill worker, believes that African Americans are underrepresented at Harvard today because they do not have the aspirations, perseverance, and hope of their West Indian counterparts. Like some policy analysts of the 1970s, Gates urges African Americans to view West Indians as a model minority. If African Americans accepted West Indians as their role model, he opines, many of their difficulties would disappear.

But Gates would do better to separate West Indian performance from African American performance. The one offers no lesson for the other. As the analyses in this book have shown, to the extent that West Indians are a success story, they are an *immigrant* success story, not a *black* success story. Yet race is such a socially meaningful trait that it obscures all other characteristics. As Philip Kasinitz (2001, 257) has written, West Indians "are almost always seen relative to other blacks—and only rarely relative to other immigrants." The message of this book is that at least as much can be learned from comparing West Indians to other immigrants as can be learned from comparing them to other blacks.

Methodological Appendix

This appendix offers a description and evaluation of the data and methods used in this study. The main sources of data are censuses, gathered both in the United States and elsewhere, and three waves of the Sociale Positie en Voorzieningengebruick Allochtonen (SPVA), an ongoing study of ethnic minorities in the Netherlands. In addition, a few survey data sets contributed in a minor way—for instance, the "Immigrants and Out-groups" module of Eurobarometer 30 (Reif and Melich 1991) and the Fourth National Survey of Ethnic Minorities in Britain (Smith and Prior 1996). Short comments on these sources appear at appropriate points in the text.

This appendix is organized in the following manner. U.S. census data are considered first, then non–U.S. census data, and finally the SPVA. Each source is evaluated initially in terms of external validity, that is, in terms of how well the respondents represent the population they purport to represent. Next, each source is evaluated in terms of how well the questions and coding permit the researcher to identify the ethnic minorities of interest. After the information on race and ethnicity has been assessed, the focus shifts to methodology. The methodological technique of greatest interest is regression analysis. It forms the basis for the adjusted means used throughout the book. A justification for the choice of dependent and then of independent variables is offered. The discussion then returns to the data and asks: how well do the variables in the data measure the concepts whose relationships the regression analysis seeks to test? The appendix concludes by considering the implications of the shortcomings of these data sets for the central conclusions of the book.

The U.S. Decennial Census

All U.S. census data for this study were downloaded from the website of the Integrated Public Use Microdata Series (IPUMS) (Ruggles et al. 2004).[1] For the years 1920, 1930, and 1940, IPUMS makes available a 1 percent random sample of all American households. In 1920 and 1930, identical information was obtained from each household; in 1940 the main schedule was truncated and additional questions were asked of one member of the household.[2] In 1970 the U.S. Census Bureau fielded two different "long-form" questionnaires. The long form, issued to 15 percent of the population, contained queries about the respondent's birthplace and parents' birthplaces. These permitted the identification of the second generation. The 15 percent long form, however, did not inquire about the year of immigration. Rather, this question appeared on a different long form, administered to 5 percent of the population. In most other respects, the two questionnaires were similar. To support research on the second generation and on the cohort of arrival, West Indians responding to both forms were included in this study.[3]

Starting in 1980, the U.S. Census Bureau began offering two independently drawn microdata samples for each decennial census: a 5 percent sample and a 1 percent sample. To maximize the case size, this study includes all foreign- and native-born English-speaking West Indians in both samples for the years 1980, 1990, and 2000 and all foreign-born sub-Saharan black Africans in both samples for the years 1990 and 2000. Only a subsample of African Americans was included, however, because of their large numbers. The fraction varied from census to census because some of the African American cases used in this study were originally drawn for other purposes. In fact, the fraction does not matter so long as the absolute number is reasonably large. There is little worry on this score: all years contained at least eight thousand (four thousand of each sex).

The External Validity of U.S. Census Data

The greatest source of inaccuracy in censuses is that individuals absent from the data differ in some systematic way from individuals present. The converse also occurs: censuses include persons who should be excluded, but that problem is less severe. Since the 1950s, the U.S. Census Bureau has supported research to identify overlooked populations and to enhance their inclusion. A particularly relevant strategy is demographic analysis, a technique that estimates coverage by comparing census results with results obtained from "demographic data essentially independent of the census, such as birth, death and immigration estimates, as well as emigration estimates, and Medicare data" (Hogan and Robinson 1993, 3). In the case of African Americans, this method uncovers more people external than internal to the census; in the case of the foreign-born, the method uncovers more people internal than external to the census. In other words, some undocumented individuals and other aliens not registered with civil authorities (students, for instance) are responding to the census. Studying the characteristics of this "residual" population provides insight into the characteristics of both legal and illegal aliens (Passel and Fix 2001).

This strand of research has uncovered two trends relevant to a census-based comparison of African Americans and West Indians. First, a substantial improvement in the coverage of African Americans occurred between 1970 and 1980 and again between 1990 and 2000 (Farley and Allen 1987; Robinson and Adlakha 2002). In 2000 native-born black women were hardly undercounted at all. On the other hand, over the last three censuses the number of foreign-born non-Hispanic blacks not counted by the census has grown. The main reason, of course, is that the number of undocumented black immigrants has grown (INS, *Statistical Yearbook*, various years). These contrary tendencies pose a problem. Moving forward in time, censuses describe African Americans with more accuracy and West Indian immigrants with less (Costanzo et al. 2001; Warren and Passel 1987).

Of course, factors besides race, nativity, and legality also affect inclusion. Research shows that men are more likely to be missed than women and that young adults are underrepresented more often than children or the elderly. Family composition, housing tenure, and type of residence also matter (Word 1997).

To date, U.S. scholars have not linked underrepresentation with any specific labor market outcome, but ethnographers conclude that undercounts occur more often in neighborhoods with a high vacancy rate or gang activity (Brownrigg and de la Puente 2003). Moreover, as discussed later, researchers in Canada have linked underrepresentation in the census with joblessness and poverty. Thus, it seems plausible to assume that many persons absent from the U.S. census have weaker labor market outcomes than those present. However, undocumented immigrants should be as likely to be in the labor force as their documented compatriots—perhaps more so, because most come to the United States to work (Mehta et al. 2002; Samers 2001). With respect to unemployment, the study conducted by Chirag Mehta and his colleagues found that undocumented Latina women suffered higher unemployment than their documented compatriots but that members of other subgroups (mostly Eastern Europeans) did not. Quantitative work on undocumented West Indians has not yet emerged, but a qualitative study shows that undocumented women work in occupations for which they are overqualified and underpaid (Colen 1990, 1995).

As indicated in chapter 2, there is a straightforward way to evaluate whether a portion of West Indian advantage is an artifact of bias in census data. It exploits the knowledge that undocumented West Indians are concentrated in only a few states: New York, New Jersey, Connecticut (at least the New York metropolitan area portion), and Florida (Passel and Woodrow 1984). As a result, the basic comparisons for this study (see table 2.3) were reestimated on a sample that excluded residents from these four states. The results, which appear in table 2.4, continue to confirm West Indian advantage over African Americans. Indeed, the two sets of results are statistically indistinguishable. This is not to say that the undercount is of no importance, but only that, when its influence is minimized, a significant West Indian advantage is still evident.

Group Definition in U.S. Censuses

The discussion so far has skirted the matter of how censuses define group membership. Since race and ethnicity are social constructions, there is no "correct" definition. In addition, difficulties can arise when group membership is not defined consistently. Unfortunately, census variables and their coding change over time, forcing the definition of group membership to change as well.

To define British West Indian immigrants in the national census, four criteria were used: birthplace, race, Hispanicity, and language.[4] Persons born in any present or past British Caribbean colony, as well as in Belize, Guyana, Bermuda, or the U.S. Virgin Islands, were eligible for inclusion. In 1970 neither Barbados nor Guyana were identifiable; most likely the former was included under the residual category "British West Indies Associated States" or "Other West Indies," both of which were assumed to be British. Guyana, however, is lost to the census analysis until 1980.[5]

The decision by the Census Bureau to substitute an ancestry question for parents' birthplace in 1980 is the single most troublesome aspect of group definition. The year 1970 was the first census year to contain enough second-generation West Indians to justify study. In that year, second-generation West Indians were persons described as black on race, non-Hispanic, and U.S.-born. They reported English as their mother tongue and claimed that one or both of their parents were born in the British West Indies. The absence of a question on parental birthplace after 1970 meant that the native-born were identified on the basis of the new ancestry question first fielded in 1980. The question asks: "What is this person's ancestry or ethnic origin?"[6] In 1980 the Census Bureau reported some triple ancestries, but only double ancestries were reported thereafter. Given these constraints, native-born West Indian Americans were defined as persons described as black on race, non-Hispanic, born in the United States, reporting an English mother tongue, and selecting at least one British West Indian background as a first or second ancestry. Note that *native-born West Indians could be second- or later-generation*, though most were probably the children of immigrants.

Because of the change in the way the census inquired about the ethnic background of native-born persons, those identified as second-generation West Indians in 1970 are not entirely comparable to native-born blacks of British West Indian ancestry after 1970. The former are defined involuntarily; the latter chose a Caribbean ancestry in the presence of other options. Qualitative studies of West Indians in the United States suggest that a fair number identify as African Americans rather than as West Indians. In her interviews with young 1.5- and second-generation West Indians, Waters (1999, 2002) observed that teens from middle class families, prosperous neighborhoods, and good schools were more likely to emphasize their Caribbean background than teens from lower-class families, poor neighborhoods, and deprived schools. In explaining the disparity, Waters noted that middle class youth perceived their Caribbean heritage as an asset; lower-class youth rarely made this association. Though quantitative research has not confirmed these relationships, the problem can be circumvented with a fairly simply strategy: substituting for the second generation persons who arrived as children (Hirschman 1994). This is the strategy used in chapter 2 to test whether segmented assimilation theory applies to West Indian Americans.

Although the introduction of the ancestry question reduces the accuracy associated with identifying second-generation Americans, it probably enhances the accuracy associated with identifying African Americans. This follows because the 1970 census only recorded race and parents' birthplace; because blacks of mixed heritage are often the children of native-born parents, additional questions, such as about ancestry, are useful for identifying mixed-heritage persons. Therefore, African Americans were identified in the 1970 census as black, non-Hispanic children of U.S.-born blacks; thereafter, they were black, non-Hispanic respondents who selected ancestries compatible with an African American heritage. Following Kalmijn (1996), these heritages were defined as "American," "Afro American," or the absence of a response. Again, the motive for this restriction is to exclude persons of mixed background.

Another black group included in this study is foreign-born black Africans. They appear in some tests of the all-black society hypothesis in chapter 5. To be included in this category, individuals had to select black on the race question, non-Hispanic on the ethnicity question, and a sub-Saharan African nation on the place-of-birth question.[7] Sufficient numbers of black Africans appear only in the 1990 and 2000 censuses.

Methodology

This book compares West Indians and African Americans on four conventional outcomes: labor market participation, unemployment, occupational prestige, and log of hourly earnings. Their construction is summarized in table 2A.1.

Dependent Variables (Economic Outcomes)

Because earnings often receive exclusive attention, the decision to include additional outcomes deserves some justification. One reason for studying outcomes other than earnings is that earnings inequality has increased substantially over the last three decades. This increase in earnings inequality may be related to the discovery that, relative to the "less-skilled" immigrants who arrived earlier, the more recently arrived earn less. Researchers have attempted to correct for the bias that income inequality might impart, but there is no consensus on the best way to achieve this goal. Perusing other economic outcomes is a good solution.

A second reason to study outcomes other than earnings is to give both agency and structure a place in the analysis. Among labor market outcomes, individuals have the most discretion over the labor force participation decision and the least discretion over unemployment. To be sure, the labor force participation decision is also affected by family need, economic opportunity, and cultural expectations. Still, it is a good indicator of causal processes that operate at the level of individuals, such as emotions, values, and motives. These characteristics are relevant to hypotheses about cultural differences and about the selectivity of migration. Unemployment, on the other hand, reflects a more complex causal process. To some degree, unemployment is also an indicator of individuals' values and motives. For instance, if they lowered their "reservation wage" (the lowest rate of remuneration they are willing to accept), some unemployed persons would be employed. Indeed, because living standards are generally lower at origin than at destination, most immigrants have a lower reservation wage than natives. But unemployment can also be an indicator of employers' responses to particular applicants. When applicants are members of a stigmatized group, unemployment also reflects employers' stereotypes about that group. For this reason, it makes sense to think about unemployment as a better indicator than labor force participation of discrimination (or of favoritism).

In terms of the causal forces they reflect, occupational outcomes and earnings fall somewhere between labor force participation and unemployment. Because everyone wants to maximize their earnings but not everyone seeks the most skilled occupations, people exercise more discretion over their occupations than over their earnings. Some occupational choices are made in school; others involve apprenticeships or on-the-job training. Young people often make compromises along the way, especially if they belong to subordinate groups or come from economically disadvantaged families. A final reason for including occupation in this study is that the U.S. census did not inquire about earnings until 1940. Thus, occupation becomes an important indicator of change in the attainment of West Indians relative to African Americans over time.

There is one final question with respect to the choice of outcome variables: which indicator of occupation is best? Substantively, occupational prestige score was selected rather than occupational status because prestige is independent of earnings, and earnings are already included. Among prestige scores, Treiman's Standard International Occupational Prestige Scale (SIOPS) was selected because it is compatible with the occupational coding in all U.S. censuses as well as with many non-U.S. data sets (Ganzeboom, de Graaf, and Treiman 1992; Ganzeboom and Treiman 1996).

Earnings include all receipts from wages, salaries, or self-employment. The variable appears in two forms: raw annual earnings and log hourly earnings. For ease of comprehension, the raw annual format is used when descriptive statistics are presented; however, because of the skewed nature of raw earnings, log hourly earnings are preferred when adjusted means are calculated. In addition, control for time worked is crucial if earnings are to be modeled effectively. For this reason, hours worked per week and weeks worked per year, the two standard controls, are incorporated directly into the dependent variable rather than introduced as control variables.

Models

The variables used to predict these four labor market outcomes vary slightly across dependent variables, but in every case they include the contribution of human capital, family obligations, and geography. The main indicators of human capital are age, education, and years since migration; indicators of family obligations include whether or not head of household, marital status, and number of children; indicators of geography are whether or not living in a metropolitan area, in the New York metropolitan area, and in the South. These predictors are summarized in table 2A.3. Certainly some models of West Indian attainment have incorporated variables drawn from perspectives other than human capital theory—for instance, labor market segmentation theory or ethnic niche theory (Model 1991, 1997). However, this strategy was not pursued here for two reasons. First, employment in labor market segments or niches is partly a consequence of racial and ethnic group membership. Hence, the inclusion of such variables would prematurely attenuate the effect of being African American or West Indian. Second, to the extent that the models used in this book replicate previous work—for instance, work on the selectivity of migration—the specifications ought to be comparable. This logic is also the motive for excluding occupational prestige from earnings models.

Although multivariate regression is the procedure that underlies all the statistical comparisons in this book, in order to reach a nontechnical audience, the results are presented as ratios of adjusted to actual means.[8] This procedure can be applied to any two groups. The first step is to estimate a regression on one of the groups; in chapter 2 it is West Indians. Second, for each independent variable in the regression, actual means are obtained for the other group, for example, African Americans. Next, the dependent variable is predicted by multiplying the West Indian coefficient of each independent variable by the actual African American mean on that independent variable. This prediction is called the adjusted mean (Bluestone and Stevenson 1999; Farley and Allen 1987; Treiman and Terrill 1975). Its interpretation is very straightforward. It is the outcome the average West Indian would have on the dependent variable were he or she to have the same values on the independent variables (age, schooling, and so on) that the average African American has. However, without a benchmark, this adjusted mean is not very informative. Is it high or is it low? One solution is to provide two numbers for each outcome: the West Indian adjusted mean and the African American actual mean. But then the reader must constantly compare two numbers. A simpler solution is to present just one number: the ratio of the two means (Xie and Goyette 2005).

A brief description of the contents of each of the four regression models follows.

1. Models of *labor force participation* include age, age squared, educa-
    tion, the unemployment rate for persons of the same sex in the
    same state, and a set of dummy variables that capture racial-ethnic
    group membership, school attendance, the presence of a disability,
    the presence of a spouse, the status of household head, residence in
    the New York metropolitan area, in the South, and in a metropoli-
    tan area. Models for women also include the number of children
    ever borne (in 2000 the number of children ever borne was not
    asked; hence, the number of children in the home under age eight-
    een was substituted) and the number of children in the home un-
    der age five. The model is estimated separately by census year and
    gender on persons age eighteen to sixty-four. Robust standard er-
    rors were used because of the inclusion of the contextual variable
    measuring the unemployment rate.

2. Models of *unemployment* include age, age squared, education, and
    a set of dummy variables that capture racial-ethnic group member-
    ship, the presence of a spouse, the status of household head, resi-
    dence in the New York metropolitan area, and in the South, or in a
    metropolitan area. Models for women also include the number of
    children under age five in the home. The model is estimated sepa-
    rately by census year and gender on persons age eighteen to sixty-
    four.

3. Models of *occupational prestige* include age, age squared, education,
    and a set of dummy variables that capture racial-ethnic group
    membership, the presence of a spouse, residence in the New York
    metropolitan area, in the South, and in a metropolitan area. Models
    for women also include the number of children ever borne (in 2000
    the number of children in the home under age eighteen was substi-
    tuted). The model is estimated separately by census year and gen-
    der on persons age twenty-five to sixty-four.

4. Models of *the natural log of weekly earnings* include age, age
    squared, education, and a set of dummy variables that capture
    racial-ethnic group membership, the presence of a spouse, resi-
    dence in the New York metropolitan area, in the South, and in a
    metropolitan area. Models for women also include the number of
    children ever borne (in 2000 the number of children in the home
    under age eighteen was substituted). The model is estimated sepa-
    rately by census year and gender on persons age twenty-five to
    sixty-four. Persons earning under $500 annually were excluded
    from the analysis.

When models diverge from this description, the text explicitly identifies the modification. The most common variant, of course, is the addition of years since migration and its square. A less common but equally important variant is the pooled model. Although the majority of estimates are limited to a single census year, a data set containing observations from 1970 to 2000 was constructed to test Borjas's theories about the selectivity of migration. This model differs from those previously described by the inclusion of dummy variables for cohort of arrival (6) and for census year (3). At the same time, the pooled model excludes some variables. As will be explained shortly, the census obtained no information on earned degrees before 1990; in addition, census questions on family size are not comparable across years. Hence, these independent variables are absent from the pooled model. Because children are secondary (tied) movers and selectivity theory applies only to primary movers, persons arriving under age eighteen are dropped from the pooled model. See chapter 4 for further information on the pooled model.

Independent Variables

Another matter of concern is the internal validity of the data—that is, the effectiveness of each independent variable at conveying the theoretically expected effects. The difficulties attendant to defining racial-ethnic group membership have already been discussed. Two other variables that are especially problematic in terms of validity are education and years since migration. One difficulty is that a year of schooling does not impart the same amount of knowledge to every student, even controlling for mental ability. Shortcomings in the way the Census Bureau codes education add to the difficulties. Before 1990, years of schooling were obtained directly. This information is of interest, but, in the absence of coding for credentials, it is impossible to know whether persons with twelve years of schooling have a high school diploma, whether persons with sixteen years of schooling have a college degree, and so on. In 1990 the Census Bureau changed the coding for schooling, creating intervals for one to four years and for five to eight years, then shifting to a combination of years of schooling and credentials. Although the information on credentials is useful, the new coding scheme elides meaningful differences among persons with less than eight years of schooling.

The confusion associated with the year of arrival is that many foreign-born residents cannot identify the exact date when they entered the United States with the expectation of staying permanently (Jasso

2004; Jasso and Rosenzweig 1990a; Redstone and Massey 2004). Short-comings in the way the Census Bureau codes the year of arrival add to the difficulties. Before 2000, the census questionnaire offered only a range of dates; for example, in 1990 the codes included intervals like 1965 to 1969, 1970 to 1974, and 1975 to 1979. A range of dates might make sense if the intervals mirrored policy shifts in admission regulations. But the intervals have no substantive meaning. Because of the need for a single digit, the year of arrival was recoded following the procedure used by Borjas (1991).

Poorly designed intervals likewise plagued the 1970 census with regard to weeks worked in 1969 and hours worked the week before the census questionnaire was answered. These were recoded to their respective midpoints.[9] Changes in census-defined city boundaries also presented problems. The desire to maintain a geographic definition of New York harmonious with each census meant that the counties—later the PUMAs, and later still the super-PUMAs used to define "greater New York area"—encompassed an increasingly large area. Finally, inconsistencies in the measurement of offspring deserve mention. Until 2000, the census questionnaire asked every woman how many children she had borne. This number was included in all the equations for women because it captures some of the variation in work experience typical of mothers.[10] In 2000, however, the fertility question was not asked. As a result, the number of children under age eighteen at home, a variable supplied by the Census Bureau, was substituted.

Non-U.S. Data Sources

As part of the hypothesis-testing effort, the multivariate analyses also draw on samples of black immigrants living outside the United States. Hence, the discussion now reviews the three non-U.S. data sets chosen for that purpose. These were all created in the 1990s; hence, the American comparison rests on the 1990 U.S. census. For all countries, only persons age eighteen to sixty-four are included in analyses of labor force participation and unemployment; only persons age twenty-five to sixty-four are included in analyses of occupational prestige and earnings. Some of these comparisons operate at the national level, and others operate at the level of cities (New York, Toronto, and so on).

The following sections offer a country-by-country description of each data source, including an evaluation of the data's external validity and a description of the variables selected for analysis. To convey these in summary form, each section ends with a list of the predictors for that country's labor force participation equation. Because the predictors of the three other dependent variables are subsets of the variables in the labor force participation equation, it would be redundant to list the predictors of all four outcomes.

Canada

The Canadian data source is the 1991 Public Use Microdata File Individuals (PUMFI), a 3 percent sample of the returns in that year. Statistics Canada, like the U.S. Census Bureau, undertakes research to determine the undercount. In 1991 demographic analysis indicated that 3.02 percent of the population was missed; the comparable figure for the 1990 U.S. census was 1.65 percent (Robinson and Adlakha 2002; Statistics Canada 1994a). Conclusions from follow-ups to the census show that persons age twenty to twenty-four, males, never-married persons, tenants, and persons living in nontraditional structures were undercounted. Additional characteristics that Statistics Canada associated with nonresponse include internal migration, annual incomes of under $10,000, and residence in the Northwest Territories. The estimated net undercount of persons who resided outside Canada a year before the census was 19.99 percent; the estimated net undercount of persons who resided outside Canada five years before the census was 13.87 percent (Statistics Canada 1994a). In other words, the undercount of recent foreign-born residents is extremely high.

As for undocumented immigrants, according to a 2003 newspaper article, they number between 100,000 and 200,000, and unlike their American counterparts, most have overstayed their visa or failed to receive refugee status (Jimenez 2003). Evidently not much is known about Canada's clandestine immigrants. Still, given the greater distance from the Caribbean, it seems safe to assume that the United States houses far more West Indian illegal entrants than does Canada.

The 1991 Canadian census inquires about place of birth and ethnicity but not about parents' birthplace or race. A question instead asks whether the respondent is a "visible minority." Regrettably, the codes for birthplace are extremely broad. English-speaking West Indians were defined as visible minorities born in "Central America, Caribbean, Bermuda [or] South America" whose ethnic response was coded "Black/Caribbean" and whose primary language was English. Native-born whites were Canadian-born persons whose primary language was English and who were not members of the Canadian census category "visible minorities." Blacks were included in their entirety, but to keep the case base of manageable size, native whites were limited to a 2 percent sample.

The dependent variables and coding schemes in the 1991 Canadian census are broadly similar to those in the 1990 U.S. census. The most salient difference concerns occupational prestige. The Canadian census offers only fourteen "major occupations," and these major occupations could not easily be assigned a Treiman prestige score (SIOPS) because each was composed of several minor occupations. Following the observation of Harry Ganzeboom and his colleagues (1992) that "the costs of being crude" are severe only when the number of occupations falls below six, weighted average SIOPS were computed for each of the fourteen Canadian occupations. Calculating these averages required three pieces of information: the detailed occupational codes ("minor occupations") associated with each of the fourteen categories (Statistics Canada 1994b); the titles and number of persons in each minor occupation (Statistics Canada 1995); and the SIOPS for each minor occupation (Ganzeboom and Treiman 1996). To facilitate the mapping process, Ganzeboom and Treiman's "numerical dominance rule" was followed. When a major occupation contained minor occupations associated with more than one SIOPS, the major occupation was assigned the SIOPS of its largest title. After the minor occupations associated with each of the fourteen major occupations had been identified, their respective SIOPS were weighted by the number of their incumbents. Each individual then was assigned a SIOPS equal to the weighted average associated with his or her major occupation.

Reminiscent of an early practice by the U.S. Census Bureau, Statistics Canada offers only hours worked during the week before the census rather than usual weeks worked the previous year. This discrepancy produced minor differences between the U.S. and Canadian earnings variables, even though both censuses provided figures for wage, salary, and self-employment income. In regression analyses, persons earning less than $500 per annum were omitted because of potential distortion of the results.

As for independent variables, the 1991 Canadian census is superior to the 1990 U.S. census in having solicited the exact year of arrival. Another strength of the Canadian data is that they record the legal status of the foreign-born. Though "undocumented" is not one of the choices, the variable does allow researchers to distinguish "landed immigrants" from "non-permanent immigrants." The latter is a person who is "in Canada on a student authorization, employment authorization, a Minister's permit or who is a refugee claimant" (Statistics Canada 1994b, 45). Among all foreign-born eighteen- to sixty-four-year-olds, 5.5 percent fit this description; among the West Indian–born, 4.8 percent do. One variable present in the U.S. census but not the Canadian census is the presence of a disability. Finally, instead of number of children ever born, two dummies convey the presence of children ages zero to six and ages six to seventeen, respectively.

In the Toronto case, the labor force participation equation includes age, age squared, years of schooling, the unemployment rate for persons of the same sex in the same province, years since migration, years since migration squared, and a set of dummy variables that capture racial-ethnic group membership, school attendance, a college degree, an advanced degree, the presence of a spouse, and the status of household head. Models for women also include a dummy for the presence of a child under age six and another for the presence of a child age six to seventeen. Subsets of these variables were used to predict the three other dependent variables.

Great Britain

The British data come from the 1991 SARs (Sample of Anonymized Records) of the U.K. census. There are two SARs files: a household-level file that contains 1 percent of the population and an individual-level file that contains 2 percent of the population. To maximize cases, individuals were drawn from both files. This decision costs some loss of detail; for example, occupations are assigned three-digit codes in the 1 percent file but only two-digit codes in the 3 percent file. However, the files contain a large number of derived variables in addition to those generated directly from the census questionnaire.

Britain too sought to gauge the accuracy of coverage in its 1991 census; to this end, analysts used both demographic analysis and a post-enumeration survey (Bulmer 1996; Simpson 1996). The official undercount is 2.1 percent (compared to 1.65 percent in the United States in 1990). According to the Census Validation Survey, the characteristics most strongly associated with omission include being unmarried, living in a large household, moving within the past year, being unemployed, and living in a nontraditional structure. In addition, race was paramount, with 5.2 percent of blacks missed (Simpson and Middleton 1997). This is slightly higher than the 4.4 percent of blacks that the 1990 post-enumeration survey concluded were absent from the 1990 U.S. census (Hogan and Robinson 1993). But of course, blacks in Britain and blacks in the United States are not the same. Approximately half the blacks in the 1991 British census were foreign-born, but only 5.1 percent of blacks in the 1990 U.S. census were foreign-born (Gibson and Lennon 1999; Peach 1996). Moreover, very few of Britain's foreign-born blacks are undocumented immigrants.[11]

As for who was "black" in the 1991 British census, the questionnaire asked respondents to choose from among eight ethnic groups, including black Caribbean, black African, and "black other." Persons selecting the option "black other" were prompted to "please describe" that choice in an open-ended way (Bulmer 1996). A study of the original returns showed that one-third of persons coded as "black other" described themselves as black British; 14 percent wrote "black/white"; the remainder used a plethora of terms to describe themselves. When Angela Dale and Clare Holdsworth (1997) traced individuals from the 1991 census to the 1971 census, they found that 79 percent of the 1991 black British were coded West Indian in 1971, a time when the "black other" option was not offered. As a result, in this research West Indians—or, as they are called in Britain, black Caribbeans—were defined as persons who identified as either black Caribbean or "black other" on the ethnic group question and who selected either Jamaica or "other Commonwealth Caribbean" for their birthplace. Not surprisingly, only 2.5 percent of Caribbean-born blacks identified as "black other." As for native-born whites, they were defined as persons born in the United Kingdom who identified as white on the ethnic group question. Owing to their large size, only a 2 percent sample of whites was extracted.

With respect to dependent variables, the SARs permits the construction of only three; earnings are not reported. Still, assigning each occupation a Treiman prestige score (SIOPS) proved a challenge. The 1988 International Standard Classification of Occupations (ISCO) is the usual conduit between data-specific occupational codes and data-invariant prestige scores (Ganzeboom and Treiman 1996). Moreover, the 1 percent household SARs already contained ISCO codes for each of its three-digit occupations. Thus, the first step was to assign each of these occupations an occupational prestige score. Unfortunately, no SIOPS were available for the two-digit occupations in the 2 percent individual sample. Thus, the next step was to map the three-digit occupations in the 1 percent sample into the two-digit occupations in the 2 percent sample. Then, each two-digit occupation's SIOPS was defined as the weighted average of its respective SIOPS. Finally, each individual in the 2 percent sample was assigned the weighted average SIOPS associated with his or her two-digit occupation.

The British models predicting labor force participation, unemployment, and occupational prestige contain fewer independent variables than the American or Canadian models; furthermore, many of the British variables lack the detail of their North American counterparts. Reflecting the relatively small immigrant presence in Britain, the 1991 U.K. census did not ask about year of arrival or mother tongue. Indicators of family size were inadvertently omitted. Marital status was available, but spousal presence or absence was not noted; geographical detail identified one urban area and one suburban area: London and outer London. Still, the most disappointing feature of the British census is its coarse educational coding. Only three levels of schooling are distinguished: certificates obtained after age eighteen (that is, after high school), bachelor's degrees, and post-bachelor's degrees. No postsecondary credentials were held by 85.8 percent of the British sample, and 75.9 percent of the matching American sample likewise had no postsecondary credentials. In this data-impoverished situation, much of the variance in labor market outcomes goes unexplained.

In the London case, the labor force participation equation includes age, age squared, the unemployment rate for persons of the same sex in the same region, and a set of dummy variables that capture racial-ethnic group membership, school attendance, educational credentials (4), the presence of a disability, and the status of household head. Subsets of these variables were used to predict the other two dependent variables.

The Netherlands

In 1971 the Dutch Central Bureau of Statistics (CBS) fielded its last census. For political and social reasons, the government decided to terminate the decennial census, substituting instead a comprehensive system of municipal data collection practices (Guiraudon, Phalet, and ter Wal 2005). To be sure, a variety of surveys are undertaken in the Netherlands, some of which contain information about the labor force outcomes of immigrants. Only one, however, distinguishes Surinamese Creoles (African-origin Surinamese) from Hindustanis (Indian-origin Surinamese): the Sociale Positie en Voorzieningengebruick Allochtonen (Social Position and the Use of Provisions by Ethnic Minorities), or SPVA. Since Surinamese Creoles are a theoretically critical group to this study, the SPVA is the data set of choice. First fielded in 1988, it is an ongoing survey of the four largest minorities in Holland: Turks, Moroccans, Surinamese, and (Dutch) Antilleans. This study draws on the 1991, 1994, and 1998 waves. Some waves have a small panel component; households interviewed a second time were excluded from the present study.[12] The 1988 wave was excluded because it does not distinguish Surinamese by ethnicity. In general, the household head is the informant, but data are collected on all family members. More recent waves solicit additional information from other members.[13]

Because ethnic minorities are highly concentrated in particular geographic areas, the SPVA's sampling frame is limited to a few cities: ten in 1988, thirteen in 1998. The best-known are Amsterdam, Rotterdam, and The Hague, but midsize and smaller towns are also included. In the selected locales, researchers sample the municipal registers to obtain the addresses of household heads of the desired ethnicities. Efforts are made to sample groups in proportion to their estimated size. A sample of native white Dutch persons ("autochtonen," or "indigenous Dutch") is also obtained in each city (Niesing 1993). Note that the Antillean-Creole comparison in chapter 5 has no geographic restrictions but the cross-national comparison in chapter 6 is limited to Amsterdam residents.

The main shortcoming of the SPVA is its response rate. Among Antilleans and Surinamese Creoles, only about half the households initially identified in municipal registries were interviewed. Interestingly, response rates for Turks and Moroccans are slightly higher. On the plus side, the proportion of illegal Creoles is probably small, and all Antilleans are legal by definition. So the causes of nonresponse are unlikely to be linked to visa status. Edwin Martens (1999) undertook some comparisons between the 1998 SPVA and published tabulations from the 1997 Enquête Beroepsbevolking (EB, Labor Market Survey). Unfortunately, little can be concluded from this undertaking because the two data sets differ substantially in their generational composition; moreover, the EB contained very few native-born ethnics, but the SPVA was not modified to reflect the disparity. An additional difficulty with the SPVA is that there was no imputation of missing data; therefore, a goodly number of responses are "missing" on some questions.[14]

In terms of defining group membership, an initial determination is made at the municipal registry; that is, the household is assigned a sampling frame on the basis of the ethnicity of the household head as listed in the register. Determination of the ethnicity within groups of Surinamese national origin required an additional step. In the 1991 wave, Surinamese household heads were asked whether they identified with an ethnic group. Those who said yes were asked the name of the group. The responses were coded as Hindustani, Creole, Javanese, and "other." In 1991, 73.8 percent of the Surinamese household heads answered this question. In 1994 it was decided that all household heads should be asked an ethnicity question directly; 87.8 percent of Surinamese answered in 1994, and 99.8 percent in 1998.[15] It should be noted that this approach gives all household members the ethnicity of the head; in fact, however, adjustments were made in process. For instance, the "autochtonen" (white native Dutch) spouses of household heads and nonrelatives of the head were assigned an ethnicity on the basis of their own characteristics.

In terms of variables, the SPVA is very rich. There was no difficulty locating all the variables available in the 1990 U.S. census. Respondent's present occupation is coded to four or five digits following standard usage by the CBS, and files are available to assign ISCO codes to these occupations. However, in 1992 the official occupational codes were revised; hence, assignments of ISCO codes in the 1991 SPVA were based on a 1984 mapping, while assignments of ISCO codes in the 1994 and 1998 waves took advantage of the 1992 mapping.[16] With respect to earnings, respondents were first asked a current net monthly figure; those who declined to answer were asked to select an interval-based response. Across the three waves, 55.8 percent of the replies come from the interval form of the question; these were recoded to their respective midpoints.

The construction of the independent variables was straightforward. As elsewhere in Europe, surveys inquire about educational credentials, not years of completed schooling. The SPVA distinguishes eight levels of education, from no credentials to postgraduate credentials. These were reduced to four categories as follows: primary school or less (bao [Bassisonderwijs, or primary education]), lower credentials (lbo/vbo [Lager beroepsonderwijs, or lower level vocational training, and Voorbereidend beroepsonderwijs, or preparatory vocational training], mavo [Middelbaar algemeen voortgezet onderwijs]), middle credentials (mbo [Middelbaar beroepsonderwijs, or middle level vocational training], havo [Hoger algemeen voortgezet onderwijs, or higher level general secondary education], vwo [Vorbereidend wetenschappelijk onderwijz, or pre-university education]), and high credentials (hbo [Hoger beroepsonderwijs, or higher level vocational training], wo [Wetenschappelijk onderwijs, or university education]). Their respective U.S. counterparts were less than high school, high school diploma, some college, and a bachelor's degree or higher. In addition, it was necessary to obtain regional unemployment rates for each year of the survey. Unfortunately, gender specific rates were not obtained. Finally, to control for unobserved changes over time, each multivariate regression included two dummy variables for the year of the survey (1991 was the omitted category).

In the Dutch SPVA, the labor force participation equation includes age, age squared, the regional unemployment rate for the year of the survey, years since migration, years since migration squared, and a set of dummy variables that capture racial-ethnic group membership, school attendance, educational credentials (4), the presence of a spouse, the status of household head, the presence of a disability, and the year of the survey (3). For the Antillean-Creole comparison, a dummy for residence in Amsterdam and eight dummies for region of residence were also included. Models for women also contain the number of children in the household under eighteen years of age. Subsets of these variables were used to predict the three other dependent variables.

Conclusion

Of the many implications to be drawn from this discussion, one stands out above the rest: sample selection bias. The insights of Jeffrey Passel and his colleagues with respect to inclusion in the census show that, during the late twentieth century, coverage of both foreign-born and native-born blacks changed in significant ways. In 1980 and again in 2000, coverage of African Americans took a quantum leap forward. Conversely, in the 1980s, and even more in the 1990s, coverage of immigrants (including black immigrants) took a quantum leap backward.

At first glance, it seemed that these changes in coverage might explain a portion of the West Indian advantage demonstrated in table 2.3. As it happens, this was not the case. Nevertheless, a complete understanding of the position of the two groups relative to one another should take sample selection bias into account.

Unfortunately, difficult as it is to "count the uncountable," this task is easier than understanding the implications of an undercount. This is so because very little research has been done on the characteristics of the undocumented, and especially on the undocumented who are absent from the census. While it is likely that uncounted African Americans have poorer labor force outcomes than counted African Americans, this conclusion may not hold for uncounted undocumented immigrants. More likely, there is variation in the consequences of legal status for different labor force outcomes. Labor force participation, for instance, is probably higher but earnings lower among the uncounted undocumented. Of course, the possibility that the uncounted undocumented differ in some systematic way from the counted undocumented cannot be ruled out. Moreover, research shows that the economic consequences of undocumented status vary by racial and ethnic background (Mehta et al. 2002). Thus, uncounted undocumented West Indians may have different labor market experiences than uncounted undocumented Mexicans. Finally, the undercount of black Caribbeans in Britain has implications for the undercount of West Indians in the United States. In Britain, almost all black Caribbeans are legal. That they are undercounted at a rate slightly higher than the rate for African Americans suggests that a myriad of factors are responsible for the undercount of West Indian Americans. Worse still, as Simpson and Middleton (1997) point out, when many factors are responsible for an undercount, scholars usually do not know if their effects are additive or interactive.

On the plus side, quantitative researchers often can devise a strategy to ascertain whether the data sets they use are contaminated by sample selection bias. But if problems are found, to understand their causes and formulate a solution requires a research project in its own right. Luckily, in the present study, such a project was not needed.

Notes

Source for the map of the Caribbean on page ix: CIA Factbook.

Chapter 1: Why Study West Indians?

1. In the interest of brevity, the term "West Indies" is used in this book to refer to regions either presently or previously under the control of Great Britain. Immigrants from these regions are called "West Indians" rather than "British West Indians" or "English-speaking West Indians."

2. In the debate over reparations for slavery, the conservative David Horowitz has used West Indian achievement as evidence that an African heritage is not a handicap in the United States (Berlet 2003).

Chapter 2: Documenting the Difference Between West Indians and African Americans

1. Cases drawn from the 1920 U.S. census and obtained from the Integrated Public Use Microdata Series indicate that 52 percent of the West Indian–born population in the New York metropolitan area was male (Ruggles et al. 2004).

2. Between 1924 and 1929, the quota for Great Britain was 34,007; in 1929 a new basis for computing quotas was introduced, and the British quota jumped to 65,721 (Daniels 2004).

3. Illiterates are defined as people who cannot read or write. For the earliest period, adults are persons age fourteen and older; thereafter, adults are persons age sixteen and older.

4. These calculations are limited to persons twenty-five to sixty-four years of age. However, the 1940 census does not offer information about year of

migration; hence, some migrants obtained at least a portion of their schooling in New York.

5.   Information on the criteria used to construct these outcomes, across all census years, appears at the end of this chapter as table 2A.1.

6.   For two category outcomes like in or out of the labor force, the average is called the "rate." To illustrate, when the U.S. government announces monthly labor statistics, it provides the labor force participation "rate" and the unemployment "rate," even though these figures are actually averages calculated by counting each person in one category as 1 (for example, those *in* the labor force), counting each person in the other category as 0 (for example, those *not in* the labor force), and dividing this sum by the total number of persons.

7.   The purpose of labor certification was to reassure American labor that immigration would not undermine their livelihoods. Hart-Celler specified that "no worker shall enter the United States unless the Secretary of Labor certifies (1) that there are not sufficient workers in the United States at the alien's destination who are able, willing and qualified to perform the skilled or unskilled labor and (2) that the employment of the alien will not adversely affect wages and working conditions of U.S. citizens similarly employed" (Tomasi and Keely 1975, 8).

8.   The "correction" involved weighting the total number of immigrants by the proportion of immigrants estimated to be black. To obtain this percentage, racial identity and year of arrival were cross-tabulated for Guyanese and Trinidadians, respectively. The data came from four censuses: 1970, 1980, 1990, and 2000. The 1970 census results were used to weight persons arriving in 1969 and earlier, the 1980 results for those arriving between 1970 and 1979, and so on.

9.   Since Guyana sent relatively few immigrants to the United States before the 1965 law was implemented, it took some time for a culture of emigration to become established there. Its emigration rate in the 1967 to 1976 period averaged only 54 per 10,000, but rose to 147 between 1977 and 2000. According to David Heer (1996), who has done extensive research on emigration rates to the United States, Guyana has the highest rate in the world.

10. A historical study of West Indian "niches" or "arenas of job concentration" uncovered several female employment niches (for instance, hospitals and nursing homes) but few for men (Model 2001). This suggests that, using their friends and relatives, West Indian women can more easily find work than West Indian men.

11. In using the term "early bird," the author acknowledges a debt to Russell Williams (2004), who introduced the phrase to describe the first person applying for a job. As in the present context, Williams speculates that early birds held advantages over latecomers.

12. An extensive discussion of the factors that enhance and depress the selectivity of migration appears in chapter 3.

13. In an extensive tabular analysis, Cooper (1985) argues that white collar emigration did not escalate during this period, but the numbers in figure 2.5 say otherwise.

14. When interpreting the figures, it is important to note that, in the 1990s, both Guyana and Barbados introduced small changes in the way they reported occupations. In both cases, the changes placed more occupations under the rubric of "upper-white-collar." For information on these changes, see the web page "Caribbean Labor Statistics" at the ILO website: http://www.ilo.carib.org. The INS offers no data for 1980; hence, data for 1979 are used instead.

15. In addition, the numbers do not control for age. In general, education attainment decreases and occupational attainment increases with age. If the average age of migrants varies within and among sending countries, these fluctuations may undermine the comparability of the results.

16. Culture, opportunity, and the selectivity of migration are all plausible explanations for West Indians' educational advantage over African Americans. Because, as will shortly be shown, West Indians maintain an economic advantage over African Americans even when the immigrants are assigned the lesser educational attainment of African Americans, this volume makes no effort to explain West Indians' educational advantage.

17. In 2000 all groups showed an increase in rates of work-related disability. For instance, in 1990 the rate for all men was 9.1 percent, and in 2000 it was 13.0 percent. This suggests that changes in the census question or its tabulation contributed to the increase. At the same time, the magnitude of the West Indian increase is so great that other factors are doubtless also at work.

18. Attempts to reverse the procedure—for example, to assign African Americans the job-related characteristics of West Indians (not shown)—reveal the "cost of being African American" rather than the "benefit of being West Indian." Both approaches yield the same substantive conclusion: West Indians reap an advantage not wholly attributable to their job-related characteristics.

19. The data sets created for this study contain relatively few foreign-born whites.

20. Similar conclusions emerge in the work of Lingxin Hao (2007), who finds that Jamaican immigrants fare better than African Americans on several indicators of wealth, but not as well as whites. As for housing, Emily Rosenbaum and Samantha Friedman (2007) find that the homes and neighborhoods of foreign-born black New Yorkers are less desirable than those of native-born non-Hispanic whites, but more desirable than those of African Americans. These authors also find that the children of black immigrants endure poorer housing conditions than foreign-born blacks.

21. Contrary to popular opinion, undocumented immigrants do respond to censuses; however, their response rate is lower than that of documented immigrants (Costanzo et al. 2001; Passel and Woodrow 1984).

22. Because the "underclass" emphasizes personal behaviors rather than economic position, most scholars consider it a "class-based subculture," not a social class. For a critical history of the underclass as a concept, see Michael Katz (1993).

23. In the tests of segmented assimilation conducted by Alejandro Portes and his colleagues (2005), immigrants who arrived before age thirteen were part of the target population. They also included the native-born children of immigrants. The present analysis, however, relies on the U.S. census, which omits a parental birthplace question (see the methodological appendix). As a result, the tests of segmented assimilation in this chapter consider only the foreign-born who arrived before age thirteen.

24. Another flaw in census data is that the PUMS offers only an approximation of inner-city residence. The census variable "central city" is larger than the "inner city"; the central city is the urbanized core of a metropolitan area, not the inner-city ghetto to which Wilson (1980) and Gans (1992) refer. For instance, the five boroughs of New York constitute one central city.

Chapter 3: Three Explanations for the Difference Between West Indians and African Americans

1. The demographic consequence could as easily be education or authority or responsibility. But to keep the discussion simple, the example pursued here is skill.

2. Both Dennis Forsyth and Winston James recount an anecdote crediting West Indian women for breaking the color line in New York's garment industry in the 1920s: "They had signs saying colored were not wanted. We took them down and marched right in to apply. You bet, we got the jobs" (Forsyth 1983, 75; James 1998, 85).

3. If the entire population flees—for instance, because of war or natural disaster—then selection does not occur at all.

4. Actually, Borjas uses the term "cohort of arrival," not "year of arrival," because he examines the effect of year of arrival by pooling together persons arriving within five-year intervals, grouping together those who arrived before 1961, those who arrived between 1961 and 1965, those who arrived between 1966 and 1970, and so on. He calls these groupings "cohorts of arrival."

5. Scholars in the United States have extended Borjas's approach to other labor market outcomes, as well as to women; so far the pattern has held (Fry 1996; Funkhouser and Trejo 1998).

6. Although not advocating white favoritism as an explanation for West Indian economic attainment, Violet Johnson (2006, 66) stresses the significance of a British affiliation for Boston's West Indians: "A British identity was more than a match for the White American status quo, for they had been taught that everything British was superior." For evidence of white Americans' Anglophilia, see Jones (2001).

Chapter 4: Testing the Hypothesis of Selectivity

1. The example of the residual method of causal attribution in chapter 2 is Paul Siegel's (1965) comparison of black and white earnings. After making the two groups the same on as many job-related characteristics as he could measure, Siegel attributed the remaining gap to discrimination (though conceding that differences in the *quality* of blacks' and whites' educations and occupations might also be at work).

2. Borjas prefers to use native-born white males (1987, 1991) or all native-born males (2000) as a benchmark. He defends the choice on the ground that native-born Mexicans do not experience discrimination. For a different conclusion, see Model and Fisher (2007).

3. Chiswick's (1979) published results for black men in 1970 are not compa-

rable to those in table 4.1 because his sample includes all black male immigrants, not just those from the English-speaking West Indies.

4. Only a portion of respondents to the 1970 census received a questionnaire inquiring about immigrants' year of arrival. As a result, the 1970 figures in table 4.1 rest on 262 black male and 322 black female immigrants from the English-speaking West Indies.

5. Changes in the size of West Indian immigrant flows correspond closely with Borjas's expectations. According to the U.S. Immigration and Naturalization Service (INS), between 1961 and 1966 only 6,500 English-speaking West Indians entered the United States annually. In contrast, between 1967 and 1976 the annual average was 23,500; between 1977 and 1985 the average was higher still: 37,177 (U.S. Census Bureau 1969, 1972, 1976; U.S. Census Bureau 1980, fig. 2.2). After peaking in the late 1980s, the official influx declined, but recent numbers are underestimates because a growing number of immigrants are undocumented.

6. Borjas creates cohorts by aggregating arrivals at five-year intervals: for example, before 1960, 1960 to 1965, 1966 to 1969, 1970 to 1975, and so on.

7. In interpreting the results, a few cautionary remarks are in order. First, scholars disagree regarding the accuracy of the responses to the year-of-arrival question in the U.S. census (Jasso 2004; Myers 2004; Redstone and Massey 2004). A second difficulty is that the dummies included to capture the effect of the year of the observation may be inadequate to control for period effects. There are other problems: results may vary depending on how arrival cohorts are defined, on which arrival cohort serves as the omitted category, and on which native-born group serves as the benchmark; return migrants do not appear in the sample; and the data do not take into account the length of the immigrant's projected stay, the kind of visa on which he or she arrived, or whether he or she arrived on a visa at all (Duleep and Regets 1999; Jasso and Rosenzweig 1990b; LaLonde and Topel 1991; Yuengert 1994).

8. For details regarding the variables responsible for these estimates, see table 2A.3 and the section devoted to models in the methodological appendix.

9. Similarly, researchers have found that job seekers who obtain positions through the intervention of people they know through the world of work secure better-paying jobs than those who obtain positions through the intervention of people they know through the world of family (Granovetter 1974).

10. A similar process accounts for the difference in time needed for the male 1977 to 1984 cohort to earn as much as African Americans (14.4 years) and

for the male 1985 to 1991 cohort to earn as much as African American (16.3 years).

11. Five percent of the sample were males. Phillips (1996) does not present the gender breakdown by intention to migrate.

12. For instance, Paul Siegel (1965) inferred that discrimination was the cause of the black-white earnings gap of 1960, but other scholars might argue, equally cogently, that African American cultural deficiency was the reason.

13. Studies of immigrants to Canada also detect cohort decline. Some of the drop is associated with economic conditions at the time of arrival. For instance, immigrants arriving at a time of high unemployment incur an initial earnings penalty from which they never recover. However, economic conditions at the time of arrival explain only a portion of cohort decline; the remaining unexplained shortfall in earnings may be due to a drop in the selectivity of migration (Aydemir and Skuterud 2004).

14. For a detailed discussion of the ancestry question, see the first chapter of Lieberson and Waters (1988).

15. The temporal pattern of declining advantage could mean that young second-generation West Indians are doing less well in more recent censuses. This interpretation did not withstand statistical scrutiny, however.

16. In a similar vein, the historian Jacqueline Jones (1993, 45) wrote: "Too often scholars discuss the 'selective' nature of black migration in terms of formal education. In fact, though easily quantifiable, an individual's grade-level was less a useful indicator of intelligence and 'preparation for Northern life' than the more subjective qualities we might consider 'gumption.'"

17. In his thoughtful evaluation of this work, Stanley Lieberson (1978) endorsed its empirical results but criticized Long's interpretative stance. The direction and magnitude of differences between blacks in the North and the South, Lieberson emphasized, could not be determined from data that examine only the northern experience. Moreover, in the absence of panel data, it was not possible to compare migrants and nonmigrants on traits like welfare receipt or earnings. However, comparisons on age and education were feasible. Addressing these issues, Lieberson (1973, 1978) concluded that movers were the more positively selected population.

18. Tolnay's (1998) findings regarding the educational attainment of black migrants between 1880 and 1990 support the early-bird hypothesis. Controlling for age, gender, and state of origin, early movers to the North

were substantially more educated, relative to nonmovers, than were late-comers.

19. Regression analysis was used to test this possibility; in just under half the estimates (fifteen out of thirty-two), African Americans living outside their state of birth had a significantly more advantageous outcome than those living within their state of birth. In no instance, however, did the opposite situation obtain.

Chapter 5: Testing Cultural Hypotheses

1. Chapter 2 confirms that West Indian immigrants are more educated than African Americans. West Indian culture may contribute to this advantage, or the selectivity of migration may contribute. Whatever the reasons for West Indians' educational edge, chapters 4 through 6 seek an explanation for that portion of West Indian economic advantage that remains when the two groups of blacks are similarly educated. Hence, explaining the immigrants' educational edge is not a goal of this chapter.

2. Unlike scholars such as Melville Herskovits, Kenneth Stampp, Eugene Genovese, and others, Sowell does not include malingering in his list of resistant behaviors (Craton 1997; Fogel 1989). This choice may reflect a desire to associate active, aggressive resistance with Caribbean blacks and passive, indirect resistance with American blacks.

3. According to Vincent Thompson (1987, 273), the term "Maroon" comes from the Spanish "cimarron," meaning wild and untamed. Robin Black-burn (1997) claims that the first "cimarrones" were Indian escapees, but the term soon extended to African runaways. Running away for a few days and returning was termed "petit marronage"; running away semi-permanently was "grand marronage."

4. Michael Mullin (1992, 289) estimates the following numbers of runaways between 1730 and 1805: Jamaica, 2,612; Barbados, 431; Virginia, 1,280; Maryland, 1,031; South Carolina, 3,267; and Georgia, 998.

5. For an excellent summary of research on slave revolts, see Paquette (1998).

6. The distinction between gardens and provision grounds merits elaboration. Most slaves in the plantation South who desired a small plot for their own use could secure one. This land should not be confused with provision grounds, which were both larger and usually some distance from where the slaves lived.

The division between the task system and the gang system also merits elaboration. Both were compatible with the allocation of provision grounds, though in different ways. Under the task system, slaves might be able to devote some time each day to maintaining their grounds. Under the gang system, entire days or half-days were set aside for the purpose. But here a distinction between the Caribbean and the United States emerges. By the early nineteenth century, Caribbean slaves working under the gang system had more time—Saturday and Sunday—and more land to cultivate than slaves assigned to gangs in the United States.

7. Figures based on plantation records (Olson 1992) show that rural American slaves were slightly more likely to hold skilled posts than do the figures based on mortality records (Ransom and Sutch 2001).

8. Sharecropping "in kind" did take root in a few places, like Nevis and the Windward Islands (Frucht 1971; Moore 1987).

9. The fate of Louisiana's blacks followed a different course. Though slaves on some sugar plantations had enjoyed access to provision grounds, after emancipation they became wage laborers on sugar estates, not independent producers on their old provision grounds (Shlomowitz 1992).

10. Roger Ransom and Richard Sutch's (2001) calculations based on 1880 IPUMS data show that nearly 30 percent of all southern farms were owned by blacks. This proportion ranged from 19 percent in the Deep South to 56 percent in Tennessee and western Virginia.

11. Those counties are, in South Carolina: Beauford, Berkeley, Charleston, Colleton, Chesterfield, Darlington, Dillon, Dorchester, Florence, Georgetown, Hampton, Horry, Jasper, Marion, Marlboro, and Williamsburg; and in Georgia: Bryan, Camden, Chatham, Glynn, Liberty, Long, and McIntosh.

12. Rosemarijn Hoefte (1998) reports a repatriation rate of 23.3 percent for the Javanese.

13. Glenroy Taitt (1999) holds the refusal of the Trinidadian government to invest in irrigation responsible for the relatively modest rice output in that country.

14. In British Guiana, Indians were equally distrustful of black leaders. Only in Trinidad did a black man, the charismatic intellectual Eric Williams, occasionally receive significant Indian support (Ryan 1991, 1996).

15. Several of the predictors—for example, New York residence and household headship—were perfect correlates of unemployment for both women and men.

16.   See the methodological appendix for more information on this data set.

17.   It was possible to undertake statistical tests on the complete sample to determine whether the gap between Antilleans and Creoles varied within cohorts of departure. The results of these tests (not shown) produced only one significant result: all other factors being the same, Creole women incurred an additional earnings penalty for leaving during the 1970s, a penalty the Antilleans escaped. In all other respects, the effect of cohort of arrival was similar for Creoles and Antilleans.

18.   Because the addition of an index of English ability only approximates controlling for language skill, the calculations were also estimated when the sample was limited to African immigrants who reported that they spoke only English. Relative to the findings in table 5.5, the restricted sample registered a greater African deficit in 1990 and a smaller African deficit in 2000. Yet the differences were not large enough to change the conclusion that African Americans do better economically than African immigrants.

19.   The author thanks Victor Nee for contributing this insight; see also Mason (2001) for evidence that darker skin tone affects labor market outcomes negatively.

20.   In the early 2000s, the annual per capita income (purchasing power parity) of residents of the larger sending countries of sub-Saharan Africa ranged from lows of $500 in Somalia and $900 in Nigeria to a high of $10,700 in South Africa. The analogous Caribbean figures are $3,900 in Jamaica and $15,700 in Barbados (U.S. Central Intelligence Agency 2004).

21.   The PUMS contain the following numbers of black adults born in South Africa: males, 164 (1990) and 87 (2000); females, 174 (1990) and 107 (2000). The calculations control for census year.

Chapter 6: Testing the White Favoritism Hypothesis

1.   The 1971 U.K. census counted 304,070 persons born in the West Indies; in 2001 there were only 261,667 (Peach 1996; see also Cathie Marsh Center for Census and Survey Research 2005).

2.   It is fascinating to learn that American whites purportedly don't see the chip on West Indians' shoulders that British whites do.

3. Unfortunately, Deaux (2006) provides no details about sample composition or sample size.

4. There is no information about the participants in Thomas's unpublished study.

5. In all trials of the previously described Bogardus social distance studies, if Muslims are included, they rank near the bottom of the scale.

6. Unexpectedly, Dion and Kawakami (1996) found that East Indians were *more* likely to report discrimination than Pakistanis.

7. Calculations by the author.

8. Calculations by the author.

9. Partly owing to a paucity of data, French West Indians are excluded from this discussion. However, in one of the rare opinion polls to include them, they are the highest-ranked non-European group in France (La Commission Nationale Consultative des Droits de L'Homme 1993). The results of the 1988 Eurobarometer mirror this conclusion (see table 6.1).

10. In a personal communication to the author, Dr. Bovenkerk revealed that the Surinamese were all of African descent (Creoles). For full details of this study, see Bovenkerk, Gras, and Ramsoedh (1995).

11. In the early 1970s, French scholars sent CVs and photos of equally qualified white French and black Antilleans in reply to newspaper ads seeking workers (Raveau et al. 1976). Depending on the job's status, white people were 3.6 to 10.2 times more likely to receive a positive response from the employer than were Antillean applicants.

12. A metropolitan area is a set of counties with an urban core; its residents are connected by commerce and employment. The boundaries of metropolitan areas are defined by commuting patterns and are periodically updated. For these reasons, the unit of analysis in studies of labor markets is usually metropolitan areas.

13. Significance tests involved estimating a regression for New York, then estimating the identical regression for a contrast city. Each regression included a dummy identifying West Indians as contrasted to native-born non-Hispanic whites. To test for a significant difference between cities, a Wald test compared the coefficient for West Indian group membership in New York to the coefficient for West Indian group membership in the contrast city. However, if the dependent variable is dichotomous and there are significant differences in group variances, the Wald test yields flawed results. For this reason, when labor force participation or unem-

ployment rates were examined, the models were estimated using logistic regression, then systematically tested for equivalence of group variance. If this test failed, Paul Allison's (1999) method of testing for coefficient differences was used.

14. A shortcoming in the Canadian data is a lack of information on hours worked. As a result, earnings in the New York–Toronto comparison are by the week.

15. A number of cross-national differences other than ethnic composition could be responsible for the results of the New York–Amsterdam comparison. The issue of confounding factors in cross-national comparisons receives attention in chapter 7.

16. At first glance, simply adding the proportion of African Americans in the local labor force as a control variable and measuring its effect would seem the better strategy. This proportion, however, is highly correlated with residence in the South. To measure the effect of labor market composition when southern residence is controlled, the sample was divided into two roughly equal groups on the basis of the proportion of African Americans in the local labor force.

Chapter 7: An *Immigrant* Success Story

1. David Card and Alan Krueger (1992) found that improvements in the quality of black schools accounted for 20 percent of the decline in the earnings gap between blacks and whites between 1960 and 1980.

2. In an attempt to take into account women's greater propensity for discontinuous employment, most analyses of women's outcomes include controls for number of children ever born or in the home. However, this approach is a less than ideal solution.

3. Yet another difficulty that plagues cross-national comparisons is "Galton's problem": the tendency for causal processes to ignore borders and instead to diffuse—from one city to another, from one country to another.

4. Cape Verdeans are a Portuguese-speaking, predominantly black immigrant group who originate in islands off the west coast of Africa and live mainly in Massachusetts.

5. Christine DuBois (2004) and Tecata Tormala and Kay Deaux (2006) conclude in favor of white favoritism on the basis of research by Mary Waters (1999) and by Jennifer Eberhardt and Deaux (unpublished but re-

ported in Deaux 2006). However, it is not appropriate to generalize from these studies, which are more exploratory than explanatory. Moreover, as noted in chapter 6, the preference that Waters describes may well have been a consequence rather than a cause of hiring West Indian workers.

6. In a very interesting analysis of the relationship between the race of the investigator and his or her subscription to white favoritism, DuBois (2004) concludes that more white than black scholars support it. This book is an exception to her rule.

7. Because the U.S. census does not identify persons on student visas, the foreign-born Africans and West Indians in these calculations were limited to those who had resided in the United States for at least five years. John Mollenkopf (2005) produces similar results based on the Immigrant Second Generation in Metropolitan New York Study. Reynolds Farley and Richard Alba (2002) produce similar results based on a pooled sample from the Current Population Survey (CPS).

8. The University of Massachusetts application is not without flaws. Hispanics can be of any race, and there are no subcategories within either the Hispanic or Asian options.

9. Among the relevant differences were that a higher proportion of the immigrants' fathers had at least a college degree and that the immigrants' SAT scores were significantly higher.

10. Unfortunately, the sample was not large enough to distinguish the effects of generation from the effects of identity.

11. According to the 1994 Dutch Labor Force Survey, 59 percent of Turkish men were in the labor force, and their unemployment rate was 29.6 percent (Muus 1995).

12. In the 1989 General Social Survey, in a list of fifty-eight groups, Cubans ranked fifty-fifth (Smith 1991).

13. DuBois's (2004) inquiry into the media depiction of West Indians in the late 1980s and early 1990s turned up more negative than positive representations.

14. The exception, as Borjas (1987) claims, is the case of refugees from communism, who are disproportionately drawn from the more affluent and educated tiers of society.

15. Eighty-nine percent in a 1989 survey (Apraku 1991).

16. The Immigration Act of 1990 created a quota for wealthy investors, who are called "employment creation" immigrants.

17. Further information on the New Immigrant Survey is available at http://nis.princeton.edu.

18. The 2000 census counted 281,421,906 Americans, of which 36,419,434 were black. The English-speaking West Indian American population was about 1,048,000. See http://factfinder.census.gov/servlet/Dataset MainPageServlet?_program=DEC&_submenuId=&_1ang=en&_ts=.

19. In 1944 Gunnar Myrdal published *The American Dilemma: The Negro Problem and American Democracy*. The dilemma in the title refers to the paradox that Americans affirmed a belief in equality even though whites did not grant equality to blacks.

Methodological Appendix

1. IPUMS is a data site maintained by the University of Minnesota; see http://usa.ipums.org/usa.

2. As explained in the text, the analyses for 1920, 1930, and 1940 were limited to residents of the New York–New Jersey metropolitan area.

3. For 1970, the study draws on West Indians from both the 15 percent county group and the 5 percent state public use samples.

4. Before 1980, Hispanicity was imputed by census officials on the basis of surname.

5. Interestingly, in 1990 the census questionnaire explicitly stated: "Specify the particular country or island in the Caribbean (not, for example, West Indies)." However, to be defined as West Indian in this study, individuals also had to be non-Hispanic, their mother tongue had to be English, and they needed to be black (or mulatto in 1920) on the race question. In 2000 individuals could identify with more than one racial category. In the interests of consistency, only persons who provided the single response "black" were eligible for definition as West Indian.

6. The question includes a set of examples, like German, Dominican, Jamaican, Korean, and so on. In addition, in 1980 and 1990 the following instructions were available: "Print the ancestry group. Ancestry refers to the person's ethnic origin or descent, 'roots,' or heritage. Ancestry also may refer to the country of birth of the person or the person's parents or ancestors before their arrival in the United States. *All* persons, regardless of citizenship status, should answer this question. Persons who have more than one origin and cannot identify with a single ancestry group may report two ancestry groups (for example, German-Irish). Be specific. For ex-

ample, print whether West Indian, Asian Indian, or American Indian. West Indian includes persons whose ancestors came from Jamaica, Trinidad, Haiti, etc. Distinguish Cape Verdean from Portuguese; French Canadian from Canadian; and Dominican Republic from Dominica Island. A religious group should not be reported as a person's ancestry." See http://www/ipums.

7. The sub-Saharan African region was defined as all African nations except Algeria, Egypt, Libya, Morocco, and Tunisia. North Africa was also excluded.

8. When the outcomes are dichotomies, probit regression is used; when the outcomes are continuous interval scale variables, ordinary least squares regression is used. The only exception is in the tests of white favoritism. There logistic regression is used in order to undertake Paul Allison's (1999) test of variance equivalence.

9. In 1970 the census inquired about hours worked the week before the census; after 1970, the question was revised to ask about usual hours worked per week the previous year. As a result, the measures of hourly earnings devised for 1970 are distorted: they rely on hours worked the week before the census but on weeks worked and annual earnings received the year before the census.

10. Another offspring-related variable, the number of one's own children under five years of age at home, was consistently available. It was included in only two equations, however; women's labor force participation, under the assumption that child care is costly, and women's unemployment, under the assumption that some employers may be reluctant to hire mothers of preschool-age children.

11. Only in recent years have illegal entrants become a perceptible presence in Britain; many are refugees who have been denied the right to remain. In 1991 the undocumented were an insignificant presence (Samers 2001).

12. About one-fifth of the households sampled in 1994 were interviewed in 1991; about 9 percent of households sampled in 1998 were interviewed in 1994.

13. Several waves of the SPVA are available from the Steinmetz Archive in Amsterdam, and additional information about the data sets can be found at its website: http://www.dans.knaw.nl/en/data?steinmetz_archief/.

14. Sampling problems and missing data also plague the Fourth National Survey of Ethnic Minorities in Britain. Research undertaken directly under government auspices seems to provide higher-quality data. On the other hand, the number of cases and the range of variables are far

superior in surveys whose mission is the study of immigrants and minorities.

15. This methodology yielded the following numbers of Creole heads per wave: 196 in 1991, 303 in 1994, and 884 in 1998.

16. The author gratefully acknowledges the assistance of Harry Ganzeboom, without whose intervention the occupational coding could not have been effected.

References

Adamson, Alan H. 1972. *Sugar Without Slaves*. New Haven, Conn.: Yale University Press.

Allison, Paul D. 1999. "Comparing Logit and Probit Coefficients Across Groups." *Sociological Methods and Research* 28(2): 186–208.

American Academy of Arts and Sciences. 1966. "Transcript of the American Academy Conference on the Negro American, May 14–15, 1965." *Daedalus* 95(1): 287–441.

Anderson, Jervis. 1981. *This Was Harlem, 1900–1950*. New York: Farrar, Straus & Giroux.

Antecol, Heather, and Kelly Bedard. 2002. "The Relative Earnings of Young Mexican, Black, and White Women." *Industrial and Labor Market Relations Review* 56(1): 122–36.

Aponte, Robert. 1996. "Urban Employment and the Mismatch Dilemma: Accounting for the Immigrant Exception." *Social Problems* 43(3): 268–83.

Apraku, Kofi K. 1991. *African Émigrés in the United States*. Westport, Conn.: Praeger.

Arnold, Faye W. 1984. "West Indians and London's Hierarchy of Discrimination." *Ethnic Groups* 6: 47–64.

———. 1996. "Los Angeles West Indian Immigrant Women: Claimin' De Not Black, De Jus' Tillin' De Bitter Harvest." Paper presented to the annual meeting of the American Sociological Association. New York, August 16–21, 1996.

Arthur, John A. 2000. *Invisible Sojourners*. Westport, Conn.: Praeger.

Aydemir, Abdurrahman, and Mikal Skuterud. 2004. "Family and Labor Studies Division." In *Explaining the Deteriorating Entry Earnings of Canada's Immigrant Cohorts: 1966–2000*. Ottawa: Statistics Canada.

Baker, Michael, and Dwayne Benjamin. 1997. "Ethnicity, Foreign Birth, and Earnings: A Canada/U.S. Comparison." In *Transition and Structural Change in the North American Labor Market*, edited by Michael G. Abbott, Charles M.

201

Beach, and Richard P. Chaykowski. Kingston, Ont.: Queens University, John Deutsch Institute and Industrial Relations Center.

Barro, Robert J., and Jong W. Lee. 1996. "International Measures of Schooling Years and Schooling Quality." *American Economic Review* 86(2): 218–23.

Barrow, Christine. 1996. *Family in the Caribbean*. Kingston, Jamaica: Ian Randle.

Bashi, Vilna. 2007. *Survival of the Knitted: Immigration Social Networks in a Stratified World*. Stanford, Calif.: Stanford University Press.

Bean, Frank D., and Gillian Stevens. 2003. *America's Newcomers and the Dynamics of Diversity*. New York: Russell Sage Foundation.

Becker, Gary S. 1971. *The Economics of Discrimination*. 2nd ed. Chicago, Ill.: University of Chicago Press.

Beckles, Hilary M. 1984. *Black Rebellion in Barbados*. Bridgetown, Barbados: Antilles Publications.

———. 1989. *Natural Rebels: A History of Enslaved Women in Barbados*. New Brunswick, N.J.: Rutgers University Press.

———. 1990. *A History of Barbados*. Cambridge: Cambridge University Press.

———. 2004. *Great House Rules*. Kingston, Jamaica: Ian Randle.

Beer, William R. 1986. "Real-Life Costs of Affirmative Action." *Wall Street Journal*, August 7, 12.

Berlet, Chip. 2003. "Response to David Horowitz's Complaint." *FrontPage Magazine*, September 14. Accessed March 1, 2007 at http://www.FrontPage Magazine.com.

Berlin, Ira. 1974. *Slaves Without Masters: The Free Negro in the Antebellum South*. New York: Pantheon Books.

———. 1998. *Many Thousands Gone: The First Two Centuries of Slavery in North America*. Cambridge, Mass.: Belknap Press of Harvard University Press.

Berlin, Ira, and Philip D. Morgan. 1993. "Labor and the Shaping of Slave Life in the Americas." In *Cultivation and Culture*, edited by Ira Berlin and Philip D. Morgan. Charlottesville, Va.: University of Virginia Press.

Berry, John W., and Rudolf Kalin. 1995. "Multicultural and Ethnic Attitudes in Canada: An Overview of the 1991 National Study." *Canadian Journal of Behavioral Science* 27(3): 301–20.

Berry, John W., Rudolf Kalin, and Donald M. Taylor. 1977. *Multiculturalism and Ethnic Attitudes in Canada*. Ottawa: Minister of Supply and Services Canada.

Bibby, Reginald W. 1995. *Social Trends Canadian Style*. Toronto: Stoddart Publishing.

Blackburn, Robin. 1997. *The Making of New World Slavery*. London: Verso.

Blauner, Robert. 1972. *Racial Oppression in America*. New York: Harper & Row.

Bluestone, Barry, and Mary Huff Stevenson. 1999. "Racial and Ethnic Gaps in Male Earnings in a Booming Urban Economy." *Eastern Economic Journal* 25(2): 109–238.

Borjas, George J. 1985. "Assimilation, Changes in Cohort Quality, and the Earnings of Immigrants." *Journal of Labor Economics* 3(4): 463–89.

———. 1987. "Self-Selection and the Earnings of Immigrants." *American Economic Review* 77(4): 531–53.

———. 1991. "Immigration and Self-Selection." In *Immigration, Trade, and the Labor Market*, edited by John M. Abowd and Richard B. Freeman. Chicago, Ill.: University of Chicago Press.

———. 1994. "The Economics of Immigration." *Journal of Economic Literature* 32(4): 1667–717.

———. 1995. "Assimilation and Change in Cohort Quality Revisited: What Happened to Immigrant Earnings in the 1980s?" *Journal of Labor Economics* 13(2): 201–45.

———. 2000. "The Economic Progress of Immigrants." In *Issues in the Economics of Immigration*, edited by George Borjas. Chicago, Ill.: University of Chicago Press.

Borjas, George J., and Rachel M. Friedberg. 2006. "The Immigrant Earnings Turnaround of the 1990s." National Bureau of Economic Research Summer Institute, Labor Series Workshop (July).

Bourgois, Philippe. 1995. *In Search of Respect*. Cambridge: Cambridge University Press.

Bovenkerk, Frank, Mitzi J. I. Gras, and D. Ramsoedh. 1995. *Discrimination Against Migrant Workers and Ethnic Minorities in Access to Employment in the Netherlands*. International Migration Papers 4. Geneva: International Labor Office.

Boyd, Monica. 1976. "Immigration Policies and Trends: A Comparison of Canada and the United States." *Demography* 13(1): 83–104.

———. 2005. "Diverse Fortunes in Different Countries? Earnings of White and Black Immigrant Generations in Canada and the United States." Paper presented to the annual meeting of the Population Association of America. Philadelphia, Pa., March 31–April 2, 2005.

Breton, Raymond, Wsevolod W. Isajiw, Warren E. Kalbach, and Jeffrey G. Reitz. 1990. *Ethnic Identity and Equality*. Toronto: University of Toronto Press.

Broderick, Francis, and August Meier, editors. 1965. *Negro Protest Thought in the Twentieth Century*. Indianapolis, Ind.: Bobbs Merrill.

Brown, Colin. 1984. *Black and White Britain: The Third PSI Survey*. London: Heinemann.

Brown, Colin, and Pat Gay. 1994. "Racial Discrimination Seventeen Years After the Act." In *Equal Employment Opportunity: Labor Market Discrimination and Public Policy*, edited by Paul Burstein. New York: Aldine de Gruyter.

Brownrigg, Leslie A., and Manuel de la Puente. 2003. "Sociocultural Behaviors Correlated with Census Undercount." Paper presented to the annual meeting of the American Sociological Association. Atlanta, Ga., August 22, 2003. Accessed at http://www.census.gov/srd/papers/pdf/lab92-03.pdf.

Bryan, Patrick. 1991. *The Jamaican People: 1880–1902*. London: Macmillan.

Bryce-Laporte, Roy. 1972. "Black Immigrants: The Experience of Invisibility and Inequality." *Journal of Black Studies* 3(1): 29–56.

Bulmer, Martin. 1996. "The Ethnic Group Question in the 1991 Census of Population." In *Ethnicity in the 1991 Census*, vol. 1, edited by David Coleman and John Salt. London: Her Majesty's Stationery Office.

Butcher, Kristin F. 1994. "Black Immigrants in the United States: A Comparison with Native Blacks and Other Immigrants." *Industrial and Labor Relations Review* 47(2): 265–84.

Butterfield, Sherri-Ann. 2006. "To Be Young, Gifted, Black, and Somewhat Foreign: The Role of Ethnicity in Black Student Achievement." In *Beyond Acting White*, edited by Erin M. Horvat and Carla O'Connor. Lanham, Md.: Rowan & Littlefield.

Campbell, Mavis C. 1976. *The Dynamics of Change in a Slave Society*. Rutherford, N.J.: Associated University Presses.

Card, David, and Alan B. Krueger. 1992. "School Quality and Black-White Earnings: A Direct Assessment." *Quarterly Journal of Economics* 107(1): 151–200.

Carliner, Geoffrey. 1980. "Wages, Earnings, and Hours of First-, Second-, and Third-Generation American Males." *Economic Inquiry* 18(1): 87–102.

Carson, Rob. 2003. "Black, African: As Different as Black and White." *News Tribune* (Tacoma, Wash.), February 6, A01.

Cathie Marsh Center for Census and Survey Research. 2005. *2001 Individual Licensed SAR (Samples of Anonymized Records), Version 2.4: Codebook* (September 26). Accessed at http://www.ccsr.ac.uk/sars/2001/indiv/resources/ukind-v2codebook20060426.pdf.

Center for Ethnic Studies. 1993. *Ethnicity and Employment Practices in the Public and Private Sectors in Trinidad and Tobago*. St. Augustine, Trinidad: Center for Ethnic Studies.

Chiswick, Barry R. 1977. "Sons of Immigrants: Are They at an Earnings Disadvantage?" *American Economic Review: Papers and Proceedings of the 89th Annual Meeting of the American Economic Association* 67(1): 376–80.

———. 1978. "The Effect of Americanization on the Earnings of Foreign-Born Men." *Journal of Political Economy* 86(5): 897–921.

———. 1979. "The Economic Progress of Immigrants: Some Apparently Universal Patterns." In *Contemporary Economic Problems, 1979*, project director, William Fellner. Washington: American Enterprise Institute.

———. 1999. "Are Immigrants Favorably Self-Selected?" *American Economic Review* 89(2): 181–5.

Clarke, Velta J., and Emmanuel Riviere, editors. 1989. *Establishing New Lives*. New York: Caribbean Research Center, Medgar Evers College, City University of New York.

Coclanis, Peter A. 1989. *The Shadow of a Dream: Economic Life and Death in the South Carolina Low Country, 1670–1920*. New York: Oxford University Press.

———. 2000. "In Retrospect: Ransom and Sutch's One Kind of Freedom." *Reviews in American History* 28(3): 478–89.

Cohen, William. 1991. *At Freedom's Edge*. Baton Rouge, La.: Louisiana State University Press.

Colen, Shellee. 1990. "'Housekeeping' for the Green Card: West Indian Household Workers, the State, and Stratified Reproduction in New York." In *At Work in Homes*, edited by Roger Sanjek and Shellee Colen. Washington: American Anthropological Association.

———. 1995. "'Like a Mother to Them': Stratified Reproduction and West Indian Child Care Workers and Employers in New York." In *Conceiving the New World Order*, edited by Faye D. Ginsburg and Rayna Rapp. Berkeley, Calif.: University of California Press.

La Commission Nationale Consultative des Droits de l'Homme. 1993. *La Lutte contre le racism et la xénophobie* [*The Fight Against Racism and Xenophobia*]. Paper presented to the Prime Minister. Paris: La Documentation Française.

Commission for Racial Equality (CRE). 1996. *We Regret to Inform You*. London: CRE.

Conniff, Michael. 1985. *Black Labor on a White Canal*. Pittsburgh, Pa.: University of Pittsburgh Press.

Cooper, Dereck W. 1985. "Migration from Jamaica in the 1970s: Political Protest or Economic Pull?" *International Migration Review* 19(4): 728–45.

Coppin, Addington, and Reed N. Olsen. 1998. "Earnings and Ethnicity in Trinidad and Tobago." *Journal of Development Studies* 34(3): 116–34.

Corra, Mamadi K., and Sitawa R. Kimuna. Forthcoming. "The Intersection of Gender and Nativity: Female African and Caribbean Immigrants in the United States." *Journal of Ethnic and Migration Studies*.

Costanzo, Joe, Cynthia Davis, Caribert Irazi, Daniel Goodkind, and Roberto Ramirez. 2001. *Evaluating Components of International Migration: The Residual Foreign-Born*. Washington: U.S. Census Bureau.

Cox, Edward L. 1984. *Free Coloreds in the Slave Societies of St. Kitts and Grenada, 1763–1833*. Knoxville, Tenn.: University of Tennessee Press.

Craton, Michael. 1982. *Testing the Chains*. Ithaca, N.Y.: Cornell University Press.

———. 1997. "Forms of Resistance to Slavery." In *General History of the Caribbean*, vol. 3, *The Slave Societies of the Caribbean*, edited by Franklin W. Knight. London: UNESCO.

Cross, Malcolm. 1994. *Ethnic Pluralism and Racial Inequality*. Utrecht: ISOR.

Crowder, Kyle D. 1999. "Residential Segregation of West Indians in the New York/New Jersey Area: The Roles of Race and Ethnicity." *International Migration Review* 33(1): 79–113.

Crowder, Kyle D., and Lucky M. Tedrow. 2001. "West Indians and the Residential Landscape of New York." In *West Indian Migration to New York*, edited by Nancy Foner. Berkeley, Calif.: University of California Press.

Dale, Angela, and Clare Holdsworth. 1997. "Issues in the Analysis of Ethnicity in the 1991 British Census: Evidence from Microdata." *Ethnic and Racial Studies* 20(1): 160–81.

Daley, Patricia. 1996. "Black-African: Students Who Stayed." In *Ethnicity in the U.S. Census*, vol. 2, edited by Ceri Peach. London: Her Majesty's Stationery Office.

Daniels, Roger. 2004. *Guarding the Golden Door*. New York: Hill and Wang.

Deaux, Kay. 2006. *To Be an Immigrant*. New York: Russell Sage Foundation.

De Bruijne, Ad. 2001. "A City and a Nation: Demographic Trends and Socioeconomic Development in Urbanizing Suriname." In *Twentieth-Century Surinam*, edited by Rosemarijn Hoefte and Peter Meel. Kingston, Jamaica: Ian Randle.

De Groot, Silvia W., Catherine A. Christen, and Franklin W. Knight. 1997. "Maroon Communities in the Circum-Caribbean." In *General History of the Caribbean*, vol. 3, *The Slave Societies of the Caribbean*, edited by Franklin W. Knight. London: UNESCO.

Dew, Edward. 1994. *The Trouble in Suriname, 1975–1993*. Westport, Conn.: Praeger.

DiMaggio, Paul. 1994. "Culture and Economy." In *The Handbook of Economic Sociology*, edited by Neil Smelser and Richard Swedberg. Princeton, N.J.: Princeton University Press.

Dion, Kenneth, and Kerry Kawakami. 1996. "Ethnicity and Perceived Discrimination in Toronto: Another Look at the Personal/Group Discrimination Discrepancy." *Canadian Journal of Behavioral Science* 28(3): 201–13.

Dodoo, F. Nii-Amoo. 1997. "Assimilation Differences Among Africans in America." *Social Forces* 76(2): 527–46.

Dodoo, F. Nii-Amoo, and Baffour K. Takyi. 2002. "Africans in the Diaspora: Black-White Earnings Differences Among America's Africans." *Ethnic and Racial Studies* 25(6): 913–41.

Domingo, Wilfrid A. 1925. "Gift of the Black Tropics." In *The New Negro: An Interpretation*, edited by Alain Locke. New York: Johnson Reprint.

Dominguez, Virginia R. 1975. *From Neighbor to Stranger: The Dilemma of Caribbean Peoples in the United States*. New Haven, Conn.: Yale University, Antilles Research Program.

DuBois, Christine M. 2004. *Images of West Indian Immigrants in Mass Media*. New York: LFB Scholarly Publishing.

Duleep, Harriet O., and Mark C. Regets. 1999. "Immigrants and Human-Capital Investment." *American Economic Review* 89(2): 186–91.

Eberhardt, Jennifer, and Kay Deaux. 2000. Unpublished data.

The Economist. 1996. "Black Like Me." *The Economist* 339(7965): 57–58.

The Economist Intelligence Unit. 2000. *Country Report: Trinidad and Tobago, Guyana, Suriname*. London: The Unit.

Engerman, Stanley L., and Barry W. Higman. 1997. "The Demographic Structure of the Caribbean Slave Societies in the Eighteenth and Nineteenth Centuries." In *General History of the Caribbean*, vol. 3, *The Slave Societies of the Caribbean*, edited by Franklin W. Knight. London: UNESCO.

Evans, M. D. R., and Jonathan Kelley. 1991. "Prejudice, Discrimination, and the Labor Market: Attainments of Immigrants in Australia." *American Journal of Sociology* 97(3): 721–59.

Falcón, Luis M., and Edwin Melendez. 2001. "Racial and Ethnic Differences in Job Searching in Urban Centers." In *Urban Inequality: Evidence from Four Cities*, edited by Alice O'Connor, Chris Tilly, and Lawrence D. Bobo. New York: Russell Sage Foundation.

Farley, Reynolds. 1996. *The New American Reality*. New York: Russell Sage Foundation.

Farley, Reynolds, and Richard Alba. 2002. "The New Second Generation in the United States." *International Migration Review* 36(3): 669–701.

Farley, Reynolds, and Walter R. Allen. 1987. *The Color Line and the Quality of Life in America*. New York: Russell Sage Foundation.

Featherman, David L., and Robert M. Hauser. 1978. *Opportunity and Change*. New York: Academic Press.

Feliciano, Cynthia. 2006. *Unequal Origins: Immigrant Selection and the Education of the Second Generation*. New York: LFB Scholarly Publishing.

Ferguson, Tyrone. 1995. *Structural Adjustment and Good Governance: The Case of Guyana*. Georgetown, Guyana: Public Affairs Consulting Enterprise.

Fernandez, Edward, and J. Gregory Robinson. 1994. *Illustrative Ranges of the Distribution of Undocumented Immigrants by State*. Population Division Technical Working Paper No. 8. Washington: U.S. Bureau of the Census.

Fogel, Robert W. 1989. *Without Consent or Contract: The Rise and Fall of American Slavery*. New York: W. W. Norton.

Foner, Eric. 1983. *Nothing but Freedom: Emancipation and Its Legacy*. Baton Rouge, La.: Louisiana State University Press.

Foner, Nancy. 1985. "Race and Color: Jamaican Migrants in London and New York City." *International Migration Review* 19(4): 708–27.

———. 1998. "West Indian Identity in the Diaspora: Comparative and Historical Perspectives." *Latin American Perspectives* 25(3): 173–88.

Foner, Philip S. 1983. *History of Black Americans: From the Compromise of 1850 to the End of the Civil War*, vol. 3. Westport, Conn.: Greenwood Press.

Forsythe, Dennis. 1983. "Black Immigrants and the American Ethos: Theories and Observations." In *Caribbean Immigration to the United States*, edited by Roy S. Bryce-LaPorte and Delores M. Mortimer. Washington: Smithsonian Institution.

Foster, Cecil. 1996. *A Place Called Heaven: The Meaning of Being Black in Canada*. Toronto: HarperCollins.

Freeman, Gary P. 1987. "Caribbean Migration to Britain and France: From Assimilation to Selection." In *The Caribbean Exodus*, edited by Barry B. Levine. New York: Praeger.

Frisbie, W. Parker, and Lisa Neidert. 1977. "Inequality and the Relative Size of Minority Populations: A Comparative Analysis." *American Journal of Sociology* 82(5): 1007–30.

Frucht, Richard. 1971. "A Caribbean Social Type: Neither 'Peasant' nor 'Proletarian.'" In *Peoples and Cultures of the Caribbean*, edited by Michael M. Horowitz. Garden City, N.Y.: Natural History Press.

Fry, Richard. 1996. "Has the Quality of Immigrants Declined? Evidence from the Labor Market Attachment of Immigrants and Natives." *Contemporary Economic Policy* 14(3): 53–70.

Funkhouser, Edward, and Stephen J. Trejo. 1998. "Labor Market Outcomes of Female Immigrants in the United States." In *The Immigration Debate*, edited by James P. Smith and Barry Edmonston. Washington: National Academy Press.

Furlong, Patrick J. 2001. "South Africa." In *Understanding Africa*, 3rd ed., edited by April A. Gordon and Donald L. Gordon. Boulder, Colo.: Lynne Rienner.

Fussell, Elizabeth. 2004. "Migrants' Origin Nations and Communities and the Cumulative Causation of Migration." Paper presented to the annual meeting of the American Sociological Association. San Francisco, Calif., August 14–17, 2004.

Fussell, Elizabeth, and Douglas S. Massey. 2004. "The Limits to Cumulative Causation: International Migration from Mexican Urban Areas." *Demography* 41(1): 151–71.

Gans, Herbert. 1992. "Second-Generation Decline: Scenarios for the Economic and Ethnic Futures of the Post-1965 American Immigrants." *Ethnic and Racial Studies* 15(2): 173–92.

———. 1999. "The Possibility of a New Racial Hierarchy in the Twenty-first-Century United States." In *The Cultural Territories of Race*, edited by Michele Lamont. Chicago, Ill.: University of Chicago Press.

Ganzeboom, Harry B. G., and Donald J. Treiman. 1996. "Internationally Comparable Measures of Occupational Status for the 1988 International Standard of Classification of Occupations." *Social Science Research* 25(3): 201–36.

Ganzeboom, Harry B. G., Paul M. de Graaf, and Donald J. Treiman. 1992. "A Standard Socioeconomic Index of Occupational Status." *Social Science Research* 21(1): 1–56.

Gibson, Campbell J., and Emily Lennon. 1999. *Historical Statistics on the Foreign-Born Population of the United States: 1850–1990*. Population Working Paper No. 29. Washington: U.S. Bureau of the Census.

Gilder, George. 1981. *Wealth and Poverty*. New York: Basic Books.

Gladwell, Malcolm. 1996. "Black Like Them." *The New Yorker*, April 29–May 6, 74–81.

Glazer, Nathan, and Daniel P. Moynihan. 1963. *Beyond the Melting Pot: The Negroes, Puerto Ricans, Jews, Italians, and Irish of New York City*. Cambridge, Mass.: MIT Press.

Goldin, Claudia D. 1976. *Urban Slavery in the American South: 1820–1860.* Chicago, Ill.: The University of Chicago Press.

Goldthorpe, John H. 1997. "Current Issues in Comparative Macrosociology: A Debate on Methodological Issues." In *Comparative Social Research: Methodological Issues in Comparative Social Science,* vol. 16, edited by Lars Mjøset, Fredrik Engelstad, Grete Brochmann, Ragnvald Kalleberg, and Arnlaug Leira. Greenwich, Conn.: JAI Press.

Gordon, April. 1998. "The New Diaspora: African Immigration to the United States." *Journal of Third World Studies* 15(1): 79–103.

Graham, Robert E., Jr. 1971. *Personal Income in South Carolina by Type, Source, and Geographic Areas, 1929–1969.* Columbia, S. C.: University of South Carolina, College of Business Administration, Bureau of Business and Economic Research.

Granovetter, Mark. 1974. *Getting a Job.* Cambridge, Mass.: Harvard University Press.

Gras, Mitzi, and Frank Bovenkerk. 1999. "Migrants and Ethnic Minorities in the Netherlands: Discrimination in Access to Employment." In *Migrants, Ethnic Minorities, and the Labor Market,* edited by John Wrench, Andrea Rea, and Nouria Ouali. London: Palgrave Macmillan.

Greene, Jack P. 1987. "Colonial South Carolina and the Caribbean Connection." *South Carolina Historical Magazine* 88(4): 192–210.

Grosfoguel, Ramón. 2003. *Colonial Subjects.* Berkeley, Calif.: University of California Press.

———. 2004. "Race and Ethnicity or Racialized Ethnicities?" *Ethnicities* 4(3): 315–36.

Grosfoguel, Ramón, and Chloe S. Georas. 2000. "'Coloniality of Power' and Racial Dynamics: Notes Toward a Reinterpretation of Latino Caribbeans in New York City." *Identities* 7(1): 85–125.

Gudeon, Edward S. 1986. "United States Immigrant and Non-Immigrant Visas." In *Towards a Just Immigration Policy,* edited by Ann Dummett. London: Cobden Trust.

Guiraudon, Virginie, Karen Phalet, and Jessika ter Wal. 2005. "Monitoring Ethnic Minorities in the Netherlands." *International Social Science Journal* 57(183): 75–87.

Gutman, Herbert. 1976. *The Black Family in Slavery and Freedom, 1750–1925.* New York: Pantheon Books.

Hagendoorn, Louk. 2001. "Stereotypes of Ethnic Minorities in the Netherlands." In *Ethnic Minorities and Inter-Ethnic Relations in Context,* edited by Karen Phalet and Antal Örkény. Aldershot, U.K.: Ashgate.

Hagendoorn, Louk, and Joseph Hraba. 1987. "Social Distance Toward Holland's Minorities." *Ethnic and Racial Studies* 10(3): 120–33.

Handler, Jerome S., and Arnold A. Sio. 1972. "Barbados." In *Neither Slave nor Free,* edited by David W. Cohen and Jack P. Greene. Baltimore, Md.: Johns Hopkins University Press.

Hao, Lingxin. 2007. *Color Lines, Country Lines*. New York: Russell Sage Foundation.

Hargis, Peggy G., and Patrick M. Horan. 1997. "The 'Low-Country Advantage' for African Americans in Georgia, 1880–1930." *Journal of Interdisciplinary History* 28(1): 27–46.

Harvard Civil Rights Project. 2003. *Reaffirming Diversity: Legal Analysis of the University of Michigan Affirmative Action Cases: A Joint Statement of Constitutional Law Scholars*. Cambridge, Mass.: Harvard Civil Rights Project.

Harvard Magazine. 2004. "John Harvard's Journal: 'Roots' and Race." *Harvard Magazine* (September–October): 69–70.

Hauser, Robert M., and David L. Featherman. 1977. *The Process of Stratification*. New York: Academic Press.

Haynes, George. 1912/1968. *The Negro at Work in New York City*. New York: Arno Press.

Haynie, Aisha C. 2002. "Not 'Just Black' Policy Considerations: The Influence of Ethnicity on Pathways to Academic Success Amongst Black Undergraduates at Harvard University." *Journal of Public and International Affairs* 13: 40–62.

Heckman, James J. 1998. "Detecting Discrimination." *Journal of Economic Perspectives* 12(2): 101–16.

Heer, David M. 1996. *Immigration in America's Future*. Boulder, Colo.: Westview Press.

Henry, Frances, and Effie Ginzberg. 1985. *Who Gets the Work? A Test of Racial Discrimination in Employment*. Toronto: Urban Alliance on Race Relations.

Heron, Melonie P. 2001. *The Occupational Attainment of Caribbean Immigrants in the United States, Canada, and England*. New York: LFB Scholarly Publishing.

Heuman, Gad J. 1981. *Between Black and White: Race, Politics, and the Free Coloreds in Jamaica, 1792–1865*. Westport, Conn.: Greenwood Press.

Higman, B. W. 1984. *Slave Populations of the British Caribbean 1807–1834*. Baltimore, Md.: The Johns Hopkins Press.

Hintzen, Percy C. 2001. *West Indian in the West: Self-Representations in an Immigrant Community*. New York: New York University Press.

Hirschman, Charles. 1994. "Problems and Prospects Studying Immigrant Adaptation from the 1990 Population Census." *International Migration Review* 28(4): 690–713.

Hodge, Robert W. 1973. "Toward a Theory of Racial Differences in Employment." *Social Forces* 52(1): 16–31.

Hoefte, Rosemarijn. 1998. *In Place of Slavery*. Gainesville, Fla.: University Press of Florida.

Hogan, Howard, and Gregg Robinson. 1993. *What the Census Bureau's Coverage Evaluation Programs Tell Us About Differential Undercount*. Washington: U.S. Department of Commerce.

Holder, Calvin B. 1998. "Making Ends Meet: West Indian Economic Adaptation in New York City, 1900–1952." *Wadabagei: A Journal of the Caribbean and its Diaspora* 1(1): 31–84.

Huffman, Matt L., and Philip N. Cohen. 2004. "Racial Wage Inequality: Job Segregation and Devaluation Across U.S. Labor Markets." *American Journal of Sociology* 109(4): 902–36.

Hunter, Carla D. 2005. "Cultural Orientation, Perceptions of Racial Discrimination, and Collective Self-esteem Among African Americans and West Indian Americans." Ph.D. dissertation, Columbia University.

Inglis, Christine, and Suzanne Model. 2007. "Diversity and Mobility in Australia." In *Unequal Chances: Ethnic Minorities in Western Labor Markets*, edited by Anthony Heath and Sin Y. Cheung. Oxford: Oxford University Press.

James, Winston. 1998. *Holding Aloft the Banner of Ethiopia*. London: Verso.

———. 2001. "New Light on Afro-Caribbean Social Mobility in New York City." In *New Caribbean Thought: A Reader*, edited by Brian Meeks and Folke Lindhal. Mona, Jamaica: University of West Indies Press.

Jasso, Guillermina. 2004. "Have the Occupational Skills of New Immigrants to the United States Declined over Time? Evidence from the Immigrant Cohorts of 1977, 1982, and 1994." In *International Migration: Prospects and Policies in a Global Market*, edited by Douglas S. Massey and J. Edward Taylor. Oxford: Oxford University Press.

Jasso, Guillermina, and Mark R. Rosenzweig. 1990a. *The New Chosen People*. New York: Russell Sage Foundation.

———. 1990b. "Self-Selection and the Earnings of Immigrants: Comment." *American Economic Review* 80(1): 298–304.

Jasso, Guillermina, Mark R. Rosenzweig, and James Smith. 2000. "The Changing Skill of New Immigrants to the United States: Recent Trends and Their Determinants." In *Issues in the Economics of Immigration*, edited by George J. Borjas. Chicago, Ill.: University of Chicago Press.

Jaynes, Gerald D., and Robin M. Williams Jr., editors. 1989. *Common Destiny: Blacks and American Society*. Washington: National Academy Press.

Jenkins, Richard. 1986. *Racism and Recruitment*. Cambridge: Cambridge University Press.

Jewson, Nick, David Mason, Sue Waters, and Janet Harvey. 1990. *Ethnic Minorities and Employment Practice: A Study of Six Organizations*. Research paper 76. London: Employment Department.

Jimenez, Marina. 2003. "200,000 Illegal Immigrants Toiling in Canada's Underground Economy." *Globe and Mail* (Toronto), November 15, A1.

Johnson, Jason B. 2005. "Shades of Gray in Black Enrollment: Immigrants' Rising Numbers a Concern to Some Activists." *San Francisco Chronicle*, February 22, A-1.

Johnson, Violet. 2000. "Black and Foreign: The Construction and Projection of Racial and Ethnic Identities Among Black Immigrants in the United States."

In *We Are a People,* edited by Paul Spickard and Jeff Burroughs. Philadelphia, Pa.: Temple University Press.

———. 2006. *The Other Black Bostonians: West Indians in Boston, 1900–1950.* Bloomington, Ind.: Indiana University Press.

Jones, Jacqueline. 1993. "Southern Diaspora: Origins of the Northern 'Underclass.'" In *The "Underclass" Debate: Views from History,* edited by Michael B. Katz. Princeton, N.J.: Princeton University Press.

Jones, Katharine W. 2001. *Accent on Privilege: English Identities and Anglophilia in the U.S.* Philadelphia, Pa.: Temple University Press.

Jordan, Winthrop. 1968. *White over Black.* Chapel Hill, N.C.: University of North Carolina Press.

Jowell, Roger, Lindsay Brook, Gillian Prior, and Bridget Taylor. 1992. *British Social Attitudes: The Ninth Report.* Aldershot, U.K.: Dartmouth.

Kalmijn, Matthijs. 1996. "The Socioeconomic Assimilation of Caribbean American Blacks." *Social Forces* 74(3): 911–30.

Kasinitz, Philip. 2001. "Invisible No More? West Indian Americans in the Social Scientific Imagination." In *Islands in the City: West Indian Migration to New York,* edited by Nancy Foner. Berkeley, Calif.: University of California Press.

Kasinitz, Philip, John Mollenkopf, and Mary C. Waters. 2003. "Becoming Americans/Becoming New Yorkers: Immigrant Incorporation in a Majority Minority City." In *Host Societies and the Reception of Immigrants,* edited by Jeffrey J. Reitz. La Jolla, Calif.: University of California at San Diego.

Katz, Michael B., editor. 1993. *The "Underclass" Debate: Views from History.* Princeton, N.J.: Princeton University Press.

Keith, Verna N., and Cedric Herring. 1991. "Skin Tone and Stratification in the Black Community." *American Journal of Sociology* 97(3): 760–78.

Kelley, Ninette, and Michael Trebilcock. 1998. *The Making of a Mosaic.* Toronto: University of Toronto Press.

Kilbourne, Barbara, Paula England, and Kurt Beron. 1994. "Effects of Individual, Occupational, and Industrial Characteristics on Earnings." *Social Forces* 72(4): 1149–76.

Kirschenman, Joleen, and Kathryn M. Neckerman. 1991. "'We'd Love to Hire Them, but...': The Meaning of Race for Employers." In *The Urban Underclass,* edited by Christopher Jencks and Paul E. Peterson. Washington: Brookings Institution Press.

Klein, Herbert S., and Stanley L. Engerman. 1985. "The Transition from Slave to Free Labor: Notes on a Comparative Model." In *Between Slavery and Free Labor: The Spanish-Speaking Caribbean in the Nineteenth Century,* edited by Manual Fraginals, Frank Pons, and Stanley Engerman. Baltimore, Md.: Johns Hopkins University Press.

Kline, Malcolm A. 2005. "Affirmative Action Negated." *The Conservative Voice,* September 24.

Knight, Franklin W. 1997. "The Disintegration of the Caribbean Slave Systems,

1772–1886." In *General History of the Caribbean*, vol. 3, edited by Franklin W. Knight. London: UNESCO.

LaLonde, Robert J., and Robert H. Topel. 1991. "Immigrants in the American Labor Market: Quality, Assimilation, and Distributional Effects." *American Economic Review* 81(2): 297–302.

Laurence, K. O. 1994. *A Question of Labor: Indentured Immigration into Trinidad and British Guiana, 1875–1917*. New York: St. Martin's Press.

Lee, Everett S. 1966. "A Theory of Migration." *Demography* 3(1): 47–57.

Lee, Gloria, and John Wrench. 1983. *Skill Seekers: Black Youth Apprenticeships and Disadvantage*. Leicester, U.K.: National Youth Bureau.

Lewis, Oscar. 1965. *La Vida*. New York: Random House.

Lichtenstein, Alexander C. 1998. "Was the Emancipated Slave a Proletarian?" *Reviews in American History* 26(1): 124–45.

Lieberson, Stanley. 1973. "Generational Differences Among Blacks in the North." *American Journal of Sociology* 79(3): 550–65.

———. 1978. "A Reconsideration of the Income Differences Found Between Migrants and Northern-Born Blacks." *American Journal of Sociology* 83: 940–66.

———. 1980. *A Piece of the Pie*. Berkeley, Calif.: University of California Press.

Lieberson, Stanley, and Mary C. Waters. 1988. *From Many Strands: Ethnic and Racial Groups in Contemporary America*. New York: Russell Sage Foundation.

Light, Ivan. 1972. *Ethnic Enterprise in America*. Berkeley, Calif.: University of California Press.

Lim, Nelson. 2001. "On the Back of Blacks: Immigrants and the Fortunes of African Americans." In *Stranger at the Gates*, edited by Roger Waldinger. Berkeley, Calif.: University of California Press.

Lindstrom, David P., and Douglas S. Massey. 1994. "Selective Emigration, Cohort Quality, and Models of Immigrant Assimilation." *Social Science Research* 23(4): 315–49.

Logan, John L., and Glenn Deane. 2003. "Black Diversity in Metropolitan America" (August 15). Accessed at http://w3.uchastings.edu/wingate/PDF/Black_Diversity_final.pdf.

Long, Larry. 1974. "Poverty Status and Receipt of Welfare Among Migrants and Nonmigrants in Large Cities." *American Sociological Review* 39(1): 46–56.

———. 1975. "The Migration Experience of Blacks." *Integrated Education* 13: 28–31.

Long, Larry, and Lynn Heltman. 1975. "Migration and Income Differences Between Black and White Men in the North." *American Journal of Sociology* 80(6): 1391–409.

Lopez, Nancy. 2003. *Hopeful Girls, Troubled Boys*. New York: Routledge.

Mandle, Jay R. 1992. *Not Slave, Not Free*. Durham, N.C.: Duke University Press.

Mare, Robert D., and Christopher Winship. 1991. "Socioeconomic Change and the Decline of Marriage for Blacks and Whites." In *The Urban Underclass*, edited by Christopher Jencks and Paul E. Peterson. Washington: The Brookings Institution.

Marshall, Woodville K. 1993. "Provision Ground and Plantation Labor in Four Windward Islands: Competition for Resources During Slavery." In *Cultivation and Culture*, edited by Ira Berlin and Philip D. Morgan. Charlottesville: University of Virginia Press.

Martens, Edwin. 1999. *Minderheden in Beeld*. Rotterdam: ISEO/EUR.

Mason, Patrick L. 2001. "Annual Income and Identity Formation Among Persons of Mexican Descent." *American Economic Review* 91(May): 178–83.

Mason, Philip. 1970. *Patterns of Dominance*. London: Oxford University Press.

Massey, Douglas S. 1991. "Economic Development and International Migration in Comparative Perspective." In *Determinants of Emigration from Mexico, Central America, and the Caribbean*, edited by Sergio Diaz-Briquets and Sidney Weintraub. Boulder, Colo.: Westview Press.

———. 2005. "Commentary." *Federal Reserve Board of New York Economic Policy Review* 11(2): 121–2.

Massey, Douglas S., Rafael Alarcón, Jorge Durand, and Humberto González. 1986. *Return to Aztlan*. Berkeley, Calif.: University of California Press.

Massey, Douglas S., Camille Z. Charles, Garvey F. Lundy, and Mary J. Fischer. 2003. *The Source of the River*. Princeton, N.J.: Princeton University Press.

Massey, Douglas, Luin P. Goldring, and Jorge Durand. 1994. "Continuities in Transnational Migration: An Analysis of Nineteen Mexican Communities." *American Journal of Sociology* 99: 1492–533.

Massey, Douglas S., Margarita Mooney, Kimberly C. Torra, and Camille Z. Charles. 2007. "Black Immigrants and Black Natives Attending Selective Colleges and Universities in the United States." *American Journal of Education* 113(February): 243–71.

Mazumdar, Sucheta. 1984. "Punjabi Agricultural Workers in California, 1905–1920." In *Labor Immigration Under Capitalism*, edited by Lucie Cheng and Edna Bonacich. Berkeley, Calif.: University of California Press.

McClain, Paula D. 1979. *Alienation and Resistance: The Political Behavior of Afro-Canadians*. Palo Alto, Calif.: R+E Research Associates.

McDonald, Roderick A. 1993a. "Independent Economic Production by Slaves on Antebellum Louisiana Sugar Plantations." In *Cultivation and Culture*, edited by Ira Berlin and Philip D. Morgan. Charlottesville, Va.: University of Virginia Press.

———. 1993b. *The Economy and Material Culture of Slaves*. Baton Rouge, La.: Louisiana State University Press.

McKay, Claude. 1940/1968. *Harlem: Negro Metropolis*. New York: Harcourt, Brace, Jovanovich. (Orig. pub. in 1940.)

McNamee, Tom. 2004. "Who Really Benefits from Affirmative Action?" *Chicago Sun-Times*, July 19. Accessed at http://www.freerepublic.com/focus/f-news/1174562/posts.

Means, Howard B. 1992. *Colin Powell*. New York: D. I. Fine.

Mehta, Chirag, Nik Theodore, Iliana Mora, and Jennifer Wade. 2002. *Chicago's Undocumented Immigrants: An Analysis of Wages, Working Conditions, and Economic Contributions*. Chicago, Ill.: University of Illinois, Center for Urban Economic Development (February). Accessed at http://www.uic.edu/cuppa/uicued/Publications/RECENT/undoc_full.pdf.

Meier, August, editor. 1963. *Negro Thought in America, 1880–1915*. Ann Arbor, Mich.: University of Michigan Press.

Merton, Robert K. 1957. *Social Theory and Social Structure*. Glencoe, Ill.: Free Press.

Miller, Kerby A. 1985. *Emigrants and Exiles*. New York: Oxford University Press.

Miller, Steven F. 1993. "Plantation Labor Organization and Slave Life on the Cotton Frontier: The Alabama-Mississippi Black Belt, 1815–1840." In *Cultivation and Culture*, edited by Ira Berlin and Philip D. Morgan. Charlottesville, Va.: University of Virginia Press.

Mintz, Sidney W. 1985. "From Plantations to Peasantries in the Caribbean." In *Caribbean Contours*, edited by Sidney W. Mintz and Sally Price. Baltimore, Md.: Johns Hopkins University Press.

Mintz, Sidney, and Douglas Hall. 1991. "The Origins of the Jamaican Internal Market System." In *Caribbean Slave Society and Economy: A Student Reader*, edited by Hilary Beckles and Verene Shepherd. Kingston, Jamaica: Ian Randle.

Model, Suzanne. 1991. "Caribbean Immigrants: A Black Success Story?" *International Migration Review* 25(2): 248–76.

———. 1997. "An Occupational Tale of Two Cities: Minorities in London and New York." *Demography* 34(4): 539–50.

———. 2001. "Where New York's West Indians Work." In *Islands in the City*, edited by Nancy Foner. Berkeley, Calif.: University of California Press.

———. 2005. "Nonwhite Origins, Anglo Destinations: Immigrants in the U.S. and Britain." In *Ethnicity, Social Mobility, and Public Policy*, edited by Glenn C. Loury, Teriq Modood, and Steven M. Teles. Cambridge: Cambridge University Press.

Model, Suzanne, and Gene Fisher. 2007. "The New Second Generation at the Turn of the New Century." In *Unequal Chances: Ethnic Minorities in Western Labor Markets*, edited by Anthony Heath and Sin Y. Cheung. Oxford: Oxford University Press.

Model, Suzanne, and David Ladipo. 1996. "Context and Opportunity: Minorities in London and New York." *Social Forces* 75(2): 485–510.

Modood, Tariq, Richard Berthoud, Jane Lakey, James Nazroo, Patten Smith, Satnam Virdee, and Sharon Beishon. 1997. *Ethnic Minorities in Britain: Diversity and Disadvantage*. London: Policy Studies Institute.

Mollenkopf, John. 2005. "Trajectories for the Immigrant Second Generation in New York City." *Federal Reserve Bank of New York Economic Policy Review* 11(2): 105–19.

Moore, Brian L. 1987. *Race, Power, and Social Segmentation in a Colonial Society*. New York: Gordon and Breach.

Moore, Garrie W. 1913. "A Study of a Group of West Indian Negroes in New York City." Master's thesis, Columbia University.

Moore, Joan, and Raquel Pinderhughes. 1993. *In the Barrios: Latinos and the Underclass Debate*. New York: Russell Sage Foundation.

Morgan, Philip D. 1983. "The Ownership of Property by Slaves in the Midnineteenth Century Low Country." *Journal of Southern History* 49(3): 399–420.

———. 1998. *Slave Counterpoint: Black Culture in the Eighteenth-Century Chesapeake and Lowcountry*. Chapel Hill, N.C.: University of North Carolina Press.

Mortimer, Delores. 1976. "Caribbeans in America: Some Further Perspectives on Their Lives." In *Caribbean Immigration to the United States*, edited by Roy S. Bryce-LaPorte and Delores M. Mortimer. Washington: Smithsonian Institution.

Moss, Philip, and Chris Tilly. 2001. *Stories Employers Tell: Race, Skill, and Hiring in America*. New York: Russell Sage Foundation.

Mullin, Michael. 1992. *Africa in America: Slave Acculturation and Resistance in the American South and the British Caribbean, 1736–1831*. Urbana, Ill.: University of Illinois Press.

Muus, Philip J. 1995. *Migration, Immigrants, and Policy in the Netherlands*. Amsterdam: Center for Migration Research, University of Amsterdam.

Myers, Dowell. 2004. "Accuracy of Data Collected by the Census Question on Immigrants' Year of Arrival." Working paper PDRG04-01. Los Angeles, Calif.: University of Southern California, School of Policy, Planning, and Development, Population Dynamics Research Group. Accessed at http://www.usc.edu/schools/sppd/research/popdynamics.

Myrdal, Gunnar. 1944. *An American Dilemma*. New York: Harper & Brothers.

Nakao, Keiko, and Judith Treas. 1994. "Updating Occupational Prestige and Socioeconomic Scores: How the New Measures Measure Up." In *Sociological Methodology 1994*, vol. 24, edited by Peter Marsden. Cambridge, Mass.: Blackwell.

National Planning Agency. 1969–79. *Economic Survey, Jamaica*. Kingston, Jamaica: Planning Institute of Jamaica.

———. 1980–2002. *Economic and Social Survey, Jamaica*. Kingston, Jamaica: Planning Institute of Jamaica.

Neal, Derrick. 2004. "The Measured Black-White Gap Among Women Is Too Small." *Journal of Black Political Economy* 112(1): S1–28.

Neckerman, Kathryn, Prudence Carter, and Jennifer Lee. 1999. "Segmented Assimilation and Minority Cultures of Mobility." *Ethnic and Racial Studies* 22(6): 945–65.

Neidert, Lisa J., and Reynolds Farley. 1985. "Assimilation in the United States: An Analysis of Ethnic and Generation Differences in Status and Achievement." *American Sociological Review* 50(6): 840–50.

Newton, Velma. 1987. *The Silver Men: West Indian Labor Migration to Panama, 1850–1914*. Kingston, Jamaica: Institute of Social and Economic Research.

Ngai, Mae M. 2004. *Impossible Subjects: Illegal Aliens and the Making of Modern America*. Princeton, N.J.: Princeton University Press.

Niesing, Willem. 1993. *The Labor Market Position of Ethnic Minorities in the Netherlands*. Rotterdam: Proefschrift.

Ogbu, John U. 1978. *Minority Education and Caste: The American System in Cross-Cultural Perspective*. New York: Academic Press.

———. 1991. "Immigrant and Involuntary Minorities in Comparative Perspective." In *Minority Status and Schooling*, edited by Margaret Gibson and John U. Ogbu. New York: Garland.

Olson, John F. 1992 "The Occupational Structure of Southern Plantations During the Late Antebellum Era." In *Without Consent or Contract: The Rise and Fall of American Slavery: Technical Papers*, vol. 1, *Markets and Production*, edited by Robert W. Fogel and Stanley L. Engerman. New York: W. W. Norton.

Onwuachi-Willig, Angela. Forthcoming. "The Admission of Legacy Blacks." *Vanderbilt Law Review*. Available at Social Science Research Network, accessed at http://papers.ssrn.com/sol3/papers.cfm?abstract_id=957891.

Osofsky, Gilbert. 1963. *Harlem: The Making of a Ghetto*. New York: Harper & Row.

Ottley, Roi. 1943. *"New World a-Coming."* Boston, Mass.: Houghton Mifflin.

Ottley, Roi, and William Weatherby, editors. 1967. *The Negro in New York*. New York: New York Public Library.

Palmer, Ransford W. 1974. "A Decade of West Indian Migration to the United States, 1962–1972: An Economic Analysis." *Social and Economic Studies* 23(4): 571–84.

———. 1995. *Pilgrims from the Sun*. New York: Twayne Publishers.

Paquette, Robert L. 1998. "Revolts." In *A Historical Guide to World Slavery*, edited by Seymour Drescher and Stanley L. Engerman. New York: Oxford University Press.

Parascandola, Louis J., editor. 2005. *"Look for Me All Around You": Anglophone Caribbean Immigrants in the Harlem Renaissance*. Detroit, Mich.: Wayne University Press.

Parrillo, Vincent N., and Christopher Donoghue. 2005. "Updating the Bogardus Social Distance Studies: A New National Survey." *Social Science Journal* 42(2): 257–71.

Passel, Jeffrey S., and Rebecca L. Clark. 1998. *Immigrants in New York: Their Legal Status, Incomes, and Taxes*. Washington: Urban Institute. Accessed at http://www.urban.org/url.cfm?ID=407432.

Passel, Jeffrey S., and Michael Fix. 2001. "U.S. Immigration at the Beginning of the Twenty-first Century." Testimony prepared for the Subcommittee on Immigration and Claims, Committee on the Judiciary, U.S. House of Representatives (August 2). Accessed at http://www.urban.org/publications/900417.html.

Passel, Jeffrey S., and Karen A. Woodrow. 1984. "Geographic Distribution of Undocumented Immigrants: Estimates of Undocumented Aliens Counted by State." *International Migration Review* 18(3): 642–71.

Patterson, Orlando. 2006. "A Poverty of the Mind." *New York Times*, March 26, 13.

Paulle, Bowen. 2005. *Anxiety and Intimidation in the Bronx and the Bijlmer*. Amsterdam: Dutch University Press.

Peach, Ceri. 1996. "Black-Caribbeans: Class, Gender, and Geography." In *Ethnicity in the 1991 Census*, vol. 2, edited by Ceri Peach. London: Her Majesty's Stationery Office.

Phillips, Daphne. 1996. "The Internationalization of Labor: The Migration of Nurses from Trinidad and Tobago." *International Sociology* 11(1): 109–27.

Plaza, Dwaine. 2001–2002. "A Socio-Historic Examination of Caribbean Migration to Canada: Moving to the Beat of Changes in Immigration Policy." *Wadabagei: A Journal of the Caribbean and Its Diaspora* 4(1): 39–80.

Poitier, Sidney. 1980. *This Life*. New York: Alfred A. Knopf.

Porter, John. 1965. *The Vertical Mosaic*. Toronto: University of Toronto Press.

Portes, Alejandro, Patricia Fernández-Kelly, and William Haller. 2005. "Segmented Assimilation on the Ground: The New Second Generation in Early Adulthood." *Ethnic and Racial Studies* 28(6): 1000–40.

Portes, Alejandro, and Rubén G. Rumbaut. 1996. *Immigrant America: A Portrait*, 2nd ed. Berkeley, Calif.: University of California Press.

Portes, Alejandro, and Min Zhou. 1993. "The New Second Generation: Segmented Assimilation and Its Variants." *Annals of the American Academy of Political and Social Sciences* 530: 74–96.

Powell, Troy A., and Claudia Buchmann. 2002. "Racial Inequality of Occupational Status in South Africa: The Effect of Local Opportunity Structures on Occupational Outcomes." RC 28 meetings of the International Sociological Association. Oxford (April).

Premdas, Ralph R. 1995. "Ethnic Identity in the Caribbean: Decentering a Myth." Robert F. Harney Professorship and Program in Ethnic, Immigration, and Pluralism Studies 17, edited by W. Wsevolod Isajiw. Toronto: University of Toronto, Department of Sociology (November).

Ramesar, Marianne D. S. 1994. *Survivors of Another Crossing*. St. Augustine, Trinidad: University of the West Indies, School of Continuing Studies.

Ransom, Roger L., and Richard Sutch. 2001. *One Kind of Freedom*, 2nd ed. New York: Cambridge University Press.

Raveau, F., B. Kilborne, L. Frere, J. M. Lorin, and G. Trempe. 1976. "Perceptions sociale de la couleur et discrimination." *Cahiers D'Anthropologie* 4: 23–42.

Redstone, Ilana, and Douglas S. Massey. 2004. "Coming to Stay: An Analysis of the U.S. Census Question on Immigrants' Year of Arrival." *Demography* 41(4): 721–38.

Reid, Ira De Augustine. 1939/1969. *The Negro Immigrant*. New York: Arno Press.

Reidy, Joseph P. 1993. "Obligation and Right: Patterns of Labor, Subsistence, and Exchange in the Cotton Belt of Georgia, 1790–1860." In *Cultivation and Culture*, edited by Ira Berlin and Philip D. Morgan. Charlottesville, Va.: University of Virginia Press.

Reif, Karlheinz, and Anna Melich. 1991. "Eurobarometer 30: Immigrants and Out-groups in Western Europe, October–November 1988" (computer file). Conducted by Faits et Opinions, Paris. Produced and distributed by Interuniversity Consortium for Political and Social Research, Ann Arbor, Mich.

Reitz, Jeffrey G. 1988. "Less Racial Discrimination in Canada, or Simply Less Racial Conflict? Implications of Comparisons with Britain." *Canadian Public Policy* 14(4): 424–41.

———. 1998. *Warmth of the Welcome*. Boulder, Colo.: Westview Press.

Reitz, Jeffrey G., and Raymond Breton. 1994. *The Illusion of Difference*. Toronto: C. D. Howe Institute.

Riach, Peter A., and Judith Rich. 2002. "Field Experiments of Discrimination in the Marketplace." *Economic Journal* 112(483): F480–518.

Richardson, Bonham. 1985. *Panama Money in Barbados, 1900–1920*. Knoxville, Tenn.: University of Tennessee Press.

———. 1989. "Caribbean Migrations, 1838–1985." In *The Modern Caribbean*, edited by Franklin W. Knight and Colin A. Palmer. Chapel Hill, N.C.: University of North Carolina Press.

Rimer, Sarah, and Karen W. Arenson. 2004. "Top Colleges Take More Blacks, but Which Ones?" *New York Times*, June 24, A1.

Roberts, George W. 1957. *The Population of Jamaica*. Cambridge: Cambridge University Press.

Robinson, J. G., and Arjun Adlakha. 2002. *Comparison of ACE Revision II Results with Demographic Analysis*. DSSD ACE Revision II Estimates Memorandum Series PP-41. Washington: U.S. Census Bureau. Accessed at http://www.census.gov/dmd/www/pdf/pp-41r.pdf.

Rodriguez, Cindy. 2002. "Study Shows U.S. Blacks Trailing." *Boston Globe*, February 17, A3.

Rogozinski, Jan. 1992. *A Brief History of the Caribbean*. New York: Facts on File.

Rong, Xue L., and Frank Brown. 2001. "The Effects of Immigrant Generation and Ethnicity on Educational Attainment Among Young African and Caribbean Blacks in the United States." *Harvard Educational Review* 71(3): 536–65.

Rose, David L. 1994. "Twenty-five Years Later: Where Do We Stand on Equal Employment Opportunity Law Enforcement?" In *Equal Employment Opportunity*, edited by Paul Burstein. New York: Aldine de Gruyter.

Rosenbaum, Emily, and Samantha Friedman. 2007. *The Housing Divide: How Generations of Immigrants Fare in New York's Housing Market*. New York: New York University Press.

Roy, A. D. 1951. "Some Thoughts on the Distribution of Earnings." *Oxford Economic Papers* 3(2): 135–46.

Ruggles, Steven, Matthew Sobek, Trent Alexander, Catherine A. Fitch, Ronald Goeken, Patricia Kelly Hall, Miriam King, and Chad Ronnander. 2004. *Integrated Public Use Microdata Series: Version 3.0* (machine-readable database). Produced and distributed by Minnesota Population Center, Minneapolis. Accessed at http://usa.ipums.org/usa/.

Ryan, Selwyn. 1991. "Social Stratification in Trinidad and Tobago: Lloyd Braithwaite Revisited." In *Social and Occupational Stratification in Contemporary Trinidad and Tobago*, edited by Selwyn Ryan. St. Augustine, Trinidad: University of the West Indies, Institute of Social and Economic Research.

———. 1996. *Pathways to Power: Indians and the Politics of National Unity in Trinidad and Tobago*. St. Augustine, Trinidad: University of the West Indies, Institute of Social and Economic Research.

Samers, Michael. 2001. "Here to Work: Undocumented Immigration in the U.S. and Europe." *SAIS Review* 21(1): 131–45.

Schaefer, Richard T. 1998. *Racial and Ethnic Groups*, 7th ed. New York: Longman.

Schama, Simon. 2006. *Britain, the Slaves, and the American Revolution*. New York: Ecco.

Schmidt, Nelly. 1989. "Les Paradoxes du développement industriel des colonies françaises des Caraibes pendant la seconde moitié du XIXe siècle: Perspectives comparatives" ["The Paradoxes of Industrial Development in French Caribbean Colonies During the Second Half of the Nineteenth Century: Comparative Perspectives"]. *Histoire, Économie, et Société* 8(3): 313–33.

Semyonov, Moshe, Danny Hoyt, and Richard Scott. 1984. "Place, Race, and Differential Occupational Opportunities." *Demography* 21(2): 259–70.

Sheridan, Richard B. 1995. "Strategies of Slave Subsistence: The Jamaican Case Reconsidered." In *From Chattel Slaves to Wage Slaves: The Dynamics of Labor Bargaining in the Americas*, edited by Mary Turner. London: James Curry.

———. 1996. "Why the Condition of the Slaves Was 'Less Intolerable in Barbadoes Than in the Other Sugar Colonies.'" In *Inside Slavery: Process and Legacy in the Caribbean Experience*, edited by Hilary M. Beckles. Kingston, Jamaica: Canoe Press.

Shlomowitz, Ralph. 1992. "'Bound' or 'Free'? Black Labor in Cotton and Sugar Cane Farming, 1865–1880." In *Without Consent or Contract: The Rise and Fall of American Slavery: Technical Papers*, vol. 2, edited by Robert W. Fogel and Stanley L. Engerman. New York: W. W. Norton.

Siegel, Paul. 1965. "On the Cost of Being a Negro." *Sociological Inquiry* 35(1) 41–57.

Simmons, Walter O. 2003. "The Black Earnings Gap: Discrimination or Culture?" *Journal of Socioeconomics* 31(6): 647–55.

Simpson, Ludi, and Elizabeth Middleton. 1997. *Who Is Missed by a National Census? A Review of Empirical Results from Australia, Britain, Canada, and the USA*. Manchester, U.K.: Cathie Marsh Center for Census and Survey Research.

Simpson, Stephen. 1996. "Nonresponse to the 1991 Census: The Effects On Ethnic Group Enumeration." In *Demographic Characteristics of Minority Populations*, vol. 1, edited by David Coleman and John Salt. London: Her Majesty's Stationery Office.

Smith, James P., and Barry Edmonston, editors. 1997. *The New Americans*. Washington: National Academy Press.

Smith, Patten, and Gillian Prior. 1996. *The Fourth National Survey of Ethnic Minorities*. London: Social and Community Planning Research.

Smith, Stephen. 2003. *Labor Economics*, 2nd ed. London: Routledge.

Smith, Tom W. 1991. *What Do Americans Think About Jews?* New York: American Jewish Committee.

Sniderman, Paul M., and Edward G. Carmines. 1997. *Reaching Beyond Race*. Cambridge, Mass.: Harvard University Press.

Sowell, Thomas. 1975. *Race and Economics*. New York: David McKay.

———, editor. 1978a. *Essays and Data on American Ethnic Groups*. Washington: Urban Institute Press.

———. 1978b. "Three Black Histories." In *Essays and Data on American Ethnic Groups*, edited by Thomas Sowell. Washington: Urban Institute Press.

———. 1981. *Ethnic America: A History*. New York: Basic Books.

———. 1983. *The Economics and Politics of Race*. New York: William Morrow.

Statistics Canada. 1994a. *1991 Census Technical Reports Coverage*. Ottawa: Minister of Industry, Science, and Technology.

———. 1994b. *User Documentation for Public Use Microdata File on Individuals*. Ottawa: Ministry of Industry, Science, and Technology.

———. 1995. *Occupation According to the 1991 Standard Occupational Classification: 1991 Census Technical Reports, Reference Products Series*. Ottawa: Minister of Industry, Science, and Technology.

———. 2001. "2001 Census Data." Accessed at http://www12.statcan.ca/english/census01 /Products/standard/themes/DataProducts.cfm?S=1.

———. 2003. *Ethnic Diversity Survey: Portrait of a Multicultural Society*. Ottawa: Ministry of Industry.

Statistics Netherlands. Various years. "StatLine." Accessed at http://statline .cbs.nl/StatWeb/start.asp?LA=en&DM=SLEN&lp=Search%2FSearch.

Steckel, Richard H. 1995. "Stature and the Standard of Living." *Journal of Economic Literature* 33(4): 1903–40.

Stevens, C. J. 2004. "Comments: The Wrong Blacks" (June 24). Accessed November 5, 2005, at http://www.joannejacobs.com.

Stigler, George J. 1962. "Information in the Labor Market." *Journal of Political Economy* 70(5): 94–105.

Stiglitz, Joseph E. 2002. *Globalization and Its Discontents*. New York: W. W. Norton.

Taitt, Glenroy. 1999. "Rice, Culture, and Government in Trinidad, 1897–1939." In *The Colonial Caribbean in Transition*, edited by Bridget Y. K. A. Brereton. Kingston, Jamaica: University of the West Indies Press.

Thompson, Vincent B. 1987. *The Making of the African Diaspora in the Americas, 1441–1900*. Essex, U.K.: Longman.

Thomson, Colin A. 1979. *Blacks in Deep Snow: Black Pioneers in Canada*. Don Mills, Ont.: J. M. Dent and Sons.

Tigges, Leann M., and Deborah M. Tootle. 1993. "Underemployment and Racial Competition in Local Labor Markets." *Sociological Quarterly* 34(2): 279–98.

Time. 1985. "Off to a Running Start." *Time*, July 8. Accessed April 18, 2007, at www.time.com/time/magazine/article/0,9171,959569-1,00.html.

Tolnay, Stewart E. 1998. "Educational Selection in the Migration of Southern Blacks, 1880–1990." *Social Forces* 77(2): 487–514.

———. 2003. "The African American 'Great Migration' and Beyond." In *Annual Review of Sociology*, vol. 29, edited by Karen S. Cook and John Hagan. Palo Alto, Calif.: Annual Reviews.

Tomasi, S. M., and Charles B. Keely. 1975. *Whom Have We Welcomed? The Adequacy and Quality of United States Immigration Data for Policy Analysis and Evaluation*. Staten Island, N.Y.: Center for Migration Studies.

Tomich, Dale. 1993. "Une Petite Guinée: Provision Ground and Plantation in Martinique, 1830–1848." In *Cultivation and Culture*, edited by Ira Berlin and Philip D. Morgan. Charlottesville, Va.: University of Virginia Press.

Tormala, Tecata T., and Kay Deaux. 2006. "Black Immigrants to the United States: Confronting and Constructing Ethnicity and Race." In *Cultural Psychology of Immigrants*, edited by Ramaswami Mahalingam. Mahwah, N.J.: Lawrence Erlbaum.

Treiman, Donald J. 1977. *Occupational Prestige in Comparative Perspective*. New York: Academic.

Treiman, Donald J., and Kermit Terrill. 1975. "Sex and the Process of Status Attainment: A Comparison of Working Women and Men." *American Sociological Review* 40(2): 174–200.

U.S. Census Bureau. 1969–2004. *Statistical Abstract of the United States*. Washington: U.S. Government Printing Office.

U.S. Central Intelligence Agency (CIA). 1982–2002. *The World Fact Book*. Washington: U.S. Government Printing Office.

U.S. Department of Homeland Security. Office of Immigration Statistics. 2002–2004. *Yearbook of Immigration Statistics*. Accessed at http://www.uscis.gov/graphics/shared/statistics/yearbook/index.htm.

U.S. Department of Labor. Bureau of Immigration. 1900–1933. *Annual Report of the Commissioner General of Immigration to the Secretary of Labor (1899–1932)*. Washington: U.S. Government Printing Office.

U.S. Immigration and Naturalization Service (INS). 1957–1977. *Annual Report of the Immigration and Naturalization Service*. Washington: U.S. Government Printing Office.

———. 1978–2001. *Statistical Yearbook of the Immigration and Naturalization Service*. Washington: U.S. Government Printing Office.

Ueda, Reed. 1980. "West Indians." In *The Harvard Encyclopedia of Ethnic Groups*, edited by Stephan Thernstrom. Cambridge, Mass.: Belknap Press of Harvard University Press.

Van Niekerk, Mies. 2000. "Paradoxes in Paradise: Integration and Social Mobility of the Surinamese in the Netherlands." In *Immigrant Integration: The Dutch Case*, edited by Hans Vemeulen and Rinus Penninx. Amsterdam: Het Spinhuis.

———. 2005. *Surinam Country Study*. Oxford: ESRC Center on Migration, Policy, and Society.

Vertovec, Steven. 1992. *Hindu Trinidad*. London: Macmillan.

Vialet, Joyce C. 1997. "Immigration: Reasons for Growth, 1981–1995." CRS Report for Congress (February 12). Accessed at http://www.cnie.org/NLE/CRSreports/Population/pop-2.cfm.

Vickerman, Milton. 1994. "The Responses of West Indians to African-Americans: Distancing and Identification." In *Research in Race and Ethnic Relations*, vol. 7, edited by Dennis Routledge. Greenwich, Conn.: JAI Press.

———. 1999. *Crosscurrents: West Indian Immigrants and Race*. New York: Oxford University Press.

Warren, Robert, and Jeffrey S. Passel. 1987. "A Count of the Uncountable: Estimates of Undocumented Aliens Counted in the 1980 United States Census." *Demography* 24(3): 375–93.

Waters, Mary C. 1993. "West Indian Immigrants, African Americans, and Whites in the Workplace: Different Perspectives on American Race Relations." Unpublished paper, Harvard University.

———. 1996. "The Intersection of Gender, Race, and Ethnicity in the Identity Development of Caribbean American Teens." In *Urban Girls*, edited by Bonnie J. R. Leadbeater and Niobe Way. New York: New York University Press.

———. 1997. "The Impact of Racial Segregation on the Education and Work Outcomes of Second-Generation West Indians in New York City." Paper presented to Jerome Levy Institute Conference on the Second Generation. Bard College, October 25, 1997.

———. 1999. *Black Identities: West Indian Immigrant Dreams and American Realities*. New York: Russell Sage Foundation.

———. 2002. "The Social Construction of Race and Ethnicity: Some Examples from Demography." In *American Diversity*, edited by Nancy A. Denton and Stewart E. Tolnay. Albany, N.Y.: State University of New York Press.

Watkins-Owens, Irma. 1996. *Blood Relations*. Bloomington: Indiana University Press.

Williams, Eric. 1962. *History of the People of Trinidad and Tobago*. London: Andre Deutsch.

Williams, Russell E. 2004. "Social Networks and Labor Market Outcomes." Ph.D. dissertation, University of Massachusetts at Amherst.

Wilson, William Julius. 1980. *The Declining Significance of Race*, 2nd ed. Chicago, Ill.: University of Chicago Press.

Word, David L. 1997. "Who Responds/Who Doesn't? Analyzing Variation in Mail Response Rates During the 1990 Census." Population Division working paper 19 (July). Washington. U.S. Census Bureau.

Wright, Gavin. 1986. *Old South, New South*. New York: Basic Books.

Xie, Yu, and Kimberly A. Goyette. 2005. "A Demographic Portrait of Asian Americans ." In *The American People: Census 2000*, edited by Reynolds Farley and John Haaga. New York: Russell Sage Foundation.

Yancey, George. 2003. *Who Is White? Latinos, Asians, and the New Black/Non-Black Divide*. Boulder, Colo.: Lynne Rienner.

Yuengert, A. M. 1994. "Immigrant Earnings, Relative to What? The Importance of Earnings Function Specification and Comparison Points." *Journal of Applied Econometrics* 9(1): 71–90.

Index